John Kartje
Wisdom Epistemology in the Psalter

Beihefte zur Zeitschrift für die alttestamentliche Wissenschaft

———

Edited by
John Barton, Ronald Hendel,
Reinhard G. Kratz and Markus Witte

Volume 472

John Kartje

Wisdom Epistemology in the Psalter

—

A Study of Psalms 1, 73, 90, and 107

DE GRUYTER

G

ISBN 978-3-11-035053-1
e-ISBN 978-3-11-035296-2
ISSN 0934-2575

Library of Congress Cataloging-in-Publication Data
A CIP catalog record for this book has been applied for at the Library of Congress.

Bibliographic Information published by the Deutsche Nationalbibliothek
The Deutsche Nationalbibliothek lists this publication in the Deutsche Nationalbibliografie;
detailed bibliographic data are available on the Internet at http://dnb.dnb.de.

© 2014 Walter de Gruyter GmbH, Berlin/Boston
Printing and binding: CPI books GmbH, Leck
♾ Printed on acid-free paper
Printed in Germany

www.degruyter.com

MIX
Papier aus verantwor-
tungsvollen Quellen
FSC
www.fsc.org   FSC® C003147

Acknowledgements

It is a pleasure to thank Dr. David Bosworth and Dr. Alexander Di Lella for numerous insightful comments, suggestions, and encouragements. I especially thank Dr. Christopher Begg, who accompanied me with patience, generosity, and wisdom throughout my years at The Catholic University of America. I am also deeply grateful to my parents and family for all of their tireless support.

Contents

Abbreviations

AB	Anchor Bible
ABRL	Anchor Bible Reference Library
Anton	*Antonianum*
ATANT	Abhandlungen zur Theologie des Alten und Neuen Testaments
ATSAT	Arbeiten zu Text und Sprache im Alten Testament
BA	*Biblical Archaeologist*
BBB	Bonner biblische Beiträge
BETL	Bibliotheca Ephemeridum theologicarum Lovaniensium
Bib	*Biblica*
BIS	Biblical Interpretation Series
BK	*Bibel und Kirche*
BKAT	Biblischer Kommentar, Altes Testament
BL	Berger and Luckmann
BN	*Biblische Notizen*
BSac	*Bibliotheca Sacra*
BTB	*Biblical Theology Bulletin*
BWANT	Beiträge zur Wissenschaft vom Alten (und Neuen) Testament
BZ	*Biblische Zeitschrift*
BZAW	Beihefte zur ZAW
CBQ	*Catholic Biblical Quarterly*
CBQMS	CBQ, Monograph Series
CMT	Conceptual Metaphor Theory
ConBOT	*Coniectanea biblica, Old Testament*
EstBib	*Estudios bíblicos*
EvQ	*Evangelical Quarterly*
ExpTim	*Expository Times*
FAT	Forschungen zum Alten Testament
FOTL	Forms of the Old Testament Literature
FRLANT	Forschungen zur Religion und Literatur des Alten und Neuen Testaments
HAT	Handbuch zum Alten Testament
Hen	*Henoch*
HS	*Hebrew Studies*
HSM	Harvard Semitic Monographs
HThKAT	Herders theologischer Kommentar zum Alten Testament
HTR	*Harvard Theological Review*
HUCA	*Hebrew Union College Annual*
ICC	International Critical Commentary
Int	*Interpretation*
JAOS	*Journal of the American Oriental Society*
JBL	*Journal of Biblical Literature*
JBQ	*Jewish Bible Quarterly*
JETS	*Journal of the Evangelical Theological Society*
JR	*Journal of Religion*
JRT	*Journal of Religious Thought*

JSJ	*Journal for the Study of Judaism in the Persian, Hellenistic, and Roman Periods*
JSJSup	Supplements to JSJ
JSOT	*Journal for the Study of the Old Testament*
JSOTSup	JSOT, Supplement Series
JSS	*Journal of Semitic Studies*
JTS	*Journal of Theological Studies*
LHBOTS	Library of Hebrew Bible/Old Testament Studies
LQ	Lutheran Quarterly
NEchtB	Neue Echter Bibel
NIB	*New Interpreter's Bible*
OBO	Orbis biblicus et orientalis
OBT	Overtures to Biblical Theology
OTE	*Old Testament Essays*
OTG	Old Testament Guides
OTL	Old Testament Library
PTMS	Pittsburgh Theological Monograph Series
RB	*Revue biblique*
RelS	*Religious Studies*
RelSRev	*Religious Studies Review*
ResQ	*Restoration Quarterly*
RevistB	*Revista bíblica*
RHPR	Revue d'histoire et de philosophie religieuses
RSR	*Recherches de science religieuse*
SBLDS	SBL Dissertation Series
SBLMS	SBL Monograph Series
SBLSP	*SBL Seminar Papers*
SBS	Stuttgarter Bibelstudien
SOTSMS	Society for Old Testament Study Monograph Series
STDJ	Studies on the Texts of the Desert of Judah
TTZ	*Trierer theologische Zeitschrift*
TynBul	*Tyndale Bulletin*
TZ	*Theologische Zeitschrift*
VT	*Vetus Testamentum*
VTSup	VT, Supplements
WBC	Word Biblical Commentary
WMANT	Wissenschaftliche Monographien zum Alten und Neuen Testament
WTJ	*Westminster Theological Journal*
ZAH	*Zeitschrift für Althebraistik*
ZAS	*Zeitschrift für Aegyptische Sprache*
ZAW	*Zeitschrift für die alttestamentliche Wissenschaft*
ZTK	*Zeitschrift für Theologie und Kirche*

Introduction

Epistemology in the Bible

Epistemology, the theory of knowledge, constitutes one of the oldest subdivisions of philosophy. Yet its application within biblical studies has only recently been explored. This is partly because the traditional field of "religious epistemology" has largely focused on the question of how we can know that God exists. For the biblical authors, that existence is presumed. Nevertheless, scriptural texts give rise to numerous epistemological questions concerning what we can know about God and how we can know it. Beyond the realm of knowledge about the divine, these texts also provide rich opportunities for the exploration of our knowledge of the world and human nature.

While the formal philosophical term "epistemology" is obviously not to be found within the Bible, it is nevertheless the case that many of the central questions which epistemology treats are addressed by Biblical Wisdom Literature. Indeed, recent scholarship has increasingly focused upon the epistemology that is implicitly represented in these texts. For example, Qoheleth proclaims that he will actively search for wisdom (Qoh 1:13); a father teaches his son to follow the path of wisdom (Proverbs 4); and Job laments that, despite intense seeking, wisdom is ultimately hidden from human minds (Job 28).

Scholarly discussion of biblical epistemology has explored such questions as how new knowledge is acquired, how it is transmitted from one generation to the next, and how its truth value can be tested. There has been something of a traditional scholarly consensus that Biblical Wisdom Literature contains a primarily empirical epistemology (i. e., knowledge is acquired by abstracting generalized truths from observations of the world at large). More recent scholarship, however, has increasingly employed methodologies drawn from the field of epistemic philosophy that move beyond the basic assumption of empirical observation to explore other possibilities of how human beings acquire knowledge (while being cautious not to artificially impose later intellectual constructs onto the biblical *Sitz-im-Leben*).

So far, this ongoing discussion within the scholarly community has given relatively little consideration to the inherent epistemology of the wisdom motifs in the Psalter. While much attention has focused on attempts to identify a unique genre of "Wisdom Psalms," these efforts have yielded scant consensus as to which psalms ought to be so classified. Beyond such classification efforts, there is a need to situate the wisdom components in the Psalter within the overall context of Biblical Wisdom Literature. These components (such as vocabulary, themes, syntactic structures, etc.) are found throughout the psalms and are not limited to a specific "wisdom" genre. An epistemological analysis of how a psalmist employs such components would help to explain the function and purpose of a given psalm.

Focus of the Present Study

The purpose of this study is to provide a comparative analysis of the epistemology of Psalms 1, 73, 90, and 107, and to explore the implications of their respective epistemological features for our understanding of the canonical structure of the Psalter. Given this purpose, I have selected these texts on the basis of two primary criteria: (1) epistemological content, and (2) canonical placement within the Psalter.

Of these four texts, only Psalm 1 (a "Torah psalm") is consistently classified as a wisdom psalm, although the three others have been acknowledged as possessing wisdom qualities. Each of these texts, in its own way, addresses the fundamental problem of why people suffer and what they can do to make sense out of their suffering and perhaps alleviate it. Hence, there is a shared focus among the four psalms on one of the great questions about the human condition. This common thread ought to facilitate the comparison of the function of the wisdom elements in each text. Through the psalmist's use of metaphor and narrative, as well as the extent of his acknowledgement of divine intervention within human life, each poem presents a unique worldview that helps to shape the meaning of knowledge within the text.

These texts are also significant insofar as each one stands at the beginning of one of the five "Books" within the Psalter (Psalms 1, 73, 90, and 107 begin Books I, III, IV, and V, respectively). This analysis will therefore provide a heretofore unexplored synchronic epistemological perspective to help advance our understanding of the canonical structure of the Psalter.

In Chapter 1, I shall discuss the philosophical underpinnings of epistemology that are most relevant to the study of biblical texts and develop a diagnostic method for the identification and analysis of the epistemological features within a biblical text.

Chapter 2 will present a "case study" of Proverbs 1–9, a text that has been the focus of considerable epistemological study. After a detailed literature review, I shall apply my own diagnostic methodology to this text as a prelude to the following analysis of the chosen psalms.

Chapter 3 will provide a discussion of the scholarly debate over the meaning of "Wisdom Psalm" as a genre within form-critical Psalter studies, followed by a literature review of recent scholarship on the wisdom qualities of selected psalms. Such scholarship is directly relevant to my epistemological analysis of psalm texts.

Chapter 4 will present the Masoretic text of Psalm 1 with my translation, text-critical analysis, and comments on select poetic features (with a particular focus on the use of metaphor). The wisdom motifs within the psalm will be identified and the diagnostic method developed in Chapter 1 will be applied in evaluating the epistemology of these motifs.

Chapters 5 through 7 will repeat the analysis of Chapter 4 for Psalms 73, 90, and 107, respectively.

A concluding chapter will compare and contrast the epistemologies of the four psalms. I shall likewise employ that comparative analysis to explore the placement of these psalms within the canonical structure of the Psalter.

Chapter I.
Basic Issues in Epistemology and the Sociology of Knowledge

In this chapter I will elucidate the basic theoretical framework of the epistemological analysis to be followed in this study. The level of detail presented here is rudimentary and only covers those aspects that are germane to the biblical analysis I will be pursuing. The interested reader who wishes to conduct a more thorough exploration of the issues discussed below is referred to the current epistemological literature (particularly, "social epistemology").[1] This chapter will treat of epistemological questions solely within the context of the philosophy and sociology of knowledge. The following chapter will situate such questions within the context of the biblical world, and will review some of the applications of this discipline to biblical studies by previous scholars.

Preliminaries

Although this study treats of epistemological issues with reference to biblical texts, it is nevertheless important to stress that it should not be situated within the sub-discipline known as "religious epistemology," which primarily concerns itself with questions about whether God exists, and, if so, what we can know about the divine being (and how we can know it). The following quotation from a recent important monograph in this field displays the vast disparity between the worldview of a religious epistemologist and that of the authors of biblical texts: "...we'll use the overused term 'God' as a maximally honorific *title* that connotes an authoritatively and morally perfect being who is inherently worthy of worship as wholehearted adoration, love, and trust, even if God doesn't actually exist."[2] Contrary to the inherent skepticism of religious epistemology, my assumption throughout this study is that, unless I state otherwise, the existence of God is presumed by the biblical authors (how well God can be known or understood differs, of course, from one biblical text to another).

---

1 See, for example, Richard Feldman, *Epistemology* (Upper Saddle River, NJ: Prentice Hall, 2003), and references therein.
2 Paul K. Moser, *The Elusive God: Reorienting Religious Epistemology* (Cambridge: Cambridge University Press, 2008) 1 (original emphasis).

By "epistemology of a biblical text," I do not mean what the text can teach us about the existence and nature of God, but rather how the author of the text (or the characters within the text) conceives of knowledge and the process of acquiring and teaching it. That knowledge need not be solely about God, but may also concern the physical world or human nature. It should be noted that the epistemology of a biblical text will generally not be stated explicitly, but must be discerned from the content of its literary components such as narrative, dialogue, gnomic sayings, and poetry. The purpose of this chapter is to develop the tools that will make such discernment possible.

Finally, while it may appear that the present chapter is overly technical and not obviously relevant to the discipline of biblical studies, I contend that any effective epistemological exploration of biblical texts requires a precise analytical lexicon and methodology, particularly when multiple texts are being compared (as different biblical authors may employ diverse vocabularies or styles of expression).[3]

Theory of Knowledge

What does it mean to know something? The act of knowing comprises numerous types of knowledge. For example, there is acquaintance knowledge ("I know that woman" – which may imply either that I have a personal relationship with her, or simply that I am aware of several public facts about her life) and technical knowledge ("I know *how* to do something"). Epistemology, however, primarily concerns itself with "propositional knowledge:" "I know *that*..." ("I know that the sky is blue;" "I know that there is a cat in the next room;" etc.). Six possible sources of propositional knowledge are generally recognized: (1) perception by the physical senses; (2) memory recall; (3) testimony of others; (4) introspection (e. g., knowledge of one's own internal state – "I am tired," etc.); (5) reason (e. g., deriving scientific knowledge from observed data); and (6) rational insight (e. g., deduction from *a priori* arithmetical or logical axioms). While these sources need not be mutually exclusive, certain epistemological schools claim primacy for a

---

3 The advantage of developing such diagnostic tools will become apparent in the following chapter, in which it will be seen that prior studies of epistemological issues by biblical scholars sometimes employ a confusing variety of philosophical and literary terms that are used with different meanings by different authors. For an exploration of the qualities of analytic epistemology (similar to those discussed in the present study) inherent in those of the Hebrew scriptures found outside of the wisdom tradition, see J. Gericke, "The Epistemology of Israelite Religion: Introductory Proposals for a Descriptive Approach," *OTE* 24 (2011) 49–73.

given source of knowledge over others. Empiricism, for example, contends (at least in its strongest form) that all knowledge ultimately derives only from sensory experience, while various schools of Rationalism hold that some propositions are known by intuition alone, and that all other propositions can be deduced from these.

But what does it mean for one to know a proposition? Traditional epistemological analysis defines knowledge as a "justified, true, belief."[4] More precisely, a subject S can be said to know a proposition p if:

i.   p is true,
ii. S believes p,
iii. S is justified in believing p,
iv. S's justification for believing p does not essentially depend on any falsehood.[5]

The third condition requires that knowledge be based upon reasonable grounds. Thus, a man may know that his wife is flipping a coin in the next room, and he may believe that the coin has come up heads. Perhaps the coin actually did come up heads (i.e., his belief is true), nevertheless, he cannot be said to "know" this result, for he has no sound reason for holding that belief. The fourth condition is meant to insure that S does not hold his belief primarily because of another's attempt to deceive him, or because of his own faulty judgment (while, say, under the influence of medication).

Given such an understanding of knowledge, a central question posed by epistemology is: under what conditions can a belief be said to be justified? Standard epistemological analysis holds that S's belief in proposition p at time t is justified (i.e., well founded) if, and only if:

i.   believing p is justified for S at t,
ii. S believes p on the basis of evidence that supports p.[6]

For example, suppose Sue listens to the weather report and comes to believe that it will rain this afternoon (note that we are concerned here with *belief* only, not

---

4 The philosophically astute reader will recall that, since Edmund Gettier's seminal critique of this definition, it is no longer held to be an adequate description of the elements of knowledge (see E. Gettier, "Is Justified True Belief Knowledge?" *Analysis* 23 [1963] 121–23). The subtle nuances of Gettier's analysis, however, need not concern us here, insofar as the traditional definition of knowledge is adequate for the degree of epistemological exploration that I will be undertaking with respect to select biblical texts.
5 See Feldman, *Epistemology*, 37. This definition partly addresses Gettier's objections.
6 Ibid., 45–47.

with whether or not it actually does rain). Her act of believing the weather service is justified insofar as she has come to know that the weather service is generally a reliable source of scientific information (condition i), while her belief that it will rain is based on the evidence that the weather service has amassed in producing its prediction (rain clouds to the west, barometric pressure, etc.; condition ii).

It follows from the above definition that justified belief depends critically upon the structure of one's justifying evidence. Traditionally, epistemology has been broadly divided between two approaches to justification of belief: foundationalism and coherentism.[7]

Foundationalism

Foundationalism is grounded upon two fundamental claims:
i.   there exist justified basic beliefs,
ii.   all justified non-basic beliefs are justified by virtue of their relation to justified basic beliefs.[8]

A justified belief, b, is a "justified basic belief" if it is not justified on the basis of any other beliefs. For example, some would claim (like Descartes) that awareness of one's own existence is a justified basic belief. The challenge for any foundationalist theory of justification is threefold: (1) do justified basic beliefs in fact exist, and, if so, what sort of knowledge do they concern; (2) how is one able to justify such beliefs, if not on the basis of any other beliefs; (3) how are non-basic beliefs related to basic beliefs, such that the former can be justified by the latter? In practice, it is exceedingly difficult to prove that any non-trivial beliefs are truly both justified and basic (the interested reader is referred to the vast philosophical literature on this question).

If, however, one is willing to relax the strict definition of a basic belief (i.e., that it not be based upon any other belief), then it is possible to formulate a "modest foundationalism" that is both plausible and practically useful. Modest foundationalism is based upon three principles:

---

7 Modern epistemological research has substantially expanded the possible foundations for evidentiary justification beyond these two alternatives – see, for example, P. K. Moser, *The Oxford Handbook of Epistemology* (Oxford: Oxford University Press, 2002). For our purposes, however, the above simple dichotomy will suffice.
8 Feldman, *Epistemology*, 52.

i.   basic beliefs are those beliefs that are spontaneously formed – these are typically beliefs about the external world that result from sensory experience,
ii. a spontaneously formed belief is justified provided that it constitutes a proper response to experience and that it cannot be falsified by any other evidence that the believer has,
iii. non-basic beliefs are justified when they are supported by strong inductive inferences.[9]

The second condition ensures that spontaneous beliefs are not considered as justified in the face of contrary evidence. More precisely, suppose that a proposition p is supported by a piece of evidence e (i.e., e is evidence for believing p). Then an additional piece of evidence d "defeats" e if $(e+d)$ does not constitute evidence for believing p. For example, a colorblind person may genuinely "see" a red ball that he has drawn out of a bag, but he would not be justified in believing that the ball was red if he also knew that only yellow balls were in the bag.

The third condition relaxes the demand that non-basic beliefs can only be arrived at by deductive reasoning, beginning from basic beliefs. Strict foundationalism adheres to such a requirement for deduction. Yet most people do not arrive at their beliefs through pure deduction (i.e., beginning with basic, *a priori* beliefs and then carefully deducing, step by step, subsequent beliefs that are linked in a dependent chain with the prior beliefs). In actuality, beliefs are held on the grounds of such non-basic justifications as probability or reasonable inference based upon one's past experiences (that is, upon inductive reasoning, rather than deductive).

Two important types of strong inductive inference included in modest foundationalism are "enumerative inference" and "inference to the best explanation."[10] The former is a type of probability argument: if one observes that a large number of things of a given type all display a particular property, then one infers that the next thing of that same type encountered will display the same property (for example, drawing fifty red balls from a bag in succession leads one to infer that the fifty-first ball drawn will also be red). The latter form of inference obtains when one considers a proposition to be justified because it is part of the best explanation available to explain one's justified basic beliefs. To cite a trivial example: if one were to directly observe falling drops of water, black clouds overhead, and to hear the sound of thunder, one would be justified in inferring that a rainstorm was occurring – such a belief provides the best explan-

---

9 Ibid., 70 – 75.
10 Ibid., 72.

ation for the observed data (although no effort was made to trace either the drops of water or the thunderous sound to the precise location of the black clouds).

Coherentism

As an alternative to foundationalism, which is grounded upon justified basic beliefs, coherentism considers the entire system of all beliefs, taken as a whole, without any particular beliefs being privileged as "basic." Within such a scheme, a belief is justified to the degree that it is more or less consonant ("coheres") with the entire belief system. More precisely, coherentism rests upon two central ideas:

i. only beliefs can justify other beliefs – i.e., nothing other than a belief can contribute to justification,
ii. every justified belief depends in part on other beliefs for its justification (i.e., there are no justified basic beliefs).[11]

The first condition establishes that knowledge cannot be absolutely grounded upon such things as sensory experience or expert testimony (only upon one's *belief* about the nature of such experience or testimony, which might well be false). The second condition establishes that the only way to determine whether a belief might in fact constitute knowledge is to consider the entire range of beliefs upon which it depends.

Consider the following example. Suppose a person generally believes that the science of meteorology yields reliable weather predictions. He holds this based on a wide range of personal beliefs: he studied meteorology in college, he has amassed a lifetime of experience of checking the daily weather against the weather service's predictions, he keeps a barometer in his backyard and practices amateur meteorology, etc. Now suppose that he has planned a picnic for the coming weekend and strongly hopes for fair weather. During the week, a co-worker tells him that she has a hunch that it will be sunny on Saturday. He is delighted by the news and believes it to be true. According to a coherentist analysis, his belief about Saturday's weather is not justified. One could summarize his coherent belief about weather prediction as: "meteorological science provides the best means for determining likely weather patterns." His belief in an unscientific hunch does not cohere with his overall belief system, and thus

---

11 Ibid., 61–62.

is not justified. Hence, even if it were sunny on that particular Saturday, his belief would not constitute actual knowledge.

Although this simple example appears fairly straightforward, more complex situations raise a series of challenging issues for coherentist systems of justification. In particular, Feldman notes that coherentism must address two primary questions: (1) how is a "system of beliefs" actually defined, how does one determine its constituent members; (2) what does it mean for a belief to cohere with a system of beliefs, how is coherence actually defined? While coherentist epistemology does not provide a conclusive answer to such questions, Feldman offers a helpful criterion that I will adopt as the basic requirement for accepting a belief as justified within a coherentist system. Consider a subject S and a proposition p, then: "S is justified in believing p if and only if the coherence value of S's system of beliefs would be greater if it included a belief in p than it would be if it did not include that belief."[12] In the above example, the person's belief about Saturday's weather does not strengthen, but rather helps to undermine, the coherence of his overall belief system about the reliability of meteorological science. It is apparent that, as one gains wider experience, a belief system may change (for example, if the person were to encounter enough accurate "hunches" about the weather, he may well come to conclude that a hunch is as accurate, or even more so, in predicting weather patterns than the weather service's science). It is precisely this capacity for evolution and change in a belief system that makes it attractive to coherentists. Over time, that evolution ought to approach the true state of affairs with greater and greater accuracy. Furthermore, it is not bound by the foundationalist requirement that one has correctly identified the corpus of justified basic beliefs upon which all knowledge depends.

As the epistemological literature makes clear, foundationalism and coherentism need not be understood as mutually exclusive. For example, the coherentist justification for a given belief might serve as the grounds for that belief's being accepted as a justified basic belief within a (moderate) foundationalist system. In the epistemological discussion of the biblical texts to be explored in this study, I will often have occasion to reference both coherentist and foundationalist features within a given text. Indeed, each of these epistemological traditions provides helpful diagnostic tools to advance both literary and theological comparisons of the writings I will be considering.

---

12 Ibid., 65.

The Sociology of Knowledge

The discussion thus far of the theory of knowledge may imply that one's holding of a justified, basic belief is a purely individual process, dependent solely, for example, upon one's own sensory experience or personal system of beliefs. In fact, however, even a cursory reflection reveals that the acquisition of knowledge relies upon an extensive network of interpersonal relations.

When the foundationalist attempts to proceed by induction from a basic belief to a non-basic one, he draws on a vast array of personal experiences that he has gained largely through interaction with other people: family, teachers, coworkers, etc. For most (likely, all) people, the laws of probability ("enumerative inference") are not first deduced purely from mathematical axioms, but are learned matter-of-factly through the expectations of given outcomes in everyday life (e. g., the fact that father has come home from work every day at six o'clock makes it highly likely that he will do so tomorrow). The understanding of a "best explanation" to account for non-basic beliefs is even more socially dependent. We learn, largely through being taught by others, what the most likely explanation for a series of observations might be. But the content of that explanation is socially qualified: the same rainstorm from which one society infers the presence of clouds with high water density is used by another society to infer the activity of benevolent gods.

The coherentist is also dependent upon the belief systems of others. In the weather example cited above, the person's trust in the validity of meteorological science relies upon the beliefs of the science teachers who taught him about the weather, upon the beliefs of the meteorologists (whose forecasts he listens to) about their scientific techniques, and so forth.

While it appears beyond question that knowledge has a social dimension, to what extent may one contend that knowledge is *socially constructed?* That question has been extensively addressed in the seminal works of P. Berger and T. Luckmann (hereafter, BL).[13] In this section I will summarize their views on the sociology of knowledge; these views will be substantially employed in the epistemological analyses of this study. In doing so, I do not claim that their approach is either unique among – or superior to – those of other researchers in the discipline of social epistemology. They do, however, provide an epistemological

---

13 See especially P. L. Berger and T. Luckmann, *The Social Construction of Reality: A Treatise in the Sociology of Knowledge* (New York: Anchor Books, 1966); P. L. Berger, *The Precarious Vision: A Sociologist Looks at Social Fictions and Christian Faith* (Garden City, NY: Doubleday, 1961); ibid., *The Sacred Canopy: Elements of a Sociological Theory of Religion* (Garden City, NY: Doubleday, 1967).

framework that is particularly useful (largely because of its clarity) for the biblical study I will be pursuing.

Social Stock of Knowledge

BL use the term "social stock of knowledge" to refer to all knowledge that encompasses a particular situation of one's life. It is "social" in the sense that it is shared by all people who participate in that situation (e. g., all of the residents of a town, all skilled metalworkers, all of the members of the middle class, etc.). Furthermore, it constitutes knowledge that has meaning only insofar as it is collectively believed. For example, a "poor" man knows that he is poor, and a wealthy man also knows that the same man is poor, so long as they are both members of the same society. The social stock of knowledge provides the justified belief that certain criteria define "poverty." But were the same man to be observed by a resident of a different society, he might well be classified as "middle class," or even "wealthy."[14]

Much of the social stock of knowledge is what BL term "recipe knowledge," that is, knowledge that helps one attain basic goals in life and solve practical problems. For most people, such knowledge is not acquired through structured lessons, but is simply "absorbed" as one is raised within a given community. Nor is such knowledge the product of extensive reflection, but rather it seems to the inhabitants of a particular community to be just "the way things have always been done or thought."

One of the consequences of recipe knowledge is that people tend to be "type cast" into preset roles. These roles can be defined, for example, by familial relations (mother, father, etc.) or occupation. No one consciously sets out to learn what a father is, or what a baker does; rather, these roles are observed and experienced in the persons one interacts with, and such interactions provide implicit education concerning those roles. BL stress that, because of these preset roles, people within a society tend to apprehend each other via "typificatory schemes."[15] Thus, a member of a given society need not develop a significant interpersonal relationship with most members of that society in order to place them within a well-ordered social structure.

That structure is both maintained with considerable stability over several generations and is readily absorbed because of the use of symbols and symbol-

---

14 Berger and Luckmann, *Social Construction*, 41–46.
15 Ibid., 30–32.

ism, of which language is the primary representative.[16] Language provides the framework by which typificatory schemes take on an abstract reality all their own (e. g., the concept of "father," the concept of "baker"). The abstraction can often be grasped without the need for an extensive body of personal experience (i. e., one need not personally know many fathers or many bakers in order to understand their function). In addition to language's ability to represent abstract qualities derived from particular, real experiences, it can also translate abstract qualities into objectively real elements of everyday life. For example, the purely lexical distinction between "familiar" and "formal" address within certain languages (e. g., "du" and "Sie" in German) has the capacity to convey the level of intimacy governing all the elements within an entire social sphere – that level of presumed intimacy (which involves much more than just the choice of pronouns in a conversation) becomes a reality for the speaker/listener as soon as the relevant language is employed. In my study of the epistemological qualities of the language of the psalms, I will particularly focus on the power of poetic metaphor to create an objectively real world for the speaker/listener.[17]

So long as there is relatively little intimate human interaction among the members of a society, language (and other social symbols) allows people to be confidently typecast and fit into their proper roles, and the validity of the language used for this purpose is not questioned. When, however, there is face-to-face encounter and growing familiarity, the typificatory schemes are opened to question and challenge: no longer can members simply be reduced to fairly one-dimensional roles. What had previously been uncritically accepted as justified, true, belief (i. e., knowledge) may now be doubted or altogether rejected.

According to BL, the process by which any society develops, maintains, and defends its social stock of knowledge is a highly dialectic interplay among three movements which they designate as "externalization," "objectivation," and "internalization."

Externalization

By "externalization," BL refer to that process by which the social stock of knowledge is originally built up. While not attempting a detailed anthropological analysis, they hypothesize that in the earliest stages of the development of society,

---

16 Ibid., 40 – 41.
17 The importance of metaphor to the basic perception of reality is discussed in a later section of this chapter.

simple activities necessary for survival (hunting, building, etc.) eventually become habitual and give rise to social roles among the various members. While such roles are the forerunners of the typificatory schemes referred to above, for the first generation of the society, there was a clear, first-hand awareness of how these roles were created. The division of the roles among the various members is neither seen as inevitable nor as "the way things have always been."

Over time, however, certain experiences are selectively retained by memory with greater detail than other experiences. Those experiences most directly connected to one's survival and wellbeing become, as BL term it, "sedimented" in the memory.[18] Just as, in a fully formed society, language is the means for preserving and transmitting the definition of social roles, so also in a proto-society language is the principal way in which sedimentation is both preserved in the mind of the first generation and becomes the foundation for more permanent social structures that can endure for subsequent generations. The formation of such structures is the focus of objectivation.

Objectivation

Because of language, the information preserved by sedimentation can be effectively communicated to later generations without the need for them to re-experience the original formative events of their forbears. Eventually, roles become established and society becomes "institutionalized": roles make it possible for social institutions to exist.[19] These institutions (e. g., class structures, divisions of labor, legal systems, etc.) are perceived by new generations as the objective reality into which one is simply born. There is no longer any awareness that such institutions are the products of human effort; BL term this the "reification" of social reality. The epistemological implication of reification is that many social beliefs which one might consider as justified and *basic* (i. e., part of the perceived "permanent reality" of society) may in fact have originated in a complex system of *coherent* beliefs held by the founders of the society.

When an institutional order is passed from one generation to the next, it is necessary for that order to be received as acceptable and "correct"; otherwise, it may be threatened by those who question its legitimacy. The process by which the members of a society attempt to explain the social order that they are pass-

---

18 Berger and Luckmann, *Social Construction*, 67–70.
19 Ibid., 74.

ing on to the next generation is termed "legitimation" by BL.[20] Insofar as its primary function is to convincingly transmit the stock of socially constructed knowledge from a more experienced group to a less experienced one, legitimation is an important component of social pedagogy. As such, it must accomplish four goals: (1) to establish the relationships among the various roles of the institutional order at any given time ("horizontal" integration); (2) to situate the entire lifespan of an individual within the total institutional order ("vertical" integration); (3) to explain why the social institution is organized the way that it is (cognitive goal); and (4) to explain why one ought to perform the role he has been given or has taken on (normative goal).

BL describe four progressive stages of legitimation which emerge as a society develops.[21] The first stage occurs as soon as language arises. This incipient legitimation is almost automatic, without any conscious attempt to justify the nature of society: as one learns his native tongue he is implicitly exposed to the structure of the society which has produced that language. The second level of legitimation proceeds via simple explanatory schemes that attempt to describe why things are the way they are. Through proverbs, maxims, legends, and folk tales (often conveyed via poetry), numerous examples are provided which reveal different individual facets of the institutional order, rather than presenting an all-encompassing view. In the third level, explicit theories are developed to explain why the different sectors of the institutional order exist and special personnel are trained to perform highly specific roles. This is the level that accounts for the development of such groups as a priestly class, a ruling class, etc. The highest, and most sophisticated, level of legitimation occurs when an overarching scheme is constructed that situates every member and every aspect of the social institution within a coherent whole: everything can be "put into its proper place." BL refer to such complete schemes as "symbolic universes."[22]

A symbolic universe represents an entire conceptual world that encompasses all socially constructed knowledge. One example of such a symbolic universe is a "divinely established order," in which everything is believed to be created and structured by the gods. Within this scheme, the nature of every conceivable entity can be explained and accounted for.

Because of its all-encompassing character, a symbolic universe is able to order and structure the perception of reality by means of what BL term *nomic* (i.e., ordering) processes. "Experiences belonging to different spheres of reality

---

20 Ibid., 92.
21 Ibid., 94–99.
22 Ibid., 99–104. See also Z. Zevit, *The Religions of Ancient Israel: A Synthesis of Parallactic Approaches* (London/New York: Continuum, 2001) 18–22.

[can be] integrated by incorporation in the same, overarching universe of meaning."[23] For example, although the experience of the realm of one's night-time dreams can seem quite real to the dreamer, the symbolic universe of "everyday life" is capable of situating that dream realm as a temporary subset of reality, caused merely by one's subconscious mental processes during sleep, etc. "In this way, the symbolic universe orders and thereby legitimates everyday roles, priorities, and operating procedures by placing them *sub specie universi*, that is, in the context of the most general frame of reference conceivable."[24]

The symbolic universe can also order the temporal stages of one's life: what it "means" (i.e., how one ought to behave, how one can expect to be perceived by others, etc.) to be a child, an adolescent, etc., while making one's past intelligible to him and ameliorating the fearful uncertainty regarding one's future. In this regard, an important function of the symbolic universe for the individual is to help him give meaning to his mortality. In the face of the inevitability of death (one's own and that of others), one needs to continue to function "normally" within society. Here, the symbolic universe exercises a transcendent power, allowing one to see beyond the limits of his personal horizon. For example, within a divinely established symbolic universe one may be encouraged by the hope of an afterlife; within an atheistic, utilitarian symbolic universe, on the other hand, one may be comforted by the knowledge of one's useful contribution to the improvement of society for future generations, and so on.

At the collective level, the symbolic universe orders social history itself. All collective events of a given society are located within a coherent whole that properly situates the relative roles of past, present, and future. The symbolic universe provides a common memory that is shared by all members of the society: everyone belongs to a meaningful universe that existed long before them and that will perdure long after them. For example, a society with a divinely established symbolic universe may represent its past in such a way that all former events are understood as being irresistibly directed by the gods toward the establishment of both present reality and a future goal.

A symbolic universe is thus the highest expression of the interplay between externalization – whereby social institutions are formed by human actions – and objectivation – whereby those same institutions are eventually perceived as permanent realities that have always existed. BL summarize this interplay thus: "Human existence is, *ab initio*, an ongoing externalization. As man externalizes himself, he constructs the world *into* which he externalizes himself. In the proc-

---

23 Berger and Luckmann, *Social Construction*, 97.
24 Ibid., 99.

ess of externalization, he projects his own meanings into reality. Symbolic universes, which proclaim that *all* reality is humanly meaningful and call upon the *entire* cosmos to signify the validity of human existence, constitute the furthest reaches of this projection."[25]

Internalization

The final movement of the dialectic interplay responsible for the social construction of reality is termed internalization by BL. If legitimation concerns the attempt by a society to explain why it is structured as it is, then internalization describes the process by which such explanations are actually received and absorbed.[26] Legitimation and internalization are thus the two moments of that pedagogical enterprise by which the self-understanding of a society is conveyed from one generation to the next.

BL identify two principal aspects of internalization: primary and secondary socialization. Primary socialization refers to the process whereby a child is born into a world that is already the product of the externalization and objectivation of others. The child not only takes on the roles and attitudes of his birth society, he takes on its entire *world*, and he does so in an automatic, non-reflective manner. One's native language is both the most important content and the most important instrument of this initial socialization. At this stage, there is no problem with identification of either oneself or of others: society presents the child with pre-defined roles and social definitions, and these are accepted without question – they constitute the only world he knows. In the language of legitimation, primary socialization provides a symbolic universe for the child which is never completely lost, even in adulthood. And yet, as BL note, such a universe makes appear as *necessity*, what is in fact "a bundle of contingencies."[27] These contingent relations can be, and often are, subject to challenge as one grows

---

25 Ibid., 104.
26 Berger (*The Sacred Canopy*, 4) summarizes the three principal movements as follows: "Externalization is the ongoing outpouring of human being into the world, both in the physical and the mental activity of men. Objectivation is the attainment by the products of this activity (again both physical and mental) of a reality that confronts its original producers as a facticity external to and other than themselves. Internalization is the reappropriation by men of this same reality, transforming it once again from structures of the objective world into structures of the subjective consciousness. It is through externalization that society is a human product. It is through objectivation that society becomes a reality *sui generis*. It is through internalization that man is a product of society."
27 Ibid., 135.

in experience. Such stresses are potentially threatening to the stability of the society. For example, a person raised in poverty and initially imbued with the identity of a "poor person," may realize that he need not remain so. While it may well be in the interest of society that such a person increase his standing by learning a trade, it is not desirable that he do so by learning how to steal.

In order to prevent such stresses from fracturing society, a secondary socialization process becomes necessary as members mature. Secondary socialization is basically any process subsequent to primary socialization that serves to integrate an individual into new roles in his society. This is the means, for example, by which one acquires the special skills resulting from the social division of labor: one learns a trade, acquires specialized education, becomes a member of a particular class (priest, ruler, artisan, etc.), and so forth. Because secondary socialization is not nearly so deeply embedded in one's life as primary socialization, it requires constant maintenance and reinforcement. The primary agents of such maintenance are the "significant others" in one's life: family, friends, employers, etc. The primary activity by which they accomplish their goal is conversation. Face-to-face conversation is the process whereby the legitimating power of language is actualized in one's life.[28] Questions that arise which might threaten one's identity or purpose can be raised and addressed by more experienced experts who perform the same social role toward which the novice aspires. In most cases, doubts or criticisms can be quelled via ordinary conversation with one's significant others (the authority of an expert's opinion or ridicule by one's peers are examples of how this might happen).

If, however, one's doubts about the correctness of a given social institution become strong enough, he may begin publicly espousing such views and criticizing the status quo.[29] Such a person is likely to be dubbed a "deviant" or "heretic" by the society, which will attempt to eliminate (or at least minimize) his challenge to its structure. BL identify two principal self-preservation techniques that social institutions employ in this effort: "therapy" and "nihilation."[30]

In therapy, the prevailing social institution seeks to recast the views of the deviant as perversions or denials of the principles of the reigning symbolic universe. For example, a confirmed capitalist living in a socialist society might be accused of failing to appreciate the fundamental human desire for the common good because of the skewed ethical values he absorbed during a troubled child-

---

28 Ibid., 153.
29 BL (*Social Construction*, 156) refer to the situation in which one's primary socialization is genuinely transformed into a different perception of reality as "alternation."
30 Ibid., 112–18.

hood. In such cases, the techniques of legitimation are employed to "re-social-ize" the deviant as a compliant member of society.

These techniques must be both explicit and intensive insofar as they essen-tially aim to reproduce the effects of primary socialization on the deviant individ-ual. BL note that the power of ritual acts – drawing on, for example, the histor-ical tradition of the society, or the transcendent power of the divine – is often employed as part of this process. So, too, is the mediation of significant others in the deviant's life. In order for their influence on him to be effective and last-ing, it is necessary that he maintain a strong sense of identification with them, and they need to provide a supportive community that closely embraces the prin-ciples of the prevailing symbolic universe. If the impact of "alternation" (see n. 29) is successfully to be reversed, then the former deviant must be segregated from his prior world of existence. For example: he will need new conversation partners (to reinforce the standard social views); his past will have to be "rein-terpreted" in such a way that he comes to understand his prior views as naturally evolving into the standard social views he now endorses (BL cite the example of early Christians interpreting the Hebrew scriptures as the "Old Testament," lead-ing up to the "New"), etc.

Nihilation entails a much stronger form of corrective action. In this case, all views other than those sanctioned by the regnant symbolic universe are concep-tually "liquidated" and their proponents are denied any existence within that universe. A deviant holding such views is deemed "sub-human" or "barbarian" and considered to be beyond the reach of legitimating influences. BL note that nihilation is most readily practiced against groups that are foreign to a given so-ciety (i.e, members of a different society that collectively endorse a view consid-ered deviant by the native society, rather than a deviant individual within the native society). In the case of the above example, nihilation might be practiced by a socialist society against a neighboring capitalist society: rather than attempt therapeutic reform of the capitalists, socialists simply consider them incapable of ever being socially acceptable.

It is apparent from the above discussion that externalization, objectivation, and internalization do not follow one another in a linear fashion. All three are usually in evidence within a given society at any one time. In the analysis of the psalm texts to be presented in subsequent chapters, I shall have occasion to identify and evaluate the interplay of each of these three movements within the worldview of the psalmist. Such identifications and evaluations will be ben-eficial for comparing and contrasting the texts under discussion and for helping to understand their placement within the Psalter.

While BL stress the role of language in the legitimation and internalization processes within a society's worldview, they do not provide an explicit analysis of how various linguistic features help to achieve those ends. In the following section I shall consider the significance of *metaphor*—both as an explicit construction of the spoken/written word, and as a societal concept that underlies a culture's self-understanding—for the structuring of one's perception of reality.

How a Society Constructs and Understands Its Worldview: Epistemological Significance of Metaphor

M. Kearney, in his anthropological study of the worldviews of disparate cultures, defines the worldview of a people as "their way of looking at reality. It consists of basic assumptions and images that provide a more or less coherent, though not necessarily accurate, way of thinking about the world."[31] Such "basic assumptions and images" are largely reflected in, and conveyed by, a society's foundational texts (e.g., its myths, histories, sacred writings, etc.). Indeed, every written text operates within a particular worldview which provides an explanation for why the world seems to be the way that it is.

Furthermore, within lengthy or composite texts, multiple worldviews may be represented. Consider, for example, the Book of Genesis. While the two creation stories in Genesis (Gen 1:1–2:4a; 2:4b-25) both represent a worldview in which the natural world is the product of God's deliberate ordering, the two stories portray a different worldview understanding of the origin of human beings (Gen 1:27 versus Gen 2:7, 21–22). Other worldview perspectives that can be found within Genesis include the idea that human beings are fundamentally prone to sinfulness (3:1–7; 4:5–8) but equally fundamentally oriented toward relationship with one another (2:18–24), and the supposition that the human will and the divine will are in continuous and direct interaction (e.g., 2:15–17; 3:16–19; 11:5–9).

These worldviews help to define the shared body of knowledge among the members of a society. From within the worldviews portrayed in Genesis, for example, human beings can "know" (after the time of Noah) that whenever they

---

31 M. Kearney, *World View* (Novato, CA: Chandler and Sharp, 1984) 41. For extensive discussions of the concept of worldview, see, for example: N. Smart, *Worldviews: Crosscultural Explorations of Human Beliefs* (New York: Charles Scribner's Sons, 1983); R. A. Simkins, *Creator and Creation: Nature in the Worldview of Ancient Israel* (Peabody, MA: Hendrickson, 1994); D. Liu, *Metaphor, Culture, and Worldview: The Case of American English and the Chinese Language* (Lanham, MD: University Press of America, 2002); D. K. Naugle, *Worldview: The History of a Concept* (Grand Rapids: Eerdmans, 2002); J. W. Sire, *Naming the Elephant: Worldview as a Concept* (Downers Grove, IL: InterVarsity, 2004); J. M. Bertrand, *(Re)Thinking Worldview: Learning to Think, Live, and Speak in This World* (Wheaton, IL: Crossway Books, 2007).

experience a rainstorm, they need not fear that it will lead to a universal flood (8:21). Joseph's brothers can "know" that to kill him would not only be a physical act of violence but would violate the order of the created world (4:9–12; 37:21–22). To be sure, a cosmogony such as Genesis will generally be much more explicit in presenting its worldviews than might, say, a brief psalm of petition, but in either case a worldview is operative.

If we now turn to explore the worldviews represented within biblical poetry, we soon encounter the prominence of metaphorical expression. Indeed, A. Berlin, a strong advocate of literary parallelism as the defining quality of biblical poetry, stresses that parallelism and metaphor are intimately connected: "I would use the term 'parallelism' to explain metaphor; and I mean it quite literally. The basic form of metaphor is parallelism, in the sense of the contiguous or syntagmatic arrangement of paradigmatic elements such that unlikes become alike. The inevitable conclusion is that both parallelism and metaphor are the defining characteristics of biblical poetry."[32]

Berlin points out that metaphor not only structures biblical poetry but also structures the society that produces and receives the poems: "Every society has its common, or stock, metaphors, and they are a window onto that society's world-view."[33] She cites as an example the pervasive metaphorical use of the sky throughout the Psalter: the personified sky which has the ability to praise, speak, and listen (Pss 19:2; 50:6; 69:35; 89:6; 96:11), or the sky as a material that can be shaped (Ps 104:2), and so forth. Such metaphors reinforce a worldview in which Yhwh is truly lord of the cosmos that he forms. At the same time, they stress an understanding of creation such that the role of every created thing is to glorify the creator. This is hardly the only way in which humanity might view creation, and hence the psalmic metaphor serves to define a unique perception of reality. Berlin concludes: "to understand the Bible's use of imagery is to perceive the network of relationships in the biblical text and in the view of the world that it represents."[34]

In a study of the treatment of creation in biblical Wisdom Literature, L. Perdue underscores this defining quality of metaphor:

> With the ability to imagine and to think rationally and conceptually, and with the capacity to express images and thoughts in words, humans have the singular ability to construct

---

32 A. Berlin, "On Reading Biblical Poetry: The Role of Metaphor," in *Congress Volume: Cambridge 1995* (ed. J. A. Emerton; VTSup 66; Leiden: Brill, 1997) 25–36. See also idem, *The Dynamics of Biblical Parallelism* (rev. and exp. ed.; Grand Rapids: Eerdmans, 2008).
33 Berlin, "On Reading Biblical Poetry," 28.
34 Ibid., 35.

meaning systems that define and interpret their world in all of its aspects. And at the heart of this world building capacity is metaphor.... Since language, through the power of imagination, both describes and shapes reality, metaphor moves beyond the merely factual description to participate in the very process of world building. *Metaphors become the semantic building blocks in the linguistic construction of reality.*[35]

Conceptual Metaphor Theory (CMT)

These observations from Berlin and Perdue warrant a more systematic consideration of the degree to which metaphorical comparison structures one's perception of reality. The research in this field has burgeoned over the past thirty years. Here, I provide a brief summary of its rudimentary elements, limiting myself to those aspects that are most germane to this study.[36]

Research into the process by which metaphors function suggests that metaphorical comparison rests on a conceptual underpinning that extends beyond a particular metaphor's linguistic expression by the spoken or written word. Building upon the pioneering work of G. Lakoff and his collaborators, "Conceptual Metaphor Theory" (CMT; within the field of cognitive linguistics) does not restrict metaphor to the ordinary linguistic meaning of the term (i. e., the direct comparison of two things, generally without use of qualifiers such as "like" or "as"). Rather, the purely linguistic understanding of the concept is broadened to include all forms of comparison: "The essence of metaphor is understanding and experiencing one kind of thing in terms of another."[37] For example, "spatial metaphors" figuratively express the qualities of something in terms of spatial orientation ("inflation is rising," etc.); "ontological metaphors" employ such tech-

---

35 L. Perdue, *Wisdom and Creation: The Theology of Wisdom Literature* (Nashville: Abingdon, 1994) 59–60 (emphasis added); see also idem, *Wisdom Literature: A Theological History* (Louisville/London: Westminster John Knox, 2007) 8–14. For a similar conclusion, argued from within the context of cognitive linguistics, see Z. Kövecses, "Metaphor: Does It Constitute or Reflect Cultural Models?" in *Metaphor in Cognitive Linguistics* (eds. R. W. Gibbs, Jr. and G. J. Steen; Amsterdam Studies in the Theory and History of Linguistic Science 175; Amsterdam: John Benjamins, 1999) 167–88. See also: Z. Kövecses, *Metaphor in Culture: Universality and Variation* (Cambridge: Cambridge University Press, 2005) and idem, *Language, Mind, and Culture: A Practical Introduction* (Oxford: Oxford University Press, 2006).

36 A good overview of modern metaphor research is provided by Z. Kövecses, *Metaphor: A Practical Introduction* (2nd ed.; Oxford: Oxford University Press, 2010, Nook); see also R. W. Gibbs, Jr., ed., *The Cambridge Handbook of Metaphor and Thought* (Cambridge: Cambridge University Press, 2008).

37 G. Lakoff and M. Johnson, *Metaphors We Live By* (Chicago: University of Chicago Press, 1980) 5.

niques as personification ("inflation is badly hurting us," etc.). Through an extensive analysis of basic metaphor types, CMT argues that virtually all aspects of how we think and act are fundamentally metaphorical in nature.

Such a claim follows from the understanding that any metaphor can be explained in terms of a "mapping" between two domains: a "source" domain and a "target" domain. The source domain supplies the qualities and relationships that are employed to help understand or describe the target domain. Thus, in the metaphorical statement: "they have hit a dead end in their research project," the source domain (a journey that has come up against a barrier which cannot be crossed) is mapped onto the target domain (people conducting research), with the obvious inference that, for some reason or other, the research cannot proceed as planned. Underlying this simple linguistic metaphor is a much broader mapping that might be formulated as LIFE IS A JOURNEY.[38] Such broad mappings are referred to as "conceptual metaphors." Kövecses summarizes: "A conceptual metaphor consists of two conceptual domains, in which one domain is understood in terms of another. A conceptual domain is any coherent organization of experience. Thus, for example, [in the case of the LIFE IS A JOURNEY conceptual metaphor] we have coherently organized knowledge about journeys that we rely on in understanding life."[39]

According to CMT, a conceptual system acquires a metaphorical definition because certain concepts are able to "fit" given sets of experiential data.[40] Consider, for example, the set of experiences comprised by a typical conversation. These include: participants (the persons speaking); speech (which itself is composed of both words and some form of syntactical structuring); stages (conversations generally have a beginning, a central development, and some form of conclusion); linear sequence (the speakers usually alternate, one speaking after the other); causation (when one person stops speaking, that is generally the signal for the other person to begin speaking with a deliberate response to what has just been said); purpose (most conversations are intended to fulfill some desired purpose of the participants, and to achieve this end in a reasonably civil and cooperative atmosphere).

Now consider that subset of the category of conversation known as an argument. It contains the same set of experiential elements, but they are of a particular type: the participants hold differing positions (they are adversaries); the speech of the argument is structured in such a way that the adversaries employ

---

38 Contemporary metaphor research follows Lakoff's convention of writing conceptual metaphors in uppercase letters.
39 Kövecses, *Metaphor*, 24.
40 Lakoff and Johnson, *Metaphors*, 61.

certain strategies and stages (they may attack the other's position, defend or re-treat from their own position, seek some form of compromise or truce, concede defeat, etc.); the linear sequence and process of causation within the argument requires that, after a verbal attack, the opponent either retreats from his position, defends it, or resorts to counterattack; the purpose of the argument, for each of the opponents, is victory over his adversary.

From the above presentation, it can be seen that the experiential elements of an argument are similar to certain elements of the concept "warfare" (adversary, attack, retreat, victory, etc.). Thus, an argument—which is a type of conversation, but has nothing directly to do with warfare—can be described by the metaphor "ARGUMENT IS WAR." Proceeding in this manner, one may contend that one's ability to understand a given conversation as an argument depends upon the fact that certain elements of the concept of warfare can be appropriately super-imposed upon the experiential data of that conversation. The metaphorical rela-tionship "ARGUMENT IS WAR" *structures* the way in which one perceives the conversation.[41]

One of the most important consequences of this structuring power of meta-phorical relationships is that it creates a coherent system for the fundamental values of a culture. Consider, for example, a culture that is partially structured by the two metaphorical relationships "MORE IS UP" (evidenced in such sayings as "his temperature is rising," "my income rose last year," etc.) and "GOOD IS UP" ("things are looking up," "she cheered me up," etc.), and that each of these metaphors is believed equally strongly by the members of the culture. In this case, a fundamental value statement such as "more is better" is coherent with both metaphorical relationships and thus constitutes a positive value. By contrast, the value statement "less is better" is not coherent with the structuring metaphors and may not be valued by the society. This illustrates the "values-ori-enting" quality of metaphor: "The most fundamental values in a culture will be coherent with the metaphorical structure of the most fundamental concepts in the culture.... So it seems that our values are not independent but must form a coherent system with the metaphorical concepts we live by. [This does not imply] that all cultural values coherent with a metaphorical system actually

---

41 Note that the metaphor not only highlights certain properties of the conversation (e. g., the importance of strategy, the adversarial nature of the exchange, etc.), but also masks other properties (e. g., the possibility for genuine collaborative efforts to emerge from an argument, the capacity for increased respect for one's adversary, etc.). For a fuller discussion of this "revealing/ concealing" duality of any metaphor, see Lakoff and Johnson, *Metaphors*, 10 – 13.

exist, only that those that do exist and are deeply entrenched are consistent with the metaphorical system."[42]

The Epistemological Structuring Power of Metaphors

In light of the above discussion, we may posit a significant relationship between the findings of BL on the sociology of knowledge and the principles of CMT concerning the structuring power of metaphor, namely: the formation and character of a society's symbolic universe are intimately connected with the structuring metaphors that it employs in the language of its legitimation processes. Furthermore, we saw above that a society's theory of knowledge is likely to depend upon the extent to which a given belief coheres with that society's overarching system of beliefs if that given belief is to be considered justified.[43] Such a comprehensive belief system will largely be defined by the society's symbolic universe and structured by its metaphorical concepts.

We find, then, that any given *linguistic* metaphor (i.e., the actual wording of a metaphor in text or in speech) can present a specific representation of an unlimited number of possible renderings of one or more underlying *conceptual* metaphors. In the example considered above—"they have hit a dead end in their research project"—only certain elements of the domain JOURNEY are represented. The most common usage of the phrase "dead end" is in reference to drivers on a road. Thus, a particular *kind* of JOURNEY is portrayed: the participants are "drivers," they are transported by a "vehicle," their path is a "road," their goal is the "destination" toward which they are travelling, they are impeded by an "external barrier" (rather than by mechanical failure or running out of fuel). Similarly, only certain aspects of LIFE are portrayed: the participants are researchers, their activity is the study of their subject, their means of proceeding is the particular methodology they employ, their goal is increased knowledge about their subject, and so forth.

An important quality of metaphors is that they have the power to shape the way one understands the target domain. In the case of the LIFE IS A JOURNEY conceptual metaphor, there is no *necessary* reason to conceive of life as having qualities of a journey: moments of life need not be thought of as progressive steps along a prepared path, heading toward a fixed destination, propelled for-

---

42 Ibid., 22–23.
43 Such coherence may be demanded of all beliefs in the system (as in a pure coherence theory of truth), or only of certain beliefs (as in a modest foundationalist theory of truth in which some level of coherence is required in order to establish a belief as basic).

ward by some means of advance, hindered by moments of stasis, etc. Indeed, as Lakoff and his collaborator M. Turner note: "[p]art of the power of such a metaphor is its ability to *create* structure in our understanding of life."[44] Another way of expressing this point is to say that a metaphor can impart the structure of a source domain onto a target domain, even when the target domain lacks any such inherent structure.

Further Epistemological Influence of Metaphors

In addition to a metaphor's power to "structure" the manner in which one perceives a target domain, Lakoff and Turner identify four other powerful influences that metaphors exert: the "power of options," the "power of reason," the "power of evaluation," and the "power of being there."[45]

A metaphor exercises the "power of options" insofar as a specific linguistic metaphor is constructed by choosing only a limited number of qualities from all the possibilities that the source domain offers. And once that metaphor is voiced, then an infinite possibility of options from the conceptual metaphor is collapsed into a limited representation of the target domain. For example, the linguistic metaphor "life in the fast lane" implies a series of options that have been chosen from the possible range represented by the LIFE IS A JOURNEY conceptual metaphor. In this case, the generic category of "vehicle" is specified by the particular choice "car," while the generic category of "path" is specified by the particular choice "fast lane." When such options are exercised, they further illuminate the perceived characteristics of the target domain.

Similarly, a metaphor exercises the "power of reason." The patterns of inference and discernment that govern the source domain are transferred to the target domain. Within the JOURNEY domain, for example, if one hits a dead end, then several options present themselves: a decision might be made to retrace one's path and seek an alternate route, or one might attempt to break through the barrier, or one might be overcome by hopelessness and simply see no way out other than to cease the attempt to proceed. Within the LIFE IS A JOURNEY conceptual metaphor, therefore, if one sees one's situation in life as a "dead end," then one will consider similar options for assessing the situation and the future choices to be made (i.e., perhaps one could revert to a former position and seek a new

---

44 G. Lakoff and M. Turner, *More Than Cool Reason: A Field Guide to Poetic Metaphor* (Chicago: University of Chicago Press, 1989) 62.
45 Ibid., 64–65.

course of action, or devise a new method for transcending one's current limitations, or simply despair of ever making progress).

Next, a metaphor exercises the "power of evaluation." Evaluative judgments in the source domain influence how we assess situations in the target domain. For example, if one's halting on a journey is termed a "dead end," then that halting has a strongly negative connotation. Hence, a situation in life that is metaphorically labeled a "dead end" is necessarily judged to be a harmful stall or a failure. Such a negative evaluation in the target domain ("life") is the direct result of the evaluative process in the source domain (i.e., a car which has hit a dead end is necessarily in a troubled predicament). The conceptual metaphor therefore forces one to view the factual situation in the target domain (some sort of pause in one's life) in negative terms rather than, say, understanding the situation as a deliberately chosen pause for rejuvenation or the attainment of a secure position of safety.

Finally, a metaphor exercises the "power of being there." By this, Lakoff and Turner mean that because conceptual metaphors are so common and pervasive throughout a society, they exert an influence over social thought which, because it is so ubiquitous, is often hardly noticed. As such, conceptual metaphors are rarely questioned or challenged, and they often implicitly form the foundational social principles against which new observations or arguments are measured in order to ascertain whether or not they cohere with the accepted social norms.

Metaphor, then, is not simply a linguistic tool; rather, it forms the structural underpinning of one's perception of the world. "To study metaphor is to be confronted with hidden aspects of one's own mind and one's own culture.... To do so is to discover that one has a worldview, that one's imagination is constrained, and that metaphor plays an enormous role in shaping one's everyday understanding of everyday events.... Recent discoveries about the nature of metaphor suggest that metaphor is anything but peripheral to the life of the mind. It is central to our understanding of our selves, our culture, and our world at large."[46] Indeed, research in cognitive analysis even suggests that metaphorical mappings describe an inherent property of how the brain itself functions.[47]

---

46 Ibid., 214.

47 See, for example, G. Fauconnier, *Mappings in Thought and Language* (Cambridge: Cambridge University Press, 1997); G. Lakoff and M. Johnson, *Philosophy in the Flesh: The Embodied Mind and Its Challenge to Western Thought* (New York: Basic Books, 1999); G. Fauconnier and M. Turner, *The Way We Think: Conceptual Blending and the Mind's Hidden Complexities* (New York: Basic Books, 2002); G. Lakoff, "The Neural Theory of Metaphor," in *The Cambridge Handbook of Metaphor and Thought* (ed. Raymond W. Gibbs, Jr.; Cambridge: Cambridge University Press, 2008) 17–38.

Even though I shall make use of CMT in what follows, this theory is not without its critics. For example, it has been criticized for being so broadly defined as to be almost meaningless: some contend that an expression such as LIFE IS A JOURNEY is too vague and imprecise to uniquely map qualities from one domain onto another.[48] The conceptual metaphor category has also been called a forced generalization that subsumes under a simplistic heading what are, in fact, unique and complex comparisons, thus depriving them of much of their nuanced value.[49] Furthermore, the research methodology—which purports to deduce deeply entrenched cultural concepts from the assessment of a limited set of *linguistic* metaphorical statements—has been called into question.[50] Such charges have not gone unanswered in the lively debate currently being played out in the cognitive linguistic literature.[51]

In addition to these objections, cognitive linguistics has seen the development of "blending theory," which provides a broader context for the comparison of mental representations than that offered by CMT alone.[52] For example, while CMT allows for the comparison of two conceptual domains (a source and a target), blending theory can accommodate the comparison of multiple domains at once. One of the advantages of such a framework is that it permits the identification and analysis of new metaphorical relationships that can be created quickly within a linguistic environment and do not necessarily have to be particular manifestations of longstanding, socially-entrenched conceptual metaphors.

Criticisms of CMT and the rise of blending theory notwithstanding, the focus of the present study lies in the comparison of the epistemological elements (which may include, but are not limited to metaphor) present across a range of selected biblical texts. To that end, I find that the basic level of metaphorical

---

48 See, e.g., R. Jackendoff and D. Aaron, review of *More Than Cool Reason, Language* 67 (1991) 320–38.

49 See, e.g., M. S. McGlone, "Concepts as Metaphors," in *Understanding Figurative Language: From Metaphors to Idioms* (ed. Sam Glucksberg; Oxford Psychology Series 36; Oxford: Oxford University Press, 2001) 90–107.

50 See, e.g., M. S. McGlone, "What is the Explanatory Value of a Conceptual Metaphor?" *Language and Communication* 27 (2007) 109–26.

51 See, e.g., Z. Kövecses, "Conceptual Metaphor Theory: Some Criticisms and Alternative Proposals," *Annual Review of Cognitive Linguistics* 6 (2008) 168–84.

52 See, e.g., Fauconnier and Turner, *The Way We Think*; idem, "Rethinking Metaphor," in *The Cambridge Handbook of Metaphor and Thought* (ed. Raymond W. Gibbs, Jr.; Cambridge: Cambridge University Press, 2008) 53–66. See also J. E. Grady, T. Oakley, and S. Coulson, "Blending and Metaphor," in *Metaphor in Cognitive Linguistics: Selected Papers from the Fifth International Cognitive Linguistics Conference* (eds. R. W. Gibbs, Jr. and G. J. Steen; Amsterdam Studies in the Theory and History of Linguistic Science 175; Amsterdam: John Benjamins, 1999) 101–24.

analysis provided by "traditional" CMT proves adequate for my purposes. More sophisticated cognitive linguistic explorations of these texts must needs be deferred to future study.

Methodology for Epistemological Textual Analysis

If the observations of this chapter are now specifically applied to *textual* analysis, it follows that in order to identify the epistemological approach represented by a given text, one must recognize its underlying metaphors (whether explicitly or implicitly voiced) and describe the qualities of its symbolic universe (i.e., the universe of the narrator of the text and/or that of the characters portrayed in the text). I present here one such methodology constructed for achieving these aims.

Every text contains propositional information (whether the propositions are stated or assumed). These propositions have meaning within the worldview of the text and can be manifested by a myriad of forms. For example, they may consist of statements or thoughts offered by an unidentified narrator or by characters in the text; they may convey unspoken (or unstated) attitudes or prejudices that are revealed by actions and decisions of the characters; or they may impart information about the properties of the physical world or of human nature. Such propositions may or may not represent genuine knowledge in the strict epistemological sense. Nevertheless, they help describe—and thus contribute to—the worldview of the text. That worldview portrays a socially constructed reality in the sense described above.[53] Furthermore, it is through a text's propositions that the structuring metaphors of its worldview are revealed and identified. It follows, therefore, that any epistemological analytic method must address three fundamental questions: (1) what propositions does this text contain; (2) do the propositions constitute genuine knowledge; (3) how are the propositions related to the socially constructed worldview represented in the text?

The following schematic outline provides a diagnostic method for the exploration of these three issues. Note that not all of the questions posed in the outline will be relevant to every text, nor will every text contain enough information to provide answers to all of the questions.

---

[53] For a brief discussion of the relevance of the work of BL to the power of the Psalter's psalms of praise to help structure society (both ancient and contemporary), see W. Brueggemann, *Israel's Praise: Doxology Against Idolatry and Ideology* (Philadelphia: Fortress, 1988) 13–14.

Epistemological Textual Analysis

I.   What are the primary propositions presented (either explicitly or implicitly) in the text?

II. Do the propositions represent genuine knowledge?
  A. Are the propositions believed (by the narrator/speaker; by the characters within the text)?
  B. Are the propositions true?
  C. How is belief in the propositions justified?
    1. Foundationalist justification?
      a. What are the fundamental basic beliefs (either explicitly stated or assumed)?
      b. What are the inductive inferences employed to justify belief in the propositions based on the basic beliefs?
    2. Coherentist justification?
      a. What is the basic coherent belief that characterizes the overall belief system?
      b. Is the coherence value of the overall system increased by including the propositions of the text?

III. What is the nature of the socially constructed reality represented in the text?
  A. What is the presumed social stock of knowledge?
    1. How does the knowledge represented by the propositions of the text contribute to the stock of knowledge?
    2. What social roles are represented/implied by the text?
    3. What structuring metaphors are present?
  B. What is the nature of the externalization and objectivation of the social order represented in the text?
    1. What legitimation techniques are employed (or assumed)?
    2. What is the nature of the symbolic universe underlying the social order represented in the text?
    3. How are structuring metaphors employed to advance legitimation and to establish the symbolic universe?
  C. What is the nature of the internalization of the social order represented in the text?
    1. How is primary socialization achieved and what content does it convey?
    2. How is secondary socialization achieved and what content does it convey?
  D. Are there challenges to the text's assumed symbolic universe?
    1. How are challenges represented or implied?
    2. How are challenges countered?

    a.   Mildly countered (ridicule, emphatic pedagogy)?

    b.   Strongly countered (therapy, nihilation)?

In the following chapter, I will provide a detailed social-epistemological case study of Proverbs 1–9 in light of the methodology developed above. In subsequent chapters, this methodology will be applied to the study of Psalms 1, 73, 90, and 107, thus enabling a systematic comparison of their respective epistemologies that will assist our understanding of their respective placements within the canonical Psalter.

Chapter II.
Social Epistemology Case Study: Proverbs 1–9

In this chapter I will apply the methodology laid out in chapter one to a social-epistemological study of Proverbs 1–9. The purpose of this application is to contextualize the vocabulary and analysis developed above with respect to a biblical text whose epistemology has already been the focus of considerable scholarly attention. We will then be better positioned to undertake an analysis of the (heretofore little-considered) epistemology of the Psalms.[1]

Preliminaries

The study of biblical texts with respect to their specific epistemological perspective (as opposed to the study of the contributions of Scripture to the overall question of religious epistemology) has only recently become the focus of extensive scholarly research.[2] Insofar as the precise philosophical category "epistemology" is obviously foreign to the Bible, one is well advised to heed Fox's caveat that modern philosophical terms "are applicable to biblical systems of thought only by analogy to the modern philosophical concepts for which the terminology

---

1 From the vast scholarly literature on Proverbs, I here draw only upon a small subset of publications which specifically address the epistemology and worldview of this text.

2 While epistemological questions are briefly addressed in most commentaries on wisdom literature, several recent monographs and commentaries devote extensive attention to this matter; see, e.g., M. V. Fox, *A Time to Tear Down and a Time to Build Up: A Rereading of Ecclesiastes* (Grand Rapids: Eerdmans, 1999); idem, *Proverbs 1–9: A New Translation with Introduction and Commentary* (AB 18 A; New York: Doubleday, 2000); T. Frydrych, *Living Under the Sun: Examinations of Proverbs and Qoheleth* (VTSup 90; Leiden: Brill, 2002); R. O'Dowd, *The Wisdom of Torah: Epistemology in Deuteronomy and the Wisdom Literature* (FRLANT 225; Göttingen: Vandenhoeck & Ruprecht, 2009). B. U. Schipper (*Hermeneutik der Tora: Studien zur Traditionsgeschichte von Prov 2 und zur Komposition von Prov 1–9.* BZAW 432; Berlin: de Gruyter, 2012) demonstrates that the author of Proverbs 2 is confident of humanity's ability to acquire divine wisdom, while the interplay of Wisdom and Torah throughout the entire Book of Proverbs is explored in: idem, "When Wisdom is Not Enough! The Discourse on Wisdom and Torah and the Composition of the Book of Proverbs" (in *Wisdom and Torah: The Reception of 'Torah' in the Wisdom Literature of the Second Temple Period*, eds. Bernd U. Schipper, and D. Andrew Teeter, 55–79. JSJSup 163. Leiden: Brill, 2013). *The Bible and Epistemology: Biblical Soundings on the Knowledge of God* (Milton Keynes, UK: Paternoster, 2007), edited by M. Healy and R. Parry, addresses the philosophical contribution of various biblical texts to Christian theology and is not directly concerned with the epistemological focus of the texts themselves.

was devised. The application of modern labels to ancient thought is valid heuristically insofar as the basic definitions of the philosophical systems can help organize and encapsulate the ancient ideas. Rarely, however, will the subtleties and ramifications of the philosophical ideas, as developed by their modern advocates, apply precisely to the ancient concepts."[3]

Mindful of such caution, several scholars have made fruitful studies of biblical wisdom texts by exploring how their authors seem to understand the nature of knowledge, and how it can be taught or acquired. Beyond such questions, other scholars have explored the underlying worldview and assumptions about human nature that the wisdom texts seem to presuppose. The detailed methodology developed in the previous chapter for the analysis of epistemological issues is designed to facilitate the separation of questions about the nature of knowledge (i.e., why held beliefs are considered to be true) from questions about how such knowledge both contributes to, and depends upon, the social structure in which that knowledge inheres. We will see that this distinction has not always been clearly delineated in previous scholarship.

Nevertheless, as our study of the relationship between the classical questions of epistemology and the social construction of knowledge has made clear, it is impossible to analyze the nature of "knowledge" as a completely abstract, isolated entity. Knowledge is always possessed, and assessed, by individuals living within a larger social structure. What passes for knowledge helps to shape and form the social structure, while the society, in turn, develops the norms that help to determine the meaning of knowledge. It is thus necessary, as van Leeuwen observes, that students of ancient wisdom literature "become nothing less than anthropologists of antiquity. Not only must [they] pursue long gone *realia* and the elusive lineaments of ancient world views; but also, to the extent possible, [they] need to elucidate the social matrices from which the sayings arose (*Sitz im Leben*) and those in which they functioned. Unfortunately, unlike field anthropologists, scholars of ancient society cannot observe their texts in action. To a large extent, [they] are dependent upon the adequacy of [their] texts."[4] Thus, one of the primary goals of the epistemological study of a biblical text is to deduce the worldview represented within the text itself, whether explicitly expounded or implicitly assumed.

It therefore follows that throughout this study, I am concerned, not with the historical/social conditions in ancient Israel, but rather with the social world-

---

3 M. V. Fox, "The Epistemology of the Book of Proverbs," *JBL* 126 (2007) 669–84, here 675–76.
4 R. C. van Leeuwen, "Proverbs 30:21–23 and the Biblical World Upside Down," *JBL* 105 (1986) 599–610, here 599–600.

view *represented in the biblical texts themselves*. It is entirely possible that a given biblical author might have produced a text that projected a worldview in sharp contrast to the actual society in which he lived. However, extra-textual considerations will only be made in those instances in which the worldview portrayed in a text appears clearly at variance with the universal human condition (e.g., an idealized worldview in which virtuous people are always rewarded with material wealth).[5]

Case Study: Proverbs 1–9

Given its attribution to Solomon, the wisest of men (Prov 1:1; cf. 1 Kgs 5:9–14), and its opening statement of purpose, i.e., that all might grow in wisdom and understanding (Prov 1:7), it is not surprising that the Book of Proverbs has been one of the most studied of all the Wisdom books with respect to its epistemological perspective.[6] And yet, that perspective – as in all of the biblical wisdom books – is at best obliquely expressed. Fox rightly notes that although "knowledge (also called 'wisdom' and 'understanding') is at the center of Proverbs' concern, little is said about how knowledge is created, where it comes from, and how truths-claims [*sic*] are verified. Still, there must have been an implicit epistemology – ideas about what knowledge is and what its sources are....

---

5 For scholarly speculation on the historical setting of various biblical wisdom texts (with extensive literature reviews), see, for example: M. V. Fox, "The Social Location of the Book of Proverbs," in *Texts, Temples, and Traditions: A Tribute to Menahem Haran* (eds. M. V. Fox, et al.; Winona Lake, IN: Eisenbrauns, 1996) 227–39; L. G. Perdue, "Wisdom Theology and Social History in Proverbs 1–9," in *Wisdom, You Are My Sister: Studies in Honor of Roland E. Murphy, O. Carm., on the Occasion of His Eightieth Birthday* (ed. Michael L. Barré, S.S.; CBQMS 29; Washington: Catholic Biblical Association of America, 1997) 78–101; idem, *Wisdom Literature: A Theological History* (Louisville/London: Westminster John Knox, 2007); idem, *The Sword and the Stylus: An Introduction to Wisdom in the Age of Empires* (Grand Rapids: Eerdmans, 2008).

6 For extensive bibliographies of recent scholarship on Proverbs, see Fox, *Proverbs 1–9*, and O'Dowd, *Wisdom of Torah*. In addition to the works referenced in n. 2, the following studies bear directly upon the analysis presented here: L. G. Perdue, "Liminality as a Social Setting for Wisdom Instructions," *ZAW* 93 (1981) 114–26; idem, *Wisdom Literature: A Theological History* (Louisville/London: Westminster John Knox, 2007) 37–76; N. C. Habel, "The Symbolism of Wisdom in Proverbs 1–9," *Int* 26 (1972) 131–57; R. C. van Leeuwen, "Liminality and Worldview in Proverbs 1–9," *Semeia* 50 (1990) 111–44; idem, "Wealth and Poverty: System and Contradiction in Proverbs," *HS* 33 (1992) 25–36; M. V. Fox, "The Pedagogy of Proverbs 2," *JBL* 113 (1994) 233–43; idem, "Ideas of Wisdom in Proverbs 1–9," *JBL* 116 (1997) 613–33; idem, "The Epistemology of the Book of Proverbs," *JBL* 126 (2007) 669–84.

[The author of Proverbs] has an epistemology, albeit unreflective and unsystematic."[7]

Most of the previous studies of the nature of knowledge in Proverbs have tended to focus upon the structure of the worldview assumed in the text (i.e., how information is acquired and employed, given one's particular understanding of the structure of creation and of the role of God and human beings within that structure). Only recently has there been a more critical analysis of the question of how stated beliefs within Proverbs are implicitly adjudged by the biblical author to be justified or true (i.e., a focus on the classical epistemological question of whether a belief actually constitutes "knowledge"). Thus, my literature review will first focus on prior discussions of the worldview represented within the text of Proverbs, and then will consider studies on the nature of wisdom in Proverbs and the justifications apparently invoked by the biblical author for holding the beliefs expressed in the text.[8]

In this discussion, I will largely limit my treatment to Proverbs 1–9, long recognized as a distinct, unitary introduction to the rest of the book.[9] In form, these chapters are characterized by extended literary sections, as compared to the numerous, brief gnomic sayings found in chaps. 10–30. In content, the first nine chapters present a consistent, somewhat idealized worldview that lends itself well to the investigation attempted here.

Worldview: Defining Metaphors and Liminal Structure

As we saw in the previous chapter, a society's structuring metaphors help to define its prevailing worldview. In his study of Proverbs 1–9, N. C. Habel identifies a fundamental metaphor running throughout the text that gives structure and meaning to the various images and scenarios portrayed there: "among the various 'spontaneous' symbolic expressions in the wisdom materials of Proverbs 1–9, *derek*, 'the route,' 'the way,' 'the road,' is the basic or nuclear expression."[10] The principal text that illustrates this "nuclear expression" is Prov 4:10–19, in which a father exhorts his son to follow the way of wisdom (4:11), which is bright like the sun (4:18) and smooth to walk along (4:12), but to shun the way of the

---

7 Fox, "Epistemology of Proverbs," 669.
8 Throughout this chapter, unless otherwise specified, I shall use the terms "wisdom," "knowledge," and "understanding" more or less interchangeably. For a thorough discussion of the Hebrew wisdom vocabulary in Proverbs, see Fox, *Proverbs 1–9*, 28–43.
9 See, e.g., Fox, *Proverbs 1–9*, 44–45.
10 Habel, "Symbolism of Wisdom," 133.

wicked (4:14), which is dark and likely to cause stumbling (4:19). On this journey, the father, who gained wisdom from his own father (4:4), will serve as guide and provide instruction (4:11). The father leads through persuasion rather than by appeal to legal obligations, and draws his authority from prior teachings, tradition, and experience.[11]

Habel observes that the nuclear expression "the way" is further represented by "satellite" metaphors, which – like the way of wisdom and the way of the wicked – are cast as polarities. Thus, there is the polarity of the "two hearts/ minds (לב)": the wise son who takes to heart the good instruction of his father (4:20–27) and the evil man with a "perverted heart" (תהפכות בלבו) who plots evil, but will ultimately be destroyed (6:12–15). There are also the polar opposites represented by the "two women companions": personified wisdom, who will lead the son along the path of life (e. g., 4:5–9; 7:4–5), and the seductive stranger who leads one to death (e. g., 5:5–8; 6:24; 7:6–27).

In addition to identifying these satellite metaphors that complement the nuclear expression "the way" that leads to either wisdom or folly, Habel notes three fundamental levels of significance on which wisdom is operative in Proverbs 1–9: first, there is the wisdom of personal experience; next, the wisdom of Yahwistic religion; and finally, the wisdom represented by cosmic creation.

The wisdom of personal experience is that wisdom which draws upon "past human experience and reason, the validity of which each individual may verify through his own critical observation of life."[12] This type of wisdom is primarily represented in Proverbs 4–6; the images are drawn from daily life and do not overtly appeal to Yahwistic piety or cultic practice.

Beyond personal experience, Habel points out that the nuclear expression of "the way" becomes reinterpreted in certain passages throughout Proverbs 1–9 in terms of an explicitly Yahwistic perspective. "Not only does the way of wisdom become the 'way of Yahweh,' but the inner emphasis moves from personal experiential wisdom to more communal religious concerns."[13] For example, in Proverbs 3, which is presented as a long exhortation from father to son on the benefits of embracing wisdom, Yhwh is explicitly identified as the trustworthy guide along the son's path (Prov 3:26). To stray from this path is not simply an affront to human reason, but is also an "abomination to Yhwh" (3:32) and will be punished directly by him (3:33). "The disaster of the devious and wicked is not depicted as the inevitable outcome of their own actions, but as the direct result of

11 Ibid., 138.
12 Ibid., 135.
13 Ibid., 144.

Yahweh's curse."[14] Habel further notes that a Yahwistic perspective is imparted as well to the metaphors of the two hearts and the two companions.[15]

Finally, Habel observes that the nuclear expression of "the way" finds its most encompassing form within a cosmological perspective. For example, in Prov 3:13–20, wisdom's "ways" are pleasant and her "paths" are peaceful (3:17). At the same time, this same wisdom is a "tree of life" (3:18), by whom Yhwh founded the earth and heavens (3:19). The most striking illustration of this perspective is found in the cosmic interpretation of the metaphor of the "two women companions." The personification of Lady Wisdom in Prov 8:22–31 famously casts her not as the companion of the young son seeking his way in the world, but rather as the companion of Yhwh himself during the process of creation: "Yhwh created me at the beginning of his *way*" (8:22; יהוה קנני ראשית דרכו). "The way, which was previously disclosed to be integral to the character of personal human existence both in the personal and religious spheres of living, is now revealed to belong to the very character of God's being. *Derek* stands in parallelism with wisdom, the speaker. God's way is first, primordial, sovereign, and foundational. At this primal cosmological level wisdom and the way tend to coincide."[16]

Habel's analysis establishes that Proverbs 1–9 is grounded in a worldview which perceives creation to be formed according to Yhwh's wisdom. By means of a fundamental metaphor – "the way" – this worldview is communicated from parent/teacher to child/student. By employing a series of complementary metaphors, parents are able to educate children not only in the ways of human experience and wisdom, but also in the ways of Yahwistic religion and morality.

Although he does not reference Habel's work, L. G. Perdue presents a paradigmatic model for understanding all biblical wisdom literature (not only Proverbs 1–9) that largely concurs with Habel's conclusions. Drawing upon the anthropological studies of A. van Gennep and V. Turner (Habel also employed Turner's research), Perdue proposes that wisdom literature should be understood in terms of van Gennep's concept of "liminal transitions" within a

---

14 Ibid., 145.
15 For example, a father tells his son to write the fruits of wisdom, fidelity and steadfastness (חסד ואמת), upon the "tablet of his heart" (3:3), an injunction evocative of the covenant theology of Jer 31:31–33 (cf. Prov 3:5–8). Likewise, the "strange" seductive woman who leads the unwary to ruin (Prov 2:16) is one who disregards the covenant of her God (2:17).
16 Habel, "Symbolism," 155.

society.[17] Van Gennep identifies a dynamic, bi-polar tension between structure and anti-structure which is inherent in any social group. Liminal transitions mark the crossing of significant thresholds ("limina") as individuals or groups negotiate their way among events or stages of life that confront them with the boundaries between structure and anti-structure. Each such transition is characterized by three temporal and spatial phases: (1) "separation," or detachment from one's prior established place in the social structure; (2) "marginality," in which the usual social elements that once helped to orient an individual (or group) with respect to his proper role and place within the society are no longer accessible to him; and (3) "aggregation," in which the individual or group, now significantly transformed and adopting a new role, is reincorporated into the social structure.[18]

The liminal phase is an "in-between" time which is often perceived by the person in transition as a period devoid of the laws, customs, and social ceremonies of his former position in the society (i.e., a perceived shift from structure to anti-structure). As examples of liminal transitions, Turner cites birth, puberty, marriage, death, kingship installation, and the experience of changes of seasons. As one passes through such transitions in a "normal" manner, structure eventually re-emerges, accompanied by the adoption of a new identity that nevertheless fills a familiar and established social position (e.g., birth leads to infancy, puberty to young adulthood, etc.).

These transitions do not always pass smoothly, however. Turner notes that liminal phases carry a danger of "antinominalism," in which the person in transition seriously questions or rebels against the old laws, norms, and values that used to govern his role in society.[19] Because such laws and norms are critical for upholding the existing social structure, antinominalism is a behavior that can threaten society itself. To counter such threats, a society depends upon the actions of "ritual leaders" (e.g., parents and teachers) to guide the inexperienced through liminal phases. The primary goal of such guidance is for the initiate "to be reduced to *prima materia* out of which is refashioned by means of the liminal experience and instruction a 'new being,' capable of living a new life with new behavior patterns after reincorporation."[20] Perdue applies the liminal model pri-

---

17 Perdue, "Liminality." See also A. van Gennep, *The Rites of Passage* (trans. M. B. Vizedom and G. L. Caffee; Chicago: University of Chicago Press, 1960) and V. W. Turner, *The Ritual Process: Structure and Anti-Structure* (Chicago: Aldine Publishing, 1969).

18 Perdue, "Liminality," 116.

19 Recall Berger and Luckmann's observation that one of the primary functions of a symbolic universe is to provide *nomic* (ordering) processes which give structure to society.

20 Perdue, "Liminality," 117.

marily to the interpretation of Egyptian wisdom literature, but he also considers two biblical texts: David's "last testament" instruction to Solomon (1 Kgs 2:1–9) and Tobit's instruction to Tobiah (Tobit 4). In each of these two cases, a father, believing himself to be near death, offers teaching and advice to his son, who will have to assume the father's role.

One can readily draw parallels between the structure/anti-structure "bi-polarity" of Perdue's liminal transitions and the opposite polarities of Habel's "the way." The son in Proverbs 1–9 is on a liminal journey, with no obvious *a priori* adherence to either wisdom or folly: either of the two options is open to him. To ultimately side with folly would be to reject the very ordering principle of creation itself (cf. Perdue's "antinominalism"). Safe passage along this journey requires the help of a wise and experienced parent/teacher (cf. Perdue's "ritual leader").

While Perdue does not apply his model to biblical wisdom literature, R. C. van Leeuwen undertakes an extensive liminal analysis of Proverbs 1–9.[21] His primary conclusion is that the worldview represented in the text is one demarcated by clear boundaries or limits ("limina") that Yhwh has defined at creation. These boundaries separate the wise from the foolish choices represented by various polar metaphors such as the two paths, two hearts, and two women. Thus, much as Habel proposed, the qualities that Yhwh globally imparted to the universe have direct implications for how one ought to direct his life: "Love of Wisdom means staying within her prescribed cosmic-social boundaries; love of Folly, like love of another's wife, means simply the deadly pursuit of things out of bounds.... The images of Proverbs 1–9 thus create a symbolic world of good and evil where good means staying within prescribed religio-moral boundaries and evil means the trespassing of these limits. To stay 'in bounds' means life, to go 'out of bounds' entails death."[22]

The purpose of education is therefore to instill knowledge of the social boundaries that one can discern by careful observation of the ordered world. The teacher's goal is to direct the student's fundamental desires in such a way that he stays within the boundaries set by Yhwh rather than transgress those bounds in pursuit of the allurements of folly.

Van Leeuwen, borrowing the terminology of S. McFague, employs the concept of "root metaphor" to describe the worldview of Proverbs 1–9.[23] A root metaphor is a foundational metaphor "whose comprehensive character determines

---

21 Van Leeuwen, "Liminality and Worldview."
22 Ibid., 116.
23 See S. McFague, *Metaphorical Theology: Models of God in Religious Language* (Philadelphia: Fortress, 1982).

the order and coherence of the subsidiary metaphors in a system."[24] A system may, and usually does, have several root metaphors, each of which helps to reveal a different aspect of the system's prevailing worldview. While it might seem that a "root metaphor" is precisely what Habel means by "nuclear expression," Van Leeuwen is, in fact, critical of Habel's analysis, arguing that the nuclear expression "the way" is not broad enough to encompass the worldview represented in Proverbs. Rather, he contends that each of Habel's "satellite metaphors" (i. e., the two paths, two hearts, and two female companions) is itself a root metaphor and that each of them portrays a different facet of the liminal worldview in the text.

Van Leeuwen seems to be (understandably) confused by the dual manner in which Habel uses the term "way/path." On the one hand, it is Proverbs' foundational metaphor to describe the basically bipolar order of the world that Yhwh established at creation. Insofar as creation was accomplished by means of Yhwh's wisdom, the basic dichotomy in the world is that between wisdom and folly. On the other hand, Habel also uses the term to designate the specific, subsidiary metaphor of the two paths of life that the son might follow (i. e., the metaphor developed in Prov 4:10 – 19). Van Leeuwen also seems to misunderstand Habel's distinction between the three levels of wisdom represented in the text. For Habel, the worldview of Proverbs 1–9 is primarily defined by the wisdom of the created world. Operating via Yahwistic religion and personal experience, that worldview shapes the ordering of the good/wise life. Van Leeuwen's critique of Habel – that his metaphor of "the way" fails to adequately capture the liminal structure of the world order – overlooks this feature of the latter's argument.

In spite of Van Leeuwen's professed differences, both he and Habel arrive at basically the same conclusions. At this point, the value of the precise terminology developed in the previous chapter will become apparent. Employing the lexicon drawn from the social-epistemological studies of Berger, Luckmann, Lackoff, and Johnson, we can recast Habel's and Van Leeuwen's observations of Proverbs 1–9 in the following consistent manner.

The social stock of knowledge represented in the text of Proverbs 1–9 comprises the various sayings of advice, warning, and exhortation delivered by the father/teacher to his son/student. It is important to note that any single text can only partially convey the stock of knowledge embodied within a particular worldview.[25] As described above, these lessons are drawn from human experi-

---

24 Van Leeuwen, "Liminality and Worldview," 111.
25 Here, "worldview" means the same as Berger and Luckmann's "symbolic universe." The former term is retained here given its prevalent use by the biblical scholars I have referenced.

ence and lessons that the father learned from his own teachers (see, e. g., Prov 4:3–4). What is not included in this social stock of knowledge is the lesson from Lady Wisdom (Proverbs 8), for that teaching is drawn directly from divine revelation. To be sure, such teaching might *become* part of the social stock, if her words are taken to heart and passed on from father to son in future generations. But *from within the worldview of the text itself,* Lady Wisdom's words represent a new teaching, not previously known to the father and not a part of his prior stock of wisdom.

The primary social roles portrayed in the text are those of the father/teacher and the son/student. But there are also a host of other social roles which are briefly alluded to and are presumed to be familiar to both teacher and student. Examples of such roles include farmers (3:10), wives/husbands (6:26–34), thieves (6:30), kings/rulers (8:15–16), and servants (9:3). It is also apparent that the son is old enough to understand such roles as that of a committed, monogamous lover, a promiscuous seductress, or a lustful adulterer. The interactions among these various roles generally define the "proper places" for the members of a society. But they can also give rise to stresses and tensions that challenge the stability of a society's worldview. Such tensions will be addressed below in our discussion of social objectivation and internalization in Proverbs 1–9.

The studies of both Habel and Van Leeuwen clearly illustrate the power of the metaphors in Proverbs 1–9 for articulating a worldview that encompasses all aspects of existence from individual personal experience through the order of creation itself. It is not necessary to identify particular "nuclear expressions" or "root metaphors" so long as we recognize that each of the metaphors employed in the text are *structuring metaphors*, i. e., ones that do not simply reflect, but actually help to shape, the manner in which the worldview is perceived by a society's inhabitants. Furthermore, as noted in the previous chapter, the structuring power of the relationships among the various metaphors creates a coherent system that helps to define the fundamental values represented in the worldview. Thus, whether the coherent metaphorical system is described in terms of "liminality" (Van Leeuwen) or "the way" (Habel), what is clear is that – in the worldview of Proverbs – the good/wise choice is the one that follows a specific path and does not cross specified boundaries. Most of the metaphors developed in Proverbs 1–9 speak in general terms of the importance of adhering to the good/wise way, heart, or woman. The numerous gnomic sayings in the remainder of the book provide specific examples from everyday life that illustrate the particular choices by which one remains faithful to the good path. Nevertheless, such illustrative scenarios are presented in the early chapters as well. For example: good love is respectful of the boundaries of marital commitments (Prov

6:27–35); the wise management of resources and energy means following the exemplary path of the industrious ants (Prov 6:6–11); and the transgression of the bounds of the law is loathsome to Yhwh (Prov 3:31–32).

Inculcating and Preserving the Worldview: Objectivation and Internalization

As noted in the previous chapter, a society's acceptance of a given worldview (and the social roles that it defines) tends to become more stressed and challenged as the interaction among its members becomes more intimate and involved. In Proverbs 1–9, these types of stresses are introduced, for example, by the wicked woman who presents temptations that can lead to questioning whether sexual virtue is preferable to lust (Prov 7:6–27). Similarly, a father acknowledges that his son will be approached by wicked men who will tempt him to forsake a lawful life in exchange for a violent one (1:10–13).[26]

Such challenges are met by a society through the objectivation (legitimation) and internalization of its worldview, particularly as these tasks are accomplished with respect to those of its members who are undergoing significant life transitions (precisely the sort of "liminal" transitions referred to by Perdue and Van Leeuwen). Indeed, a major goal of Proverbs 1–9 is to help the young and inexperienced confirm their trust in the soundness of the prevailing worldview of the text and to successfully confront threats to that trust. "Proverbs 1–9 does not merely embody a worldview…. Rather, these chapters are primarily concerned to inculcate a particular Yahwistic worldview."[27] That "Yahwistic" worldview is one in which God has formally ordered the world according to his own design (e.g., Prov 3:19–20). As noted above, the good/wise are those who remain within the limits, and who follow the paths, that God has prescribed for them.

In Berger and Luckmann's language of objectivation, the Book of Proverbs principally addresses the need which arises from the second level of legitimation. At this level, the goal is to teach the young in a society "why things are the way they are." Fox points out that the final redactors of Proverbs had an image of society that was both programmatic and didactic: "The program does not seem to be insidious or cynical…. But it *is* didactic; it is the way the compil-

---

26 Later in the Book of Proverbs (e.g., Prov 14:20; 19:1), there are indications that the good do not always prosper and the wicked do not always suffer, a recognition which puts further stress on the well-ordered worldview prevalent in most of Proverbs 1–9.
27 Van Leeuwen, "Liminality," 113.

ers of the proverbs wished their readers to view the world and their own role within it."[28]

The pedagogical program whereby such a view could be communicated is laid out in Proverbs 2.[29] Before any teaching from the father, however, the education of the son requires the latter's possession of the "fear of Yhwh" (יראת יהוה; Prov 1:7). While closely related to wisdom, this fear is not equivalent to it. Following von Rad, Fox notes that Prov 1:7 presents a qualification of *wisdom*, rather than a qualification of the fear of Yhwh, and therefore states a fundamental axiom of the epistemology of Proverbs: "Proverbs 1:7 and similar statements (2:5; 9:10) affirm wisdom's religious validity by subordinating it in various ways to the fear of God. The fear of God is the sphere within which wisdom is possible and can be realized, the precondition for both wisdom and ethical behavior."[30]

At its most primal level, this fear is likely manifested by a young child's dread of God's punishment for bad behavior. But as the child matures, the fear evolves into a more nuanced fear of disappointing God, or a fear of the consequences of one's actions (not just the consequences for one's own life, but the consequences for others who may be hurt or otherwise negatively affected). Prov 2:5 promises that as one seeks wisdom, eventually one will come to *understand* the fear of Yhwh and not just experience it as an emotional feeling. "At this stage, the pupil has progressed from unreflective fear to a cognitive awareness of what fear of God really is, and this is equivalent to knowledge of God. This is fear of God as *conscience*."[31]

It might seem that the fear of Yhwh has no proper place in the social epistemological scheme of Berger and Luckmann. To be sure, an inherent human awareness of the presence and the will of the divine is an insight of theological anthropology (and the product of divine revelation) rather than a socially constructed human quality. Nevertheless, the fear of Yhwh can readily be situated within Berger and Luckmann's social-epistemological model, insofar as it is, *de facto*, part of the internalization (specifically, part of primary socialization) of the worldview represented in Proverbs. That is, the fear of Yhwh is a quality (like language or the existence of socio-economic roles) that every society just seems to innately possess.

---

28 Fox, "Social Location," 238.
29 The discussion here is drawn primarily from Fox, "Pedagogy," the arguments of which are reproduced in idem, *Proverbs 1–9*, 131–34, and 348–51.
30 Fox, *Proverbs 1–9*, 69.
31 Ibid., 70.

Like other internalized elements of a society, the fear of Yhwh is nurtured and developed through the education and formation that a child receives from his society. That development progresses to the extent that one seeks wisdom diligently (Prov 2:1–4). The benefits of acquired wisdom are a more developed moral awareness (Prov 2:9) and a shrewdness that protects one from wicked men and women (Prov 2:11–19).

The importance of properly seeking wisdom cannot be overstated, for the acquisition of wisdom is ultimately granted by God (Prov 2:6) to the "upright" (ישׁר) and to those who "walk blamelessly" (תמהלכי ; Prov 2:7). Thus there are two main stages to education: (1) the father's instruction, complemented by the son's study and inquiry; and (2) God's granting of wisdom (contingent upon both the moral behavior and the diligence of the son).

In Proverbs 1–9, the father relies upon several pedagogical techniques. First, he draws upon the authority that is rooted in the credibility of his paternal position and in the tradition that he keeps and passes on (e. g., Prov 4:1–3). In this capacity, he speaks in stark terms and insists that to forsake his instruction leads only to death. Next, he offers a series of promises of rewards for those who are obedient to his teachings (e. g., long life [3:1–2; 4:10], good health [3:8], the esteem of neighbors [3:4], wealth [8:18]) and dire warnings of ruin for those who are not (e. g., disgrace among their peers [3:35], living in darkness [4:19], poverty [6:11], and death [5:5; 7:27]). Furthermore, he employs a tone of intimacy and vividness with the son, that seeks to persuade him by acknowledging that he himself has known the struggles which the youth is now confronting (e. g., the father recalls that he was once a pupil himself [4:3–4], or his speaking of the sexual lure of a wanton woman with a frankness that betrays his own awareness of the power of lust [5:3; 6:27–28; 7:6–27]). Finally, he employs irony to expose the foolishness of the youth who thinks he can profit from wickedness (e. g., if one joins a band of murderous thieves, he will himself be killed [1:10–19]; if one engages in lustful promiscuity, he will in fact sacrifice his regenerative power [5:9]).

Of all the father's pedagogical techniques, the one that is most likely to be persuasive to an impetuous youth is the promise of reward for the one who heeds wise teaching.[32] Frydrych (recognizing the same fundamental bipolarity in the worldview of Proverbs that Habel identifies) rightly notes that the authors of Proverbs "had an unshakable conviction that the God who created this world, and has a complete control over it, unequivocally favors the wise and righteous just as much as he detests the fools and evil people (e. g., Prov 3:33; 10:3; 15:29).

---

32 For further discussion of this point, see Frydrych, *Living Under the Sun*, 35–36.

As a result of the role that God plays, the world of the proverbial sages is regular and predictable and those who follow the path of wisdom will succeed in it and prosper."[33] Perdue cites Prov 3:9–10, 13–18; 8:18–21 as further evidence for the book's assumption that divine providence manifests itself through the righteous' possession of wealth and power.[34]

Indeed, this concept of reward for following the right path is not simply a teacher's lure to inspire his student but is, rather, a deeply embedded truth in the worldview of Proverbs 1–9. Van Leeuwen argues that because the worldview of Proverbs assumes the fundamental goodness of creation, it is possible for wealth to be perceived as the reward of both wisdom and moral righteousness, while poverty can be understood as a marker of folly and wickedness. "The created world is good... and loss, lack, or distortion of created goods is an evil."[35]

As described in the previous chapter, at the second level of legitimation there is no attempt to explicitly teach an overarching picture of the entire worldview. Rather, simple explanatory schemes are presented (by means of proverbs, maxims, and illustrative examples) that each reveal a particular facet of the worldview. This stage can be seen in numerous sayings from the later chapters of Proverbs that seem to articulate the unqualified superiority of wealth over poverty (e. g., Prov 10:15; 13:8a; 14:20; 18:23; 22:7) and the perception that wealth is a pure gift from God (10:22). Other sayings suggest a causal relationship: namely, that righteousness leads to wealth while wickedness leads to poverty (e. g., Prov 12:3; 13:22, 25; 14:14, 19; 22:4; 28:25b), or that industriousness leads to wealth while sloth leads to poverty (e. g., 6:6; 10:4–5; 18:9; 24:30; 26:12, 16).[36]

It might seem that such an idealized view is overly naïve, for wise behavior is obviously not always followed by prosperity. If, however, the Book of Proverbs is considered as a whole, it is clear that challenges to its prevailing worldview are acknowledged within the text itself (both explicitly and implicitly). Fox terms "anomaly proverbs" those sayings that seem to contradict the view that the righteous always prosper and the wicked always fail.[37] For example: a righteous man might fall before a wicked one (Prov 25:26); a wealthy man is not nec-

---

33 Ibid., 32.
34 Perdue, "Wisdom Theology," 88–89.
35 Van Leeuwen, "Wealth and Poverty," 26.
36 Perdue finds in this scheme an overtone of Deuteronomistic theology: "In a way, we have the 'either/or' so typical of Deuteronomic preaching: obedience to the teachings of the law leads to life, while disobedience results in death. Only now it is Wisdom who is the Deuteronomic preacher who offers the radical life-changing decision or [sic] 'yes' or 'no'" ("Wisdom Theology," 99–100).
37 Fox, "Epistemology of Proverbs," 682.

essarily just (Prov 10:2; 11:16; 13:23; 21:6; 28:6); those who attain power are not always righteous (Prov 28:15–16a); and the foolish might attain luxury (Prov 19:10).[38] Such sayings, Frydrych concludes, "only make adequate sense if in the sages' world at least occasionally those who ambush the innocent fill their pockets with loot [cf. Prov 1:10–13], the righteous stagger, the wicked have the upper hand and fools live lives of luxury.... [Thus] the proverbial sages were aware that the picture of the world they paint is not entirely accurate."[39]

These types of worldview-undermining challenges pose a threat to the success of social legitimation in the life of a person undergoing a liminal transition. When such challenges arise, the parent/teacher attempts to preserve (or restore) order by what Berger and Luckmann term "secondary socialization" (i.e., the second level of internalization). The usual process by which this is accomplished is through dialogue with an authority figure or teacher. While actual dialogue between teacher and student is not represented in Proverbs, it can be approximated by the contiguous pairings of contradictory statements in which an "anomalous proverb" is immediately corrected by the following proverb. For example, Prov 14:20 ("A pauper is despised even by his peers, but a rich man has many friends") is countered by 14:21 ("He who despises his fellow is wrong; he who shows pity for the lowly is happy").[40] Similarly, Prov 22:7 touts the fact that the wealthy take advantage of the poor, only to be followed by Prov 22:8 which promises misfortune for the unjust.

Another form of secondary socialization is reflected in the so-called "better than" sayings. Here, the correction to an anomaly is not made by a following verse, but within the same verse. The form of these sayings often begins by recognizing that while some righteous people truly are poor, they are nevertheless better than those wicked who may be prosperous. For example: "Better a little with righteousness than a large income with injustice" (Prov 16:8; cf. also 15:16–17; 16:16, 19; 17:1; 19:22b; 21:3; 22:1; 28:6, 11).

As discussed in the previous chapter, stronger measures than didactic conversation are sometimes required to reform those persons ("deviants") who challenge a prevailing worldview. Berger and Luckmann refer to the milder of these

---

38 For an extended discussion of the "wealthy wicked/fools" and the "poor just/wise" in Proverbs, see Van Leeuwen, "Wealth and Poverty."

39 Frydrych, *Living Under the Sun*, 38.

40 Many commentators propose that such pairs originally existed as two independent statements, but were deliberately combined by the final redactors of Proverbs so as to create a wisdom lesson, upholding the ultimate superiority of righteous behavior. See, for example, H. C. Washington, *Wealth and Poverty in the Instruction of Amenemope and the Hebrew Proverbs* (SBLDS 142; Atlanta, GA: Scholars, 1994) 191–202.

measures as "therapy," and to the harsher as "nihilation." Examples of each of these can be found in Proverbs.

One of the techniques of therapy is to recast the discordant perspective as a denial of the principles of the prevailing worldview. A powerful illustration of this strategy is provided by Prov 30:21–23:

21 The earth shudders at three things, at four which it cannot bear:
22 a slave who becomes king; a scoundrel sated with food;
23 a loathsome woman who gets married; a slave-girl who supplants her mistress.

Van Leeuwen refers to the above as an example of a "world upside down proverb," for it equates the inversion of the social order (e. g., slaves who rule or scoundrels who are satisfied) with nothing less than a disruption of the divinely-established cosmic order (the earth shudders).[41] Another therapy technique in evidence in Proverbs is the invocation of divine approval of behavior that is consonant with the worldview, but divine condemnation of behavior that contradicts it. For example, a cheating merchant is an "abomination" to Yhwh, but an honest merchant pleases him (Prov 11:1; cf. also Prov 12:2; 15:8–9; 17:15; 20:10, 23; 27; 28:9). In a similar vein, Lady Wisdom gleefully mocks the downfall of sinners due to their own foolishness (Prov 1:22–26). Finally, the therapy technique of "reinterpretation" – in which a deviant comes to understand his prior, problematic views as evolving into an outlook which is more in line with the prevailing worldview – is employed by the father who instructs his son to redirect his sexual passion from the lustful desire for any appealing woman (which is likely to lead to adulterous affairs) to the committed, monogamous love he ought to enjoy with his own wife (Prov 5:15–20).

As Berger and Luckmann note, however, there can be deviants who so reject the worldview of their society that they are beyond reform and can only be rejected. This process is termed "nihilation" and it is reflected in Proverbs in the attitude toward certain foolish men who are incapable of being instructed. Fox cites Prov 9:7–8

7 He who chastises an impudent man (לץ) receives insult,
   he who reproves an evildoer gets hurt.
8 Don't reprove an impudent man lest he hate you;
   reprove the wise and he'll love you.

---

41 Van Leeuwen, "Proverbs 30:21–23."

These verses (along with Prov 13:1b; 15:5, 12; 23:9; 27:22) express the viewpoint that there are two types of person: "the teachable, who may not yet be wise but *can* progress in learning, and the foolish, who are incapable of learning."[42] Similarly, Frydrych notes that certain fools (כסיל), though they do not lack intellectual ability, nevertheless refuse instruction and embrace the state of folly by their own choice: they disdain knowledge (1:22); lack any desire for self-improvement (1:32); are stubborn, unteachable, and self-centered (18:2); refuse correction (17:10); and do not learn from personal experience (26:11).[43] Such as these are left to the fate of their own folly and are not the subjects to whom the parents/teachers of Proverbs address themselves.

Justification for Belief: Foundationalism or Coherentism?

The final issue to be addressed in our epistemological study of Proverbs 1–9 concerns the justification that is implied within the text for believing the various observations and proverbial statements represented there. A longstanding consensus among scholars of biblical wisdom literature is that the knowledge represented within these texts is primarily acquired empirically: that is, one gains knowledge through observing one's surrounding environment and relationships. Drawing upon examples mainly taken from Proverbs, Crenshaw summarizes this view:

> Even religious instructions and proverbial sayings emphasize personal observations as the means of acquiring knowledge.... To learn industry and to prepare for adversity, young boys and girls looked to ants as they busily laid provisions in store for future need [Prov 6:6–11]. To see the perils of wanton living, young people watched a seduction unfold and followed it to its disastrous consequences [Prov 7:6–27]. To recognize the dangers presented by excessive drinking of wine, they spied on a drunkard whose irrational conduct invited brutal beatings. To acquaint themselves with the undesirable consequences of laziness, they watched unmotivated persons sleep while their fields became unproductive [Prov 24:30–34]. In short, if these young people wished to learn how to cope with every eventuality, they studied their environment and society at large....[44]

---

42 Fox, *Proverbs 1–9*, 316.
43 Frydrych, *Living Under the Sun*, 29–34.
44 J. L. Crenshaw, *Education in Ancient Israel: Across the Deadening Silence* (ABRL; New York: Doubleday, 1998) 240–41. Similar recent stances on the empirical nature of wisdom in Proverbs can be found in, for example: D. J. Estes, *Hear, My Son: Teaching and Learning in Proverbs 1–9* (New Studies in Biblical Theology; Grand Rapids: Eerdmans, 1997) 27; J. L. Crenshaw, "Qoheleth's Understanding of Intellectual Inquiry," in *Qohelet in the Context of Wisdom* (ed. A. Schoors; BETL 136; Leuven: Leuven University Press, 1998) 205–24, here 212; R. J. Clifford,

This type of empirical approach to attaining knowledge is essentially a form of (modest) foundationalism: basic beliefs are spontaneously formed based upon sensory experience. The assumption is that one learns something new by observing ants or a seduction – these scenes are not simply illustrative examples but the conveyors of previously unknown knowledge. Within such a scheme, it is not obvious how to account for the "anomalous proverbs." For example, it would seem that the observation of a prosperous wicked man would provide "defeating evidence" against the supposedly justified basic belief that the virtuous prosper but the wicked fail.

It is also unclear how the fundamental structuring metaphors of Proverbs would relate to the book's numerous empirically-justified beliefs. How, for example, would one infer an encompassing metaphor such as the "the way" or the "liminal transition" from an observation of ants? While individual observations might provide illustrative examples or supporting evidence, they do not seem capable by themselves of giving rise to the abstract metaphors. If one were to argue that while no single observation could generate a structuring metaphor, but that the observation of many (and varied) scenes could, then one would essentially be endorsing a more coherentist scheme for justification.

It is just such coherentism that Fox proposes as the primary justificatory scheme for Proverbs. He begins by noting that none of the proverbs which seem to be grounded in experience actually *derive* their main point from the experience itself. Rather, the experience serves to reinforce a previously held belief.[45] For example, Prov 7:26–27 declares that an adulterous affair is fatal. This is considered a given truth by the parent/teacher, and he is simply using the narrated seduction (Prov 7:6–23) as a way to drive this point home to his son/student. Similarly, when a lazy son is sent to observe industrious ants (Prov 6:6–11), the parent is simply using the insects to underscore what he already "knows" to be true: hard work is profitable, while sloth leads to poverty. In general, a given anecdote "reports not the discovery of knowledge but an experience that reinforces a known principle. The observation is an occasion for reflection, not inference, and the anecdote is a testimonial to an axiomatic belief."[46] In other words, while Proverbs' anecdotes are pedagogical tools, they are not the source of new knowledge themselves.

Fox denies that a belief which is generated by a given experience is truly "basic" (i. e., that the knowledge extracted from an experience is spontaneously

---

Proverbs: A Commentary (OTL; Louisville: Westminster John Knox, 1999) 218; Frydrych, *Living Under the Sun*, 53–56.
45 Fox, "Epistemology of Proverbs," 670–74.
46 Ibid., 673.

and instantly known). Rather, he contends that the sayings of Proverbs "receive their validation by virtue of consistency with the integrated system of assumptions that inform the book.... The propositions of sapiential knowledge (or the propositions on which sapiential advice is founded) are considered valid insofar as they are concordant with each other and supported by common principles."[47] Thus, the knowledge gleaned from the sayings is not radically innovative but instead conforms to a coherence theory of truth.

As we saw in the previous chapter, one of the primary challenges for a coherence theory is to establish not only what the measure of coherence is for any given system of beliefs, but also to identify the core principle(s) with which the associated beliefs are required to agree. Fox argues that the coherence system in Proverbs is best represented by the ideal of "harmony" or "balance." "There is no prime axiom from which all ideas are spun out; the system itself is primary. But...an ideal of harmony is central to the system, and a sense for what is harmonious – the moral equivalent of a musical ear – is important in both the formation of a wise person and the validation of new wisdom."[48] For example, those proverbs that dwell on the evils of a contentious wife (e.g., Prov 21:9 = 25:24; 21:19) help to illustrate the axiom that "harmony is precious." The ideal of balance requires that hard work and industriousness ought to be handsomely repaid, while laziness ought to produce nothing (e.g., Prov 6:6–11). Social harmony and balance requires that servants not rule over their masters (e.g., Prov 19:10; 30:23). The ideal of harmony also governs justice insofar as people are repaid according to their deeds: good deeds yield good results while bad deeds yield bad results (e.g., Prov 11:6, 8; 19:17; 26:27). This harmony is often described in aesthetically charged terms such as "graceful," "beautiful," "pleasant," or "radiant" (e.g., Prov 1:9; 3:22; 4:9, 18).[49] Within this scheme, any saying that serves to promote harmony is coherent with the whole system and thus constitutes a justified belief, while any dissonant saying would not be justified. Hence, the "anomaly proverbs" should only be considered as vehicles of real knowledge to the extent that the situations they describe are seen as temporary aberrations which are rendered coherent with the whole by virtue of being paired with the situations described in the "corrective" proverbs, as discussed above.

---

47 Ibid., 676.
48 Ibid., 677.
49 For a more extensive discussion of the aesthetic beauty of wisdom in Proverbs, see G. E. Bryce, *A Legacy of Wisdom: The Egyptian Contribution to the Wisdom of Israel* (Cranbury, NJ: Associated University Presses, 1979) 151–52.

It might be argued that this "harmony/balance" is yet another structuring metaphor in addition to those already proposed. But in fact, Fox is simply using this concept to describe the fundamental order of creation with which Yhwh infused the world, and which Habel and Van Leeuwen accept as a given for Proverbs. This fundamental order is the defining quality that can be used to ascertain the justification for believing any proposition within the overall system of beliefs (to the degree that the proposition coheres or conflicts with the ordering principle of the system). It also confers qualitative value on the structuring metaphors: for example, Habel's "the way" will yield beneficial results when it marks a path towards greater harmony and balance.

But where does such a primary, defining quality as "harmony" originate? How can it be known other than by being extracted from empirical observation and experience? Fox notes that it is only Lady Wisdom herself who presents a knowledge that is something completely new and not previously possessed by human beings (Prov 8:22–36). Because men have received her revelation, they can teach their own sons that the world is created by means of wisdom (Prov 3:19) and that this wisdom is harmonious and balanced.

Fox's critics argue that, originally, it was precisely by means of such empirical exercises as watching adulterers or ants that human beings acquired the "new" knowledge that the world is harmoniously ordered.[50] Thus, empiricism alone can account for the epistemological justification scheme of Proverbs. What these critics overlook, however, is that within the text of Proverbs itself observation is not used as a means for discovering new knowledge. The results of the observational exercises that the fathers set for their sons are already known in advance by the elders. Fox's critics make the mistake of confusing pedagogy (passing knowledge from one person to another) with epistemology (ascertaining the origin and nature of knowledge).

This distinction is important, for it reveals that biblical wisdom literature may contain epistemological elements in line with both the foundationalist and the coherentist traditions. Whatever is received directly through revelation constitutes a justified basic belief (unlike modern philosophers, the biblical authors would not trouble themselves over the question of whether one could receive divine communication). And such basic beliefs can undergird a coherent core of beliefs by which to evaluate empirical observations and human statements.

Thus we see that divine revelation, while not explicitly considered in the previous chapter, can readily be treated within any epistemological scheme insofar

---

50 See, for example, Crenshaw, *Education*, 243.

as it constitutes a justified basic belief. And yet, the presence of such revelation need not imply that the associated theory of truth is purely foundationalist rather than coherentist. Proverbs, in spite of its largely coherentist character, clearly acknowledges a unique and critical function for revelation. Frydrych notes that Lady Wisdom functions like a "mediatrix" between Yhwh and humanity, providing heretofore unknown insights into the process of creation: "the sages believed that in their striving for wisdom, God provided them with a special insight, one that was observed to reach beyond what the human mind alone was able to grasp through its natural abilities, and essentially allowed the sages to see things from the divine perspective.[51]

In other words, as soon as the concept that creation has been infused with wisdom is received as knowledge, then that knowledge in turn gives rise to the various structuring metaphors through which human beings perceive and order their world. Furthermore, even the capacity to receive such knowledge is contingent upon God's initiative: "For the Lord grants wisdom, at his behest come knowledge and good sense" (Prov 2:6). Nowhere in Proverbs is it asserted that human beings originally attained this knowledge by empirical observation.

Conclusion

In this study of the social epistemology of Proverbs 1–9, we have demonstrated the complex relationships among: (1) the prevailing worldview of the society represented within a biblical text, (2) the structuring metaphors by which that society understands and describes its worldview, (3) the means by which the society employs metaphors to inculcate the worldview among its young/inexperienced members as well as to address any challenges to the acceptance of the worldview, and (4) the justification scheme by which the society accepts a given belief as actual knowledge.

While these elements have been variously investigated by scholars in the Book of Proverbs, I am aware of no such studies for the Psalms. Accordingly, in the following chapter, I shall explore the extent to which prior studies of the Psalms contain elements of epistemological analysis.

---

51 Frydrych, *Living Under the Sun*, 60–61.

Chapter III.
Wisdom Elements Within the Psalms:
Prior Studies and Present Focus

Introduction

In this chapter, after a brief review of the scholarly literature concerning the classification of a distinct genre of "wisdom psalms" within the Psalter, I shall discuss a selection of prior studies of wisdom elements within the Psalms that are particularly germane to the epistemological focus I am pursuing. Finally, I shall offer the rationale for my selection of the four psalms to be studied here.

Wisdom Psalms as a Unique Genre

The question of whether "wisdom psalms" exist as a distinct category within the Psalter remains one of the most contested issues in contemporary biblical scholarship.[1] Yet the attempt to identify such a genre based upon either a common form or content (or both) is not new.

Gunkel, while not defining wisdom psalmody as a specific *Gattung*, nevertheless identified *Weisheitsdichtung*, a broad category of wisdom poetry that includes certain psalms along with sections of Job, Proverbs, and Qoheleth.[2] He did not attempt to provide a comprehensive catalogue of such poetry, nor did he offer well-defined criteria for classifying it. But he did note qualities of form and content that wisdom poetry evidences. With regard to form, the poet often refers to his work as "wisdom" (חכמה), "instruction" (תורה), "riddle" (חידה), or "proverb" (משל). The materials in question likewise often use the formulaic marker "fear of the Lord" (יראת יהוה) and adopt the format of direct address from a wise elder to the young or inexperienced (often referred to as "son"). In content, they feature admonitions and instructions, promises of blessings to the good and warnings to the wicked, frequent comparisons between good and evil, "numerical sayings" (e.g., Ps 62:12), beatitudes (i.e., אשרי say-

---

1 See, for example the recent reviews of J. L. Crenshaw ("Wisdom Psalms?" *Currents in Research: Biblical Studies* 8 [2000] 9–17) and J. K. Kuntz ("Reclaiming Biblical Wisdom Psalms: A Response to Crenshaw," *Currents in Biblical Research* 1 [2003] 145–54).
2 H. Gunkel, *Einleitung in die Psalmen: Die Gattungen der religiösen Lyrik Israels* (HKAT; Abt. 2 Suppl.; Göttingen: Vandenhoeck & Ruprecht, 1933) 381–97.

ings), and questions of theodicy.[3] Gunkel included Psalms 1, 37, 49, 73, 91, 112, and 128 in his discussion of "wisdom poetry," but did not offer a complete listing of the psalms in this category.

Mowinckel discussed wisdom elements within what he termed "learned psalmography," but did not present a clear definition of what constitutes such psalms nor did he compile a comprehensive listing of them. He contended that these poems were not originally produced for cultic use but that "in this case we have to do with a psalmography that has originated in the circles of the 'wise men,' the learned leaders of the 'wisdom schools.'"[4] He adopted many of the same criteria that Gunkel had adduced and included within this class Psalms 1, 34, 37, 49, 73, 78, 105, 106, 111, 112, and 127.

One of the first attempts to systematically identify wisdom psalms as a distinct literary form was made by Murphy.[5] He offered seven characteristics that define the form: (1) "happy" (אשרי) sayings (e. g., Psalms 1, 128); (2) graded numerical sayings (e. g., Ps 62:12); (3) "better" (טוב...מן) sayings (e. g., Ps 37:16); (4) address of teacher to "son" (e. g., Ps 34:12); (5) acrostic patterns (e. g., Psalms 34, 37); (6) simple comparisons, often using similes (e. g., Pss 1:4; 37:2; 49:13); and (7) admonitions (e. g., Psalms 32, 34, 37). Using these criteria, he identified seven "pure" wisdom psalms (not every one of which contains all seven elements): 1, 32, 34, 37, 49, 112, and 128. In addition, he identified seven psalms that contain wisdom "elements": 25, 31, 39, 40, 62, 92, and 94. Unlike Mowinckel, Murphy dismissed as fruitless any attempt to ascertain the precise life-setting of the wisdom poems. Yet, on the basis of form and content, he concluded that "it is still feasible to speak of 'wisdom psalms' as a literary form parallel to the other psalm types."[6]

Later exegetes have employed different criteria and compiled different lists for the wisdom psalm category. Kuntz identified seven characteristics that differ from Murphy's only in that he added the criterion of "rhetorical question," while dropping Murphy's "acrostic" criterion.[7] He also attempted to identify wisdom

---

3 For an extensive discussion of אשרי sayings in the Psalter, see E. Lipinski, "Macarismes et Psaumes de congratulation," *RB* 75 (1968) 321–67, here 323–25. Lipinski questions whether the beatitude form is one of the defining characterstics of Wisdom Literature.

4 S. Mowinckel, "Psalms and Wisdom," in *Wisdom in Israel and in the Ancient Near East* (ed. M. Noth and D. W. Thomas; VTSup 3; Leiden: Brill, 1955) 205–24, here 206. See also idem, *Psalms*, 2. 104–25.

5 R. E. Murphy, "A Consideration of the Classification 'Wisdom Psalms,'" in *Congress Volume: Bonn 1962* (ed. J. A. Emerton; VTSup 9; Leiden: Brill, 1963) 156–67.

6 Ibid, 16.

7 J. K. Kuntz, "The Canonical Wisdom Psalms of Ancient Israel – Their Rhetorical, Thematic, and Formal Dimensions," in *Rhetorical Criticism: Essays in Honor of James Muilenburg* (ed. J. J.

psalms by looking for a shared vocabulary among the Psalter, Job, Proverbs, and Qoheleth.[8] His final listing of wisdom psalms included all those so identified by Murphy, plus Psalms 127 and 133. Whybray, in his study of wisdom psalms, played down the criterion of literary form and focused primarily on content, arguing that "the surest criterion is a general conformity to the concerns of the wisdom literature proper [i.e., Job, Proverbs, and Qoheleth]."[9] Such "concerns" include the psalmist's interior reflection on life (why people suffer, what is the source of happiness, etc.) and a didactic emphasis. Whybray's compilation of wisdom psalms nearly doubled that of his predecessors: Psalms 8, 14(53), 25, 34, 39, 49, 73, 90, 112, 127, 131, and 139, with wisdom elements being found in Psalms 18, 27, 32, 86, 92, 94, 105, 107, 111, 144, and 146.

Largely reacting to these disparate (and somewhat imprecise) criteria employed to identify wisdom psalms and the lack of consensus about which psalms qualify for this classification, Crenshaw concluded that there is no compelling evidence for the existence of a separate such category at all. His observations on the matter are especially relevant to the present study: "Perhaps we should limit ourselves to what can definitely be affirmed: some psalms resemble wisdom literature in stressing the importance of learning, struggling to ascertain life's meaning, and employing proverbial lore. Their authorship and provenance matter less than the accuracy and profundity of what they say."[10] In particular, the "labeling of words and expressions [in the Psalter] as sapiential serves no useful purpose. After all, labels ought to clarify or to issue vital information. Perhaps it is time to move beyond speculation to a different task, that of specifying *functional* similarities and differences among genres. After all, fools had access

---

Jackson and M. Kessler; PTMS 1; Pittsburgh: Pickwick Press, 1974) 186–222. While both Kuntz and Murphy employ several criteria that are identical to elements highlighted by Gunkel, neither of them explicitly acknowledges this aspect of the latter's work.

8 See also A. Hurvitz, "Wisdom Vocabulary in the Hebrew Psalter: A Contribution to the Study of 'Wisdom Psalms,'" *VT* 38 (1988) 41–51.

9 R. N. Whybray, *Reading the Psalms as a Book* (JSOTSup 222; Sheffield: Sheffield Academic Press, 1996) 37.

10 Crenshaw, "Wisdom Psalms?" 15. The observation of J. Luyten, in his study of Psalm 73 ("Psalm 73 and Wisdom," in *La Sagesse de l'Ancien Testament*. Nouvelle édition mise à jour [ed. M. Gilbert; BETL 51; Leuven: Leuven University Press, 1990] 59–81, here 63–64), is also helpful: "The search for a genre 'wisdom psalm' is in any case scarcely relevant to an attempt to locate the full extent and correct meaning of the relation between psalms and wisdom.... It seems more meaningful to study the dimension of wisdom in the psalms. This allows us to keep in the forefront certain characteristics of the psalm which are important for the literary, culturally historical, or theological evaluation without demanding a procrustean decision regarding the psalm's *Sitz im Leben* or literary classification."

to proverbs. It was the *use* of proverbs that distinguished the fools from the wise."[11]

In agreement with Crenshaw's suggestion, rather than pursuing the larger question of whether a particular psalm belongs to a class of wisdom psalms, I will instead simply explore how the wisdom elements of a psalm function to help structure the social epistemology represented within the poem.

Prior Research

While I am aware of no prior scholarship that specifically addresses the issue of epistemology in the Psalms, a number of recent studies have begun to explore wisdom elements in the Psalter that are confined neither to the conventional wisdom lexicon nor to those texts that have been traditionally classified as "wisdom psalms."

Weeks: Rethinking the "Wisdom Psalm" Criteria

In a critical review of the current state of wisdom psalms scholarship, S. Weeks provides a helpful clarification of the various criteria that have been employed by scholars for classifying a given psalm within the wisdom genre.[12] He dismisses as too imprecise those classification schemes that are (1) based either primarily on literary form, or (2) based on the requirement that the text be primarily didactic in nature. He ultimately decides that a psalm ought to be classified among the biblical Wisdom Literature solely on the basis of its thematic content.

Using Job, Qoheleth, and Proverbs as the defining texts for biblical wisdom themes, Weeks notes that such themes do not generally treat of the relationship between Yhwh and his people: hence, there is relatively little reference either to the origins and history of Israel, or to prophecy, the covenant, and the cult. "Wisdom literature's interest, however, can be described more precisely as an interest in the fate of individuals: both the ways in which those individuals are able to

---

11 J. L. Crenshaw, "A Proverb in the Mouth of a Fool," in *Seeking Out the Wisdom of the Ancients: Essays Offered to Honor Michael V. Fox on the Occasion of His Sixty-Fifth Birthday* (eds. R. L. Troxel, K. G. Friebel, and D. R. Magary; Winona Lake, IN: Eisenbrauns, 2005) 103–15, here 115 (original emphasis).
12 S. Weeks, "Wisdom Psalms," in *Temple and Worship in Biblical Israel* (ed. John Day; Library of Hebrew Bible/Old Testament Studies (formerly JSOTSup) 422; London: T&T Clark, 2005) 293–307.

shape their future, and the extent to which they are able to do so. Associated with this interest, of course, is a concern with the guidance which individuals can receive, and the authoritativeness of that guidance.... [Wisdom] literature is concerned with how individuals discover what they should do to survive and prosper in their own, individual lives, or with exhorting them to follow the guidance which they have received."[13]

Using such thematic content as a defining criterion, Weeks concludes: "If a psalm is meaningfully to be described as a 'wisdom psalm,' we would expect to find that it has a primary interest in the way individuals act to ensure their future well-being, the guidance they receive in doing so, or the obstacles that they face in deciding how to act best."[14] Basing himself on such standards, Weeks finds that among those psalms which have traditionally been classified as wisdom psalms, some (such as Psalms 1 and 37) clearly fit his definition, but others do not. Psalm 119, for example, although it focuses upon the Torah, is not specifically concerned with the role of the Law in directing one in living a good life. Thus, while thematic content is important, it is not only the subject matter, but also the psalmist's application of this, which must be carefully considered.

Geller and Van Leeuwen: Function Over Form

While Weeks provides a broad overview of psalms research and offers general suggestions for how such research ought to advance, it is noteworthy that a number of contemporary (though unrelated) studies, undertaking detailed analyses of specific psalms, largely adopt Weeks's approach of concentrating on the *function* of the wisdom content within a psalm, rather than only upon its form or subject matter.

S. A. Geller, e. g., has investigated the function of wisdom in the Psalter by comparing the portrayal of the natural world with the portrayal of Torah piety in a series of four psalms (8, 19, 104, 139), none of which are traditionally considered to be wisdom psalms.[15] He argues that a significant shift in the fundamental Israelite worldview occurred over the course of the seventh through the fifth centuries under the influence of a developing "Deuteronomic Movement," that culminated in the reform of Josiah. "It was a radical and uncom-

---

13 Ibid., 297–98.
14 Ibid., 299.
15 S. A. Geller, "Wisdom, Nature and Piety in Some Biblical Psalms," in *Riches Hidden in Secret Places: Ancient Near Eastern Studies in Memory of Thorkild Jacobsen* (ed. Tzvi Abusch; Winona Lake, IN: Eisenbrauns, 2002) 101–21.

promising expression of absolute monotheism and cultic centralization: one God, one shrine. It demanded total devotion – in love – to God and rejection of all foreign gods and ideas." As a result of this shift, wisdom, which had previously been perceived primarily through the ordering of the natural world (which Geller terms "Old Wisdom"), was now to be acquired through focus on the Torah ("New Wisdom"). The relationship between teacher and pupil received new emphasis, but "the only right thoughts were those that centered on God's revelation [through the Law]. Nature had no role, except as witness to God's power of creation and, negatively, as an inciter to idolatry."[16]

Geller sees the tension between the worldviews engendered by Old and New Wisdom as a creative force in the Psalter, with psalmists drawing variously upon one or the other tradition (e. g., the strong Torah piety stressed in Psalm 119), and often blending the two (as in Psalm 37), in order to address concerns about such matters as suffering, theodicy, and the place of human beings in the world (particularly as worldviews were being shaped by the continuously changing fortunes of Israel).

For Geller, the strongest representative of Old Wisdom in the Psalter is Psalm 104, "with its dominant focus on nature-creation" and the role of Yhwh as creator.[17] The creation theme is also clearly present in Psalm 8, but here one finds an additional – and unexpected – focus on humanity. The glory of God is not only proclaimed by the heavens, but also by the mouths of babes and infants (v. 3). And the psalmist's pondering of the marvels of creation does not lead to praise of Yhwh, but rather to a reflection on the place of human beings in the world (vv. 4–5). Geller sees the psalmist's statement of his personal wonder and awe (as well as his reflection on the human condition) as transcending the strict nature-theology of Old Wisdom.

In Psalm 19, we find the juxtaposition of nature-theology (vv. 2–7: "The heavens are telling the glory of God...") with Torah-based piety (vv. 8–11: "The Torah of Yhwh is perfect..."). Geller sees this pairing as both complementary and conflicting as the psalmist struggles to reconcile the increasingly internalized Torah piety (as one strives to keep the Law and avoid sin) with the outward-directed praise of Yhwh in his creation (which is not generally focused on humanity). "One cannot both look at the heavens and constantly search the ground for stumbling stones [i. e., be worried about failing to properly observe Torah]."[18]

---

16 Ibid., 102.
17 Ibid., 105.
18 Ibid., 115.

Finally, Geller reads Psalm 139 as the expression of the psalmist's nearly complete inward focus. Although it is not a "Torah Psalm," it reflects the introspection that Torah piety demands. Here, however, it is not the psalmist who carefully searches and knows the Torah, but rather Yhwh who searches and knows the psalmist (vv. 2–4).

Geller concludes by noting that although Torah piety superseded Old Wisdom, it could not satisfactorily address all of the questions which beset humanity, most notably the problem of why the good suffer. While Geller does not consider the influence of the changing understanding of wisdom upon the Israelite worldview, his study suggests that such an investigation could well yield insights into how various psalms – whether they are commonly classified within a "wisdom genre" or not – address the fundamental problems with which biblical Wisdom Literature frequently contends.

R. C. Van Leeuwen, in a recent study, echoes Geller's methodology insofar as he calls for a "trans-genre" approach to exploring wisdom elements within the Psalter.[19] Drawing upon research from folklore scholarship, he notes that the practice of limiting wisdom studies in the psalms to specific genres is overly confining. Instead, one ought to concentrate on the particular use that a given genre is expected to serve: "fundamental aspects of worldview (such as Israel's 'salvation history,' covenant, laws, election traditions, cultic practices) may be entirely absent from this or that genre, simply because the genre has a different *function*."[20]

Van Leeuwen then applies this approach to Psalms 111 and 112, which are commonly assumed to have been intentionally paired in the Psalter. Form-critically, Psalm 111 is generally classified as a hymn of thanksgiving, while Psalm 112 has the form of an extended "blessing" (אשרי איש) psalm and is generally numbered among the wisdom psalms. Nevertheless, Van Leeuwen points out (as have commentators before him) that the qualities highlighted in the anthropological blessing of Psalm 112 mirror those mentioned in the theological thanksgiving of Psalm 111, and that the psalmist(s) intended each psalm to function in a complementary manner vis-à-vis its partner.

The example of Psalms 111 and 112 makes clear that it would be erroneous to assume that different genres imply different *Sitze im Leben*. If one wishes to analyze a psalm in order to discern the worldview represented within it, simply identifying the psalm's genre is not necessarily informative. "One must ask of

---

19 R. C. Van Leeuwen, "Form Criticism, Wisdom, and Psalms 111–112," in *The Changing Face of Form Criticism for the Twenty-First Century* (eds. Marvin A. Sweeney and Ehud Ben Zvi; Grand Rapids: Eerdmans, 2003) 65–84.
20 Ibid., 70 (original emphasis).

genres, What [sic] recurring human *problem*, general or particular, is this piece of communication seeking to address or solve? *Genres attach to life settings or existence in terms of a common human problem or function, broad or narrow, as the case may be.*"[21] A useful corollary to this observation is that, in trying to ascertain the worldview of a particular psalm, one is justified in comparing it to texts drawn from other genres of biblical literature (both psalms of different genres, as well as texts outside of the Psalter), so long as these comparative texts address similar questions and concerns.

Wisdom and Torah

One such example of intertextual analysis comparing various psalms with texts drawn from outside the Psalter can be found in the growing body of contemporary research on the sapiential motifs common to the Psalter and the Torah. Such studies yield a better understanding of the function of wisdom themes within each of these genres. For example, by carefully comparing the language in Psalm 119 used to describe Torah with comparable language used throughout the Pentateuch and Wisdom Literature, K. A. Reynolds finds that this psalm demonstrates that the astute study of Torah can profoundly enrich one's life.[22] Similarly, T. Arnold argues that eight key Torah-related terms ("Torabegriffe") in Psalm 119 help present the psalm as an "invitation to the happy life".[23] In her study of Psalm 19, A. Grund demonstrates the significant relationship between this psalm and post-exilic Torah wisdom themes, while A. Klein finds that Psalm 19 serves as a literary "bridge" between the Torah themes of Psalm 119 and the broader biblical Wisdom Literature.[24]

---

21 Ibid., 82 (original emphasis). Note Crenshaw's similar emphasis on the *functional* use of wisdom elements in biblical texts (see n. 11 above).

22 K. A. Reynolds, *Torah as Teacher: The Exemplary Torah Student in Psalm 119* (VTSup 137; Leiden: Brill, 2010).

23 T. Arnold, "Die Einladung zu einem "Glücklichen" Leben: Tora als Lebensraum nach Ps 119,1–3," in *The Composition of the Book of Psalms* (ed. Erich Zenger; BETL 238; Leuven: Uitgeverij Peeters, 2010) 401–12.

24 See: A. Grund, *"Die Himmel erzählen die Herrlichkeit Gottes": Psalm 19 im Kontext der nachexilischen Toraweisheit* (WMANT 103; Neukirchen-Vluyn: Neukirchener Verlag, 2004); A. Klein, "Half Way Between psalm 119 and Ben Sira: Wisdom and Torah in Psalm 19," in *Wisdom and Torah: The Recption of 'Torah' in the Wisdom Literature of the Second Temple Period* (eds. Bernd U. Schipper and D. Andrew Teeter; JSJSup 163; Leiden: Brill, 2013). For other studies of inter-textual Wisdom influences in specific psalms, see, for example, Phil J. Botha, "Psalm 91 and Its Wisdom Connections," *OTE* 25 (2012) 260–76 and *idem*, "Interpreting 'Torah' in Psalm 1

Berlin: "Creation Wisdom"

A. Berlin has made a study of the "wisdom of creation," exploring how the discussion of creation in the Psalter often embodies important wisdom themes, even in psalms not traditionally grouped within the wisdom genre.[25] Like Geller, she focuses on Psalm 104, noting that its wisdom elements include: contemplation of the cosmos and the role of humanity within it; the conviction that Yhwh creates with wisdom (v. 24; cf. Prov 3:19), this implying that creation is logical and well-ordered; and the idea that the wicked will be vanquished (v. 35; cf. Psalms 1 and 37). Berlin situates her analysis within the broader domain of Psalms scholarship by insisting, "I do not want to argue that Psalm 104 is a wisdom psalm, for its stated aim is to 'bless the Lord,' not to instruct or to inquire into matters of good and evil. Nonetheless, these [wisdom] affinities raise the question of the use of wisdom thought in the Psalms and also, by extension, the relationship of wisdom to Torah."[26]

She begins by observing that wisdom in the Psalter differs from wisdom as generally encountered in other ancient Near Eastern literature (and much of the biblical Wisdom Literature). While the latter is generally "pragmatic, universalistic, [and] 'nonsectarian,'" the former is grounded "in the context of trust in God to do justice, punish the wicked, and so forth. Success or failure in life is determined not by intellectual knowledge or by savvy behavior but by loyalty to God and to his commandments... (cf. Ps 128:1; Psalms 1, 37, and 112). In the Psalms, the path to wisdom is through following God's commandments (cf. Eccl 12:13). And knowledge of the commandments is achieved through the study of God's words – learning them, speaking them (Pss 1:2; 37: 30 – 31; 119:12 – 16, 74 – 77 et passim). That is, in the view of many psalms, the form in which wisdom is accessible to Israel is through the Torah, the textual record of God's words."[27]

In agreement with Geller, and drawing upon the research of M. Weinfeld, Berlin attributes the connection between "Psalter wisdom" and Torah to deuter-

---

in the Light of Psalm 119," *HTS Teologiese Studies/Theological Studies* 68 (2012), Art. #1274, 7 pages. http://dx.DOI.org/ 10.4102/hts.v68i1.1274.

25 A. Berlin, "The Wisdom of Creation in Psalm 104," in *Seeking Out the Wisdom of the Ancients: Essays Offered to Honor Michael V. Fox on the Occasion of His Sixty-Fifth Birthday* (eds. Ronald L. Troxel, Kelvin G. Friebel, and Dennis R. Magary; Winona Lake, IN: Eisenbrauns, 2005) 71 – 83.

26 Ibid., 71.

27 Ibid., 72.

onomistic influences.[28] Deut 4:6–8 makes the connection explicit, noting that Israel's observance of Yhwh's "laws and rules" (חקים ומשפטים) shall be proof of her "wisdom" (חכמה). Furthermore, she accepts Geller's thesis that the deuteronomistic focus on Torah displaced an older, nature-centered, wisdom in the Psalter.

And yet, she contends that Psalm 104 combines wisdom elements from both the nature-centered and the Torah traditions. Even though in this psalm the wonders of the natural world are discussed explicitly and at length, while the word "Torah" never appears, Berlin sees creation as a parallel expression of Yhwh's Law here: "The natural world is, at it were, an ongoing visual revelation, just as the Torah is an ongoing textual (or aural) revelation."[29] In addition, she understands the unfolding discussion of creation in the psalm as a poetic retelling of the Genesis creation accounts. Thus, the Torah represents the core of what the psalmist is relating. While Geller identifies Psalm 104 primarily as a representative of Old (nature-focused) Wisdom, Berlin's analysis of the same text yields the important observation that, in the Psalter, wisdom elements from both the natural world and the revealed covenant can be creatively blended. While Berlin does not address the question of worldviews, given the diverse worldviews from which these two traditions (Old Wisdom and Torah) emerge, her discussion suggests that the blending of their perspectives could have significant epistemological consequences.

Brown: Comparing Psalms to Proverbs

W. P. Brown, in a study of the wisdom elements found in several psalms (Psalms 32, 34, 37, 78, 111, and 112 – all [except Psalm 78] traditionally identified as "wisdom psalms"), offers one of the most extensive comparisons, to date, between Proverbs and the Psalms.[30] He notes that the most striking difference between the two books is the strong personification of wisdom in Proverbs, which is completely absent from the Psalter. In the former, wisdom acts as a teacher-mediator

---

28 Berlin refers to M. Weinfeld, *Deuteronomy and the Deuteronomic School* (Oxford: Clarendon, 1972; reprint, Winona Lake, IN: Eisenbrauns, 1992) 244–81 (page citations are to the reprint edition).

29 Berlin, "Wisdom of Creation," 74.

30 W. P. Brown, "'Come, O Children … I Will Teach You the Fear of the Lord' (Psalm 34:12): Comparing Psalms and Proverbs," in *Seeking Out the Wisdom of the Ancients: Essays Offered to Honor Michael V. Fox on the Occasion of His Sixty-Fifth Birthday* (eds. Ronald L. Troxel, Kelvin G. Friebel, and Dennis R. Magary; Winona Lake, IN: Eisenbrauns, 2005) 85–102.

between Yhwh and humanity (e. g., Prov 8:22–31), while in the latter, the psalmists pray directly to God, expecting to be both heard and answered.

Brown notes that while in the Psalms, Yhwh is the principal source of instruction and protection, in Proverbs that role is often filled by wisdom herself. Her "house" is a place to gather for instruction, where her disciples can partake of a rich banquet (cf. Proverbs 9). "As God has 'his' habitation on Zion, providing refuge for worship, so wisdom has 'her' domicile, a place of instruction. Sophia's house is also a house of life and serves as a refuge from death and danger (see Prov 9:18). Conversely, refuge in the Psalms is occasionally construed as a place or destination of instruction, whose source is God, the Temple's *resident* theologian (Pss 31:3–4; 43:2–3)."[31]

In addition to instruction by Yhwh in the Psalter, Brown observes that Torah is also a source of teaching there. And yet, although Torah in the Psalms is, to some extent, the counterpart of wisdom in Proverbs, Torah is never personified in the Psalter. Brown surmises that this is because the psalmists "placed great value on God's *unmediated* agency in teaching. The language of command is the exclusive prerogative of God."[32] By contrast, commandments to learn and study in Proverbs are frequently given by parents, teachers, or wisdom herself (e. g., Prov 2:1; 3:1; 4:4; 7:1–2; 8:10), but not directly by Yhwh.

In spite of the difference between the roles of wisdom (in Proverbs) and Torah (in the Psalms), they nevertheless complement each other. For example, they each operate within separate milieus, but together they cover all strata of society. If Torah belongs within the cultic domain of prayer and praise of Yhwh, often recounting the covenantal relationship with Yhwh throughout Israel's history, wisdom is celebrated for "[traversing] the domains of human intercourse that lie outside the domain of the cult: from the family to the larger corporate, particularly urban, environment defined by marketplaces, crossroads, and city gates (Prov 1:20–21; 8:2–3). But nowhere does she gain entrance to the Temple (contra Sir 24:8–11). Nowhere does she play a definitive role in the history of salvation (contra Wis 10:1–21).... Her realm lies apart from the sanctuary of praise and petition that the God of the psalmists inhabits."[33]

Furthermore, Proverbs and Psalms are complementary with respect to their ultimate aims. While the Psalter as a whole is concerned primarily with the praise of God (cf. the book's title תהלים), the goal of Proverbs is primarily to impart instruction (cf. Prov 1:2–6). "In short, praise of God in Psalms is conjoined

---

31 Ibid., 100 (original emphasis).
32 Ibid., 101 (original emphasis).
33 Ibid.

with assent to wisdom in Proverbs. 'Learning the ropes' of life through wisdom (Prov 1:5) is matched by 'singing to God with a new song' in praise (Ps 149:1)."[34]

Given the difference in focus and purpose between Proverbs and Psalms, one might expect their epistemological perspectives to differ as well. It will be recalled from the previous chapter that the principal epistemological justification scheme in Proverbs is coherentism, with a limited number of core beliefs derived directly from divine revelation. If, as several of the studies considered above contend, wisdom in the Psalter tends to be more theocentric and more directly conveyed by God (i.e., unmediated) than in other biblical Wisdom Literature, then one might expect a greater role for divine revelation and a justification scheme in the Psalms that is more foundationalist (i.e., rooted in *a priori* revealed truths) than coherentist. One of the purposes of this study is to explore such a possibility.

Kellenberger: "Realization Discovery"

Finally, it is of interest to consider here the work of J. Kellenberger, a philosopher of religion (rarely referred to by biblical scholars), who has identified an epistemological scheme that he terms "realization-discovery," of which he considers the Psalms to be an exemplar.[35] Although he is mainly concerned with how a psalmist "knows" the presence of God (or how a "fool" denies that presence), the process that he describes can be more generally applied to other types of knowledge as well.

Kellenberger begins by noting that, in the Psalms, "knowing" God is not so much a matter of reason, but of feeling; not simply observing, but beholding. Anyone can behold God's presence in the surrounding world. What impedes that beholding is not a lack of information, but rather a condition of one's heart. When the psalmist proclaims: "the fool [נבל] says in his heart, 'there is no God'" (Ps 14:1), he is not making an existential statement, but is rather averring that the fool, because of his wickedness, feels no relationship with God. God's presence is to be found among the righteous (בדור צדיק), not the wicked (Ps 14:5). Similarly, when the wicked man (רשע) declares that "there is no God" (Ps 10:4), he is not doubting God's existence. Rather, he scorns (נאץ)

34 Ibid., 102.
35 See J. Kellenberger, *The Cognitivity of Religion: Three Perspectives* (Berkeley and Los Angeles: University of California Press, 1985); idem, "Wittgenstein's Gift to Contemporary Analytic Philosophy of Religion," *Philosophy of Religion* 28 (1990) 147–72; idem, "The Fool of the Psalms and Religious Epistemology," *International Journal for Philosophy of Religion* 45 (1999) 99–113.

God (Ps 10:3), contends that God pays no attention to his wicked deeds (Ps 10:11), and imagines that God does not care about his actions (Ps 10:13).

In these psalms, "knowledge" is dependent upon a precondition of the heart. "The fool is the opposite of the Psalmist, then, not by virtue of denying a proposition the Psalmist affirms, but by virtue of having a sensibility utterly different from the Psalmist's: the fool does not find God's presence in his life. And he does not because of the disposition of his heart."[36] That disposition, Kellenberger contends, is pride and sinfulness. Pride is grounded in an attachment to self-image and a lack of self-denial (cf. Ps 73:25 in which the psalmist implicitly expresses self-denial by declaring that only God can bring him delight).[37] Because of sin, the wicked have no fear of God (cf. Psalm 36) and practice self-deception, presuming that they are immune from God's oversight (Psalms 10 and 14). In the tradition of the Psalms, there is thus a connection between (1) not finding God, (2) being blind to God's presence, and (3) sin (Kellenberger suggests NT parallels in Matt 5:8 and Rom 1:18–21).[38]

In order to find the presence he denies, the fool must overcome a kind of "moral blindness" that prevents him from beholding what has always been present before him. The process by which this happens falls under the epistemic category of "discovery" (hence, Kellenberger's term "realization-discovery"). It is not the fruit of an argument; the psalmist is not attempting to "prove" anything. Realization-discovery comes with the discovery of God's presence: for example, the discovery of God's power (Psalm 66), majesty (Psalm 93), loving-kindness (Psalm 107), faithfulness, and righteousness (Psalm 36).[39]

Realization-discovery can be achieved in a number of ways, but it always requires that the discoverer be able to transcend his own self-focus. This can happen, for example, through the experience of a personal crisis, such as the grieving over a loss which directs one's focus beyond oneself and toward God (cf. psalms of lament). Awe and wonder before nature or God's power can also provide the context for self-transcending discovery (cf. Psalms 93, 99, and 104). Other means include the acknowledgement of personal guilt for sin, as well as love or sympathy as one is moved to see another as oneself.[40]

---

36 Kellenberger, "Fool of the Psalms," 100. Compare Ps 37:30–31, in which God's Torah resides in the hearts of the just, allowing them to speak wisdom (on this point, see Brown, "'Come, O Children,'" 88–89).
37 Kellenberger, *Cognitivity of Religion*, 114–15.
38 Kellenberger, "Wittgenstein's Gift," 161. See also *Cognitivity of Religion*, 118.
39 Kellenberger, "Wittgenstein's Gift," 160.
40 Kellenberger, *Cognitivity of Religion*, 114–15.

And yet, it is not the case that any of these processes will necessarily lead to an awareness of God's presence. The fool of the Psalms, after all, has always before him the same evidence that is present to the faithful psalmist. Why should one deny God's presence and the other embrace it? Kellenberger suggests that realization-discovery in the Psalms seems to include a role for God's direct influence (a kind of "psalmic grace"). If empirical experiences are sufficient for moving one's focus away from self-centeredness, perhaps God's explicit revelation is necessary for discovering God's presence and for imparting knowledge about him. Kellenberger asks, "What does the fool lack in the way of belief? What does he or she need to believe religiously? If we answer this question from within the sensibility of the Psalms, it is not a more thorough gathering of evidence.... It is a lifting of blindness to the presence of God, which streams all about the unbeliever. A lifting that the unbeliever may not be able to do by himself or herself, and may require something happening to him or her, something being given. I do not take it to be a disadvantage of the epistemological model we find in the Psalms that it affords a role for God's grace."[41]

Kellenberger's conclusion that certain types of knowledge cannot be acquired without divine assistance is supported by Brown's observation that in the psalms explicit dependence upon Yhwh's intervention (not unlike Kellenberger's "grace") is sometimes required before one becomes capable of receiving new knowledge. In Psalm 32, for example, the psalmist receives instruction directly from Yhwh (Ps 32: 8 – 9), but only after first confessing his sins and receiving Yhwh's forgiveness (v. 5). Brown argues that this psalm "establishes the occasion of instruction within an explicitly cultic setting (that is, a setting of prayer [v. 6], refuge [v. 7], and praise [v. 11]) by situating confession and forgiveness as foundational for wise conduct."[42]

Employing the epistemology lexicon from chap. 1, we can say that while realization-discovery is firmly rooted in the foundationalist justification scheme, it constitutes a sort of hybrid between empiricism and divine revelation. Certain types of knowledge can be acquired by observing the natural and human world, but only with God's unmediated help can one fully perceive and behold what is before one's eyes.

---

41 Kellenberger, "Fool of the Psalms," 105.
42 Brown, "'Come, O Children,'" 93.

Conclusion

The preceding, partial survey of studies on wisdom elements in the Psalms, drawn from recent literature that moves beyond traditional form criticism, has revealed the potential fruitfulness of exploring such elements in psalms of varying genres. A methodology that focuses more on the function of wisdom elements within a given text, rather than solely on the text's form or *Sitz*, can free one to identify epistemological qualities that might otherwise be missed (for example, the realization that the nature imagery employed in Psalm 104 reveals a worldview that not only endorses "Old Wisdom," but can also celebrate the wisdom of Torah). Furthermore, we have seen that a full appreciation of wisdom in the Psalter will likely require a greater attentiveness to the role of God in the definition of knowledge (i.e., in the justification for holding beliefs within a particular worldview) – and in the acquisition of that knowledge – than is required in other biblical Wisdom Literature.

Four Psalms: An Epistemological Approach

The remainder of this study will present a detailed epistemological analysis of Psalms 1, 73, 90, and 107. Of these, only Psalm 1 (a "Torah psalm") is consistently classified as a wisdom psalm, although the other three have been acknowledged as possessing wisdom qualities.[43] Each of these texts, in its own way, addresses the fundamental problem of why people suffer and what they can do to make sense out of their suffering and perhaps alleviate it. They also address (at least implicitly) the difficult truth that the wicked sometimes prosper, while the righteous sometimes perish.[44] Hence, there is a shared focus among the four psalms, which ought to facilitate the comparison of the function of the wisdom elements in each text. Through the psalmist's use of metaphor and narrative, as well as the extent of his acknowledgement of divine intervention within human life, each poem presents a unique worldview that helps to shape the meaning of knowledge within the text.

---

[43] A more detailed discussion of previous classifications and understandings of these psalms will be provided in the following chapters.

[44] For a brief discussion of how various Jewish commentators have addressed the Psalter's engagement with questions of theodicy, see H. Angel, "The Differences Between the Wise and the Foolish in Psalms: Theodicy, Understanding and Providence, and Relgious Responses," *Jewish Bible Quarterly* 38 (2010) 157–65.

Psalm 1, as I shall discuss in the following chapter, constructs a fundamental worldview (shaped by a particularly strong metaphorical structure) against which the rest of the psalms can be measured. While this poem does not overtly address the question of suffering, it assumes a worldview in which the roles of both those who suffer and those who prosper are clearly defined. I shall explore the way in which this clear definition affects the very manner in which one can "know" what suffering is and in which one can perceive the character of those who endure it.

In Psalm 73, the psalmist struggles with the age-old problem that the wicked often seem to thrive, while the just suffer. He clearly acknowledges that fact and yet is not satisfied with his lack of understanding about why the world is so ordered. Thereafter, rather abruptly, and without intentionally seeking it, he attains the understanding he lacked, and comes to perceive his world from a new (and more satisfactory) perspective. I shall explore how this "new knowledge" is acquired, and of what it consists.[45]

Psalm 90 presents an introspective reflection on the brevity of life and the ubiquity of suffering throughout a typical life span. There is no attempt by the psalmist to distinguish between the righteous and the wicked, although some degree of universal culpability for the human condition is acknowledged. With noteworthy directness and precision, the psalmist asks Yhwh to impart wisdom to him so that he might better make sense of the suffering and brevity of life. I shall explore, within the context of the worldview portrayed in the psalm, what it would mean to "make sense" out of human suffering, what type of wisdom Yhwh could impart to accomplish that goal, and how the psalmist might actually acquire it from Yhwh.

In Psalm 107, the psalmist employs a rich series of metaphors to create a worldview in which a variety of persons – those with moral culpability and those without it – have to face suffering and hardship. The psalm explores the degree to which Yhwh causes/alleviates suffering, as well as the human capacity for engaging Yhwh from within the midst of suffering. At the end of the poem, the psalmist exhorts "anyone who is wise" to carefully observe and ponder all that has been recounted. I shall explore what the "new knowledge" in this psalm might be, such that even a wise man could learn something from it of which he had previously been unaware.

---

45 Weeks ("Wisdom Psalms," 303) notes that relatively little scholarly attention has been paid to "the wisdom characteristics of a small group of psalms which focus upon the hiddenness of divine retribution"; he considers Psalm 73 as the exemplar of this group.

Finally, it will be noted that each of these psalms stands at the beginning of one of the Psalter's five "Books" (Psalm 1 begins Book I; Psalm 73, Book III; Psalm 90, Book IV; and Psalm 107, Book V). While I do not contend that these psalms were so placed primarily because of their epistemological qualities, I shall nevertheless consider those qualities in view of the overall composition of the canonical Psalter. If, as some scholars contend, there is a wisdom-centered influence on the final structure of the Psalter, then aspects of that influence may be reflected in the various representations of knowledge that are found in these psalms which mark the beginnings of the Psalter's canonical segments.

Preliminary Note on the Texts[46]

My prevailing assumption throughout this study is that the MT generally represents the "original" Hebrew text, and this study is principally an analysis of that text.[47] Unless there is strong Hebrew manuscript evidence to the contrary, emen-

---

[46] I present here, for convenience, a list of all the major commentaries on the Psalms that I have consistently consulted and referred to in this work: F. Delitzsch, *Biblischer Kommentar über die Psalmen* (BKAT; 5th ed.; Leipzig: Dörffling & Franke, 1894); B. Duhm, *Die Psalmen* (Kurzer Hand-Commentar zum Alten Testament 14; Freiburg i. B.: Mohr, 1899); C. A. Briggs and E. G. Briggs, *A Critical and Exegetical Commentary on the Book of Psalms* (2 vols.; ICC; Edinburgh: T&T Clark, 1906); H. Gunkel, *Einleitung in die Psalmen: Die Gattungen der religiösen Lyrik Israels* (HKAT; Abt. 2 Suppl.; Göttingen: Vandenhoeck & Ruprecht, 1933); idem, *Die Psalmen: Übersetzt und Erklärt* (5th ed.; HKAT II/2; Göttingen: Vandenhoeck & Ruprecht, 1968); S. Mowinckel, *The Psalms in Israel's Worship* (trans. D. R. Ap-Thomas; 2 vols.; 1962; repr., Biblical Resource Series; Grand Rapids: Eerdmans, 2004); H.-J. Kraus, *Psalmen* (2 vols.; BKAT XV/2; Neukirchen-Vluyn: Neukirchener Verlag, 1960); C. Westermann, *Der Psalter* (Stuttgart: Calwer Verlag, 1967); idem, *Ausgewählte Psalmen* (Göttingen: Vandenhoeck & Ruprecht, 1984); M. Dahood, *Psalms* (3 vols.; AB 16,17, 17 A; Garden City, NY: Doubleday, 1966–1970); L. C. Allen, *Psalms 101–150* (WBC 21; Waco: Word Books, 1983); P. C. Craigie, *Psalms 1–50* (WBC 19; Waco, TX: Word Books, 1983); M. E. Tate, *Psalms 51–100* (WBC 20; Dallas: Word Books, 1990); E. S. Gerstenberger, *Psalms: Part 1, with an Introduction to Cultic Poetry* (FOTL 14; Grand Rapids: Eerdmans, 1988); idem, *Psalms: Part 2, and Lamentations* (FOTL 15; Grand Rapids: Eerdmans, 2001); F.-L. Hossfeld and E. Zenger, *Die Psalmen: Psalm 1–50* (NEchtB; Würzburg: Echter Verlag, 1993); K. Seybold, *Die Psalmen* (HAT I/15; Tübingen: Mohr, 1996); F.-L. Hossfeld and E. Zenger, *Psalmen 51–100* (HThKAT; Freiburg: Herder, 2000); idem, *Psalmen 101–150* (HThKAT; Freiburg: Herder, 2008); J. Goldingay, *Psalms* (3 vols.; Baker Commentary on the Old Testament; Grand Rapids: Baker Academic, 2006–2008).

[47] The MT is taken from K. Elliger and W. Rudolph, eds., *Biblia Hebraica Stuttgartensia*, 5th ed. (Stuttgart: Deutsche Bibelgesellschaft, 1967/77). The LXX text is taken from the critical edition by A. Rahlfs, ed., *Psalmi cum Odis* (Septuaginta: Vetus Testamentum Graecum: auctoritate Societatis Litterarum Gottingensis editum; Vol. X; Göttingen: Vandenhoeck & Ruprecht, 1979); the

dation of the MT should be rare. While significant discrepancies between the MT and the ancient versions will be identified, emendation of the MT based upon such differences will only be considered in those instances in which serious internal inconsistencies or anomalies within the Hebrew text itself might be resolved by doing so. A detailed review of the numerous emendations to the MT proposed for these psalms by various twentieth-century scholars, while of interest in its own right, is beyond the scope of this study.[48]

Peshitta text (hereafter referred to as Syr) is taken from L. G. Rignell, ed., *Psalms* (The Old Testament in Syriac according to the Peshitta Version II/3; Leiden: Brill, 1980); both the Vulgate text (*iuxta LXX*; hereafter referred to as Vg) and Jerome's translation of the Hebrew text (*iuxta Hebraicum*) are taken from R. Weber, ed., *Biblia Sacra iuxta Vulgatam Versionem, editionem quartam emendatam* (Stuttgart: Deutsche Bibelgesellschaft, 1994).

48 For extended discussions of the relationships among the ancient versions and the MT, see, for example, E. Tov, *Textual Criticism of the Hebrew Bible* (2nd rev. ed.; Minneapolis: Fortress, 1992) esp. 121–54; idem, *Text-Critical Use of the Septuagint in Biblical Research* (2nd rev. ed.; Jerusalem Biblical Studies 8; Jerusalem: Simor, 1997); E. Würthwein, *The Text of the Old Testament* (trans E. F. Rhodes; 2nd rev. ed.; Grand Rapids: Eerdmans, 1995) esp. 50–99.

Chapter IV.
Psalm 1: Social Epistemology Within a Deuteronomistic Worldview

In this chapter, after a translation of Psalm 1 and a brief discussion of text-crit-ical, structural, and dating issues, I shall apply the methodology developed in chap. 1 to explore the worldview represented within the text, with a particular focus on its use of metaphor. I shall argue that the psalm's structural metaphors are the dominant features in the poem and that they are strongly representative of the theology evinced by Deuteronomy and the Deuteronomistic History. I shall assess the influence of such a deuteronomistic worldview upon the social epis-temology of the poem and explore the justification scheme that is employed to support the fundamental propositions which the psalmist puts forth. Finally, I shall consider the canonical placement of the psalm within the Psalter in light of the poem's epistemological characteristics.

Translation and Text-Critical Issues

1 אַשְׁרֵי־הָאִישׁ אֲשֶׁר לֹא הָלַךְ בַּעֲצַת רְשָׁעִים וּבְדֶרֶךְ חַטָּאִים לֹא עָמָד וּבְמוֹשַׁב לֵצִים לֹא יָשָׁב:

2 כִּי אִם בְּתוֹרַת יהוה חֶפְצוֹ וּבְתוֹרָתוֹ יֶהְגֶּה יוֹמָם וָלָיְלָה:

3 וְהָיָה כְּעֵץ שָׁתוּל עַל־פַּלְגֵי מָיִם אֲשֶׁר פִּרְיוֹ יִתֵּן בְּעִתּוֹ וְעָלֵהוּ לֹא־יִבּוֹל וְכֹל אֲשֶׁר־יַעֲשֶׂה יַצְלִיחַ:

4 לֹא־כֵן הָרְשָׁעִים כִּי אִם־כַּמֹּץ אֲשֶׁר־תִּדְּפֶנּוּ רוּחַ:

5 עַל־כֵּן לֹא־יָקֻמוּ רְשָׁעִים בַּמִּשְׁפָּט וְחַטָּאִים בַּעֲדַת צַדִּיקִים:

6 כִּי־יוֹדֵעַ יהוה דֶּרֶךְ צַדִּיקִים וְדֶרֶךְ רְשָׁעִים תֹּאבֵד:

1   Blessed is the person who has not walked in the counsel of the wicked,
    and in the way of the sinful has not stood,
    and in the seat of scoffers has not sat.

2   But in Yhwh's Torah is his joy,
    and on his Torah he muses day and night.

3   He is like a tree, planted beside water channels,
    which gives its fruit in its season, and its leaf does not wither,
    and everything he does he makes prosper.

4   Not so, the wicked.
    Rather, (they are) like chaff that wind blows away.

5   Thus, the wicked do not rise in the judgment,
    nor sinners in an assembly of the righteous.

6   For Yhwh knows the way of the righteous,
    but the way of the wicked perishes.

There are no significant text-critical difficulties with this psalm. I shall briefly address a few of its more substantial semantic and syntactic issues; the interested reader is referred to the relevant literature for a fuller discussion.[1]

Verses 1–2

I translate עצה in v. 1 as "counsel" (thus, e. g., the NAB, NRSV, NJPSV). Dahood, on the basis of Qumran and Ugaritic evidence, argues that the *gathering* of the wicked is intended, rather than their *advice*. Thus, he translates "council."[2] I retain "counsel" insofar as it seems more consistent with the overall metaphor of following a path under the influence of a guide. Both the LXX (βουλή) and the Syr (ﺯﺩﺣ) concur with such a reading.

Later in the same verse, ליץ has the basic meaning of "babbler." But because it is parallel with רשעים and חטאים, it is usually understood here to mean some-

---

1 In addition to the commentaries cited in chap. 3 (n. 46), the following studies provide a representative sampling of text-critical and structural analyses of Psalm 1: P. Auvray, "Le Psaume 1," *RB* 53 (1946) 365–71; H. N. Richardson, "Some Notes on ליץ and Its Derivatives," *VT* 5 (1955) 163–79; J. A. Soggin, "Zum ersten Psalm," *TZ* 23 (1967) 81–96; R. Bergmeier, "Zum Ausdruck עצת רשעים in Ps 1:1; Hi 10:3; 21:16 und 22:18," *ZAW* 79 (1967) 229–32; E. Beaucamp, "Le sens de ki-im en Psaume 1, vv. 2 et 4," *RSR* 57 (1969) 435–37; W. H. Brownlee, "Psalms 1–2 as a Coronation Liturgy," *Bib* 52 (1971) 321–36; H. Bardtke, "Erwägungen zu Psalm 1 und Psalm 2," in *Symbolae Biblicae et Mesopotamicae. Festschrift Francisco Mario Theodore de Liagre Böhl* (eds. M. A. Beek, A. A. Kampman, and C. Nijland, J. Ryckmans; Leiden: Brill, 1973) 1–18; G. W. Anderson, "A Note on Psalm I 1," *VT* 24 (1974) 231–33; R. Lack, "Le psaume 1 – Une analyse structurale," *Bib* 57 (1976) 154–67; P. Auffret, "Essai sur la structure littéraire de Psaume 1," *BZ* 22 (1978) 27–45; W. Vogels, ""A Structural Analysis of Ps 1," *Bib* 60 (1979) 410–16; R. P. Merendino, "Sprachkunst in Psalm I," *VT* 29 (1979) 45–60; J. T. Willis, "Psalm 1 – An Entity," *ZAW* 91 (1979) 381–401; N. H. Snaith, "Psalm I 1 and Isaiah XL 31," *VT* 29 (1979) 363–64; J. P. Brennan, "Psalms 1–8: Some Hidden Harmonies," *BTB* 10 (1980) 25–29; G. André, "'Walk,' 'Stand,' and 'Sit' in Psalm I 1–2," *VT* 32 (1982) 327; J. A. Durlesser, "Poetic Style in Psalm 1 and Jeremiah 17:5–8: A Rhetorical Critical Study," *Semitics* 9 (1984) 30–48; S. C. Reif, "Ibn Ezra on Psalm I 1–2," *VT* 34 (1984) 232–36; P. Auffret, "Compléments sur la structure littéraire du Ps 2 et son rapport au Ps 1," *BN* 35 (1986) 7–13; J. F. D. Creach, "Like a Tree Planted by the Temple Stream: The Portrait of the Righteous in Psalm 1:3," *CBQ* 61 (1999) 34–46; J. Høgenhaven, "The Opening of the Psalter: A Study in Jewish Theology," *JSOT* 15 (2001) 169–80; R. Cole, "An Integrated Reading of Psalms 1 and 2," *JSOT* 98 (2002) 75–88; C. J. Collins, "Psalm 1: Structure and Rhetoric," *Presbyterion* 31 (2005) 37–48; E. I. Esteban, "Salmo 1: Reflexiones Teológicas y Escatológicas Acerca del Juicio," *Theologika* 26 (2011) 28–45; R. L. Cole, *Psalms 1–2: Gateway to the Psalter* (Hebrew Bible Monographs 37; Sheffield: Sheffield Phoenix Press, 2013).

2 Dahood, *Psalms*, 1. 2. See also Bergmeier ("Zum Ausdruck עצת רשעים"), who argues for the same translation, based on Qumran usage of the word.

thing like "mocker" or "scoffer." The Syr (ܡܡܝܩܢܐ) attests this understanding, but the LXX reads the stronger "pestilent/pestiferous" person (λοιμός). N. H. Richardson, surveying the lexical range of ליץ in the MT, agrees with such a stronger reading ("evil person").[3]

A syntactic question arises at the beginning of v. 2 regarding the correct interpretation of the phrase כי אם. In view of the preceding series of negations in v. 1, the most common understanding of this expression is as an adversative ("but/rather").[4] The phrase could, however, be read as the opening of the protasis of a conditional sentence, of which the apodosis begins in v. 3 with והיה (thus, "Because his joy is in Yhwh's Torah [v. 2].... Therefore he is like a tree... [v. 3]).[5] I find no compelling reason in favor of such a reading, and so adopt the adversative understanding, as will become clear in my following structural analysis.

Verses 3 – 4

כל אשר יעשׂה יצליח ("and everything he does he makes prosper") could conceivably have as its subject the tree ("and everything [i.e., fruit] it produces prospers"). However, the parallel between the blessed man in v. 3 and the wicked in v. 4 argues for keeping the blessed man as the subject in v. 3c. Goldingay points out that, in the hiphil, צלח is usually transitive (e.g., Ps 37:7; Deut 28:29; Josh 1:8; Isa 48:15); I follow his translation ("he makes prosper").[6] I find no reason to accept the suggestion in *BHS* that the entire phrase is a gloss.

At the end of v. 4, the LXX attests ἀπὸ προσώπου τῆς γῆς ("from the face of the earth"), which is present neither in any known variants of the MT nor in the Syr. Briggs and Briggs deem it an explanatory gloss, inserted "to get rid of the abruptness of the first line [i.e., v. 4a]."[7]

---

3 Richardson, "Some Notes on ליץ," 176. Contra Richardson, see Anderson ("Note on Psalm I 1"), who argues against any such tendency to progressively intensify the negative qualities of the persons mentioned in v. 1a, 1b, and 1c. Snaith ("Psalm I 1") adopts a view similar to Anderson.
4 See, e.g., B. K. Waltke and M. O'Connor, *An Introduction to Biblical Hebrew Syntax* (Winona Lake, IN: Eisenbrauns, 1990) § 39.3.5d. This is the sense reflected in the LXX and the Syr readings.
5 Such is the reading of Beaucamp, "Le sens de ki-im en Psaume 1." He argues for this on structural grounds, contending that vv. 2 and 3 form a couplet, as do vv. 4 and 5. Also employing structural analysis, Collins ("Psalm 1: Structure and Rhetoric"), contra Beaucamp, argues for the more traditional adversative reading of כי אם (as does Cole, *Psalms 1–2*, 57–58).
6 Goldingay, *Psalms*, 1. 79.
7 Briggs and Briggs, *Commentary*, 1. 9.

Verses 5–6

The expression לא יקמו רשעים במשפט ("the wicked do not rise in the judgment") is taken by some earlier scholars (e.g., Delitzsch; Duhm; Briggs and Briggs; Dahood) to suggest a kind of eschatological reckoning, comparable to such texts as Dan 7:10, 22, 26.[8] More recent exegetes, however, find a reference here not to a final event at the end of time, but rather to an ongoing judgment process to which the wicked are subjected in each generation. Tate, for example, understands "the judgment" as the *place* of judgment (cf. Deut 25:1): "the wicked will have no place, or no respect, in the courts of law, where justice and righteousness are the *modus operandi*."[9] Similarly, Goldingay understands the phrase as referring to "an assembly of the faithful," who gather to pass judgment concerning disputes (or charges of wrongdoing) within the community. Such an assembly, he compellingly argues, constitutes the counterpart to the wicked, the sinful, and the scoffers who offer bad counsel in v. 1. At the time of their judgment, the wicked will not be able to rise up and take their place in the assembly (cf. v. 1, in which the faithful "do not stand" among the sinful).[10]

אבד ("perish") has a broad lexical range. Snaith points out that, in addition to "perish," the word can also mean "to wander/be lost."[11] Perhaps the attestation that most closely parallels its usage in Ps 1:6 is Job 6:18, which describes caravans losing their way in the desert and "perishing." Thus, the word may connote not simply "perishing," but the kind of perishing which results from straying off a safe path. If this is the meaning intended by the psalmist, it would closely parallel the image used in Ps 1:1a of the blessed and the wicked following divergent ways.

---

8 An exception is Auvray ("Le Psaume 1," 368), who rejects any eschatological interpretation of v. 5. He finds no suggestion of resurrection in קום, but rather reads it as referring to the resistance of the wicked against the assembly of the righteous (i.e., "standing against"; cf. Josh 7:12, 13; Amos 7:2, 5).

9 Tate, *Psalms*, 1.58.

10 Goldingay, *Psalms*, 1.87.

11 Snaith, *Five Psalms*, 10. The word is used to describe Jacob as a "wandering" Aramean (Deut 26:5). It can also describe livestock which have been "lost": Deut 22:3; 1 Sam 9:3, 20; Jer 50:6; Ezek 34:4, 16; Ps 119:176.

Structure, Unity, and Dating

Structure

It is striking how many different structural schemes have been proposed for this brief psalm. In his survey of twenty-three scholarly studies and modern translations, C. J. Collins finds no less than thirteen suggested structural divisions for the psalm's six verses.[12] Anticipating my analysis below of the poem's metaphors, I find Collins's own proposed structure – based upon the rhetorical force of the lines – to be the most compelling. I present it here, with slight modifications:[13]

> vv. 1–2   two contrasting sources of guidance: "journey" metaphor
> vv. 3–4   two contrasting consequences: "plant" metaphor
> vv. 5–6   two contrasting final outcomes

The psalm's dominant structural feature is the antithetical comparison between the blessed man and the wicked. The first couplet defines the distinction between the two ways of life, the second couplet develops the qualities that characterize each way, while the third couplet describes the ultimate destination toward which each way leads.

Unity

Most modern commentators treat Psalm 1 as a unified whole.[14] Within the larger structure noted above, there is a chiastic sub-structure that unifies vv. 1–5:

> A   vv. 1–2   blessed man
> B   v. 3   fruitful plant
> B′ v. 4   withered plant
> A′ v. 5   wicked man

---

12 Those divisions are (according to verse number): 1–3/4–5/6; 1–3/4–6; 1–2/3–4/5–6; 1–2/ 3–4a/4b-6; 1–2/3/4–6; 1/2–3/4–6; 1/2–3/4–5/6; 1/2–3/4/5–6. See Collins, "Psalm 1," 37. Several highly detailed studies of the structure of Psalm 1 (beyond the level necessary for our purposes) can be found in: Lack, "Le Psaume 1"; Auffret, "Essai sur la structure"; Vogels, "Structural Analysis of Ps 1"; and Cole, *Psalms 1–2*, 46–52.
13 Collins, "Psalm 1," 40.
14 See, e. g., Willis, "Psalm 1 – An Entity"; Craigie, *Psalms*, 59 (and references therein); Cole, *Psalms 1–2*, 46–47.

Furthermore, the repetition of דרך ("way") in vv. 1 and 6 provides an *inclusio* for the entire poem.

This apparently self-contained character of the psalm notwithstanding, many scholars have noted lexical, thematic, and even structural similarities between Psalms 1 and 2, which have led to the suggestion that the two psalms were deliberately paired (perhaps even composed together) to serve as an introduction to the entire Psalter.[15] Lexical similarities include: the description אשרי ("blessed") in the opening line of Psalm 1 and the closing line of Psalm 2; the use of הגה ("muse") in Ps 1:2 and Ps 2:1; the warning in both Ps 1:6 and Ps 2:12 that those who do not follow the righteous "way" (דרך) will "perish" (אבד). Others have argued for strong thematic links between the two poems. W. H. Brownlee, for example, contends that there was originally no division between Psalms 1 and 2; rather, they formed a single poem as part of a coronation liturgy for the kings of Judah.[16] R. Cole, while acknowledging the two psalms as originally independent compositions, understands their pairing as a deliberate commentary on the ideal qualities of the king: the monarch of Psalm 2 *is* the blessed man of Psalm 1 who takes joy in Yhwh's torah.[17]

Additional evidence cited in support of the original unity of the two psalms is the fact that Psalm 2 is among the few psalms in Books I–III that lack a superscription (perhaps indicating that a single psalm has secondarily been split in order to form two poems). Furthermore, several ancient sources seem to support this possibility. In Acts 13:33, Paul quotes part of MT Ps 2:7, referring to it (in most manuscripts) as from the second psalm. However, there is a variant attested in Codex Bezae in which he refers to the line as coming from the "first psalm."[18] J. Høgenhaven cites additional sources (including the Babylonian Talmud and 4Q174 from Qumran) that could be interpreted as referring to the first two psalms of the canonical Psalter as a unified text.[19] None of these data provide decisive proof, however, of the original unity of the two psalms.[20]

---

15 For a review of the lexical, thematic, and structural similarities, see Cole, "An Integrated Reading," and *Psalms 1–2* (and references therein); for a particularly detailed discussion of the structural similarities, see also Auffret, "Compléments sur la structure."

16 Brownlee, "Psalms 1–2."

17 Cole, "An Integrated Reading" and *Psalms 1–2*, 63–64.

18 For a fuller discussion of this matter, see J. A. Fitzmyer, *The Acts of the Apostles* (AB 31; New York: Doubleday, 1998) 516–17.

19 Høgenhaven, "Opening of the Psalter."

20 Cole (*Psalms 1–2*, 46–78), providing an exhaustive review of the evidence for and against the original unity of the two psalms, ultimately decides against it (while strongly arguing for the likelihood that they were deliberately paired in the Psalter's final redaction).

Although the above evidence may well indicate a deliberate redactional pairing of Psalms 1 and 2, for the purposes of this study I shall treat Psalm 1 as a distinct entity. Such a move is warranted, given my focus on the epistemology operative within individual psalm texts.

Dating

While acknowledging the difficulties associated with attempts to date the psalms, most commentators agree that Psalm 1 is probably a late exilic or post-exilic text. The themes of the psalm, and even some of its language, share a strong similarity with deuteronomistic theology (this issue will be explored in greater detail below). Furthermore, it has long been noted that the image of a fruitful tree as a symbol for a blessed man (Ps 1:3) bears a striking resemblance to the similar image in Jer 17:5–8. Recently, J. A. Durlesser and J. F. D. Creach have conducted independent comparative studies of these two texts and have reached the similar conclusion that it is unlikely that the psalmist was directly quoting or paraphrasing the prophet.[21] Nevertheless, both scholars concede that the two texts clearly employ comparable images that seem to draw from a shared socio-cultural environment, thus further supporting a late/post-exilic dating for the psalm.

Metaphor Analysis

In the first chapter of this study I argued that a society's "social epistemology" is largely responsible for structuring its operative worldview. It was shown that conceptual metaphors are among the primary tools (though not the only ones) employed by a culture for the acquisition and transmission of its shared social stock of knowledge. In chap. 2 I considered the specific example of the social epistemology represented in the Book of Proverbs. While metaphor is important for defining the worldview of Proverbs, it is nevertheless not the prevailing feature of the book's literary style.

In the present and following chapters, however, I shall explicitly focus on the structuring power of metaphor as one of the dominant epistemological features of the Psalter. Writing in 2002, William Brown commented that his study of

---

21 See Durlesser, "Poetic Style in Psalm 1 and Jeremiah 17:5–8"; Creach, "Like a Tree Planted by the Temple Stream."

the use of metaphor in the Psalter "fills a yawning gap in exegetical practice. Form-critical concerns have traditionally governed critical exegesis of Psalms, and it is only recently that the poetic image has captured the professional exegete's attention."[22] The decade following Brown's observation, however, has witnessed a remarkable rise in the number of studies devoted to metaphors in the psalms.[23]

Psalm 1 contains two conceptual metaphors: LIFE IS A JOURNEY and PEOPLE ARE PLANTS (cf. vv. 3–4). The JOURNEY domain has often been noted by commentators because of the "two ways" metaphor—the way of the righteous and the way of the wicked—that echoes a theme encountered elsewhere in biblical Wisdom Literature (cf., for example, our discussion in chap. 2 of the "two paths" metaphor in Proverbs).

Referring to the powers of metaphor discussed above (i.e., the powers of structuring, of options, of reason, of evaluation, and of being there), the JOURNEY metaphor in Psalm 1 does provide a certain degree of structure to the way in which the target domain (LIFE) is perceived. The reader/listener is invited to view life as a progression from beginning to end, along particular paths. Such structuring immediately invites questions about the nature of this journey: one wonders, e.g., what are the journey's beginning/end points, who are the travelers, what is the terrain over which they traverse, what are the helps/perils they encounter along the way, and so forth.

But in Psalm 1, the LIFE IS A JOURNEY conceptual metaphor only weakly exercises the power of options. For example, besides the observation (v. 1) that the

---

22 W. P. Brown, *Seeing the Psalms: A Theology of Metaphor* (Louisville: Westminster John Knox, 2002) 14.

23 To cite just a few examples: P. van Hecke, ed., *Metaphor in the Hebrew Bible* (BETL 187; Leuven: Leuven University Press, 2005); A. Basson, *Divine Metaphors in Selected Hebrew Psalms of Lamentation* (FAT 2.15; Tübingen: Mohr, 2006); W. P. Brown, "'Here Comes the Sun!': The Metaphorical Theology of Psalms 15–24," in *The Composition of the Book of Psalms* (ed. Erich Zenger; BETL 238; Leuven: Uitgeverij Peeters, 2010) 259–77; B. Doyle, "Where is God When You Need Him Most? The Divine Metaphor of Absence and Presence as a Binding Element in the Composition of the Book of Psalms," in *The Composition of the Book of Psalms* (ed. Erich Zenger; BETL 238; Leuven: Uitgeverij Peeters, 2010) 377–90; P. van Hecke and A. Labahn, eds., *Metaphors in the Psalms* (BETL 231; Leuven: Uitgeverij Peeters, 2010); B. Weber, "'Dann wird er sein wie ein Baum...' (Psalm 1,3): Zu den Sprachbildern von Psalm 1," *OTE* 23 (2010) 406–26; A. R. Gray, *Psalm 18 in Words and Pictures: A Reading Through Metaphor* (BIS 127; Leiden: Brill, 2014). For metaphor studies prior to Brown's work, see, for example, F.-L. Hossfeld, "Die Metaphorisierung der Beziehung Israels zum Land im Frühjudentum und im Christentum," in *Zion: Ort der Begegnung: Festschrift für Laurentius Klein zur Vollendung des 65. Lebensjahres* (eds. F. Hahn, F.-L. Hossfeld, H. Jorissen, and A. Neuwirth; BBB 90; Bodenheim: Athenäum, 1993) 19–33.

traveler is well advised to reject bad counsel and to avoid loitering with scoffers, there is no reference to the means of transportation (walking, sailing, etc.), no description of what the paths are like (no reference to terrain or environment), no description of the qualities of the trip (smooth, rough, rapid, impeded, etc.), and no mention of the destination envisaged. The *travellers* are clearly differentiated (the righteous and the wicked), but the characteristics of their respective journeys, which one would expect to see developed within the LIFE IS A JOURNEY metaphor, are not. It is as if the metaphor were only employed in order to stress that there are two fundamental options in life. By comparison, Moses (Deut 30:15–20) manages to convey the same dichotomy without metaphorical language.

An important consequence of this lack of specificity is that the potential power of reason for the LIFE IS A JOURNEY metaphor is largely unrealized. Within the JOURNEY domain, one would expect that a traveler who is misguided, lost, or stalled would have recourse to seeking out a new guide, or to retracing his steps and selecting a new path, etc. However, within the weakly developed metaphor of JOURNEY in Psalm 1, there is no clear means for shifting from the path of the wicked to the path of the righteous (indeed, the psalm's use of the metaphor does not even allow for a clear evaluation of the actual paths themselves, but only of the travelers on the paths). The wicked "stand in the way of the sinful" and "sit with scoffers" (Ps 1:1), but how does the journey itself differ in the case of sinners and the righteous? And is sitting along the journey a bad thing in itself (because, for example, it represents a stalemate or a lack of ambition) or is it only the sitting with scoffers that is problematic (i.e., as a bad influence)?

While motion/travel is generally the principal distinguishing quality of the LIFE IS A JOURNEY metaphor, in Psalm 1 that quality is almost irrelevant. It is as if the righteous are automatically understood to be following a good path (and the sinful a bad path), so that the path itself—along with any possibility for a shift from one path to the other (from righteous to sinful, or from sinful to righteous)—need not be addressed. There is a kind of moral stasis in which the righteous and the sinful are fixed in their respective states, and the incomplete development of the JOURNEY metaphor only serves to underscore that condition.

By contrast, the PEOPLE ARE PLANTS conceptual metaphor is considerably more developed in the psalm. This metaphor is fairly common throughout the Psalter (and, indeed, can be found throughout the MT).[24] It refers to human be-

---

24 W. J. Urbrock ("Mortal and Miserable Man: A Form-Critical Investigation of Psalm 90," in *SBLSP 1974* [2 vols.; Atlanta: Scholars, 1974] 1. 1–33, here 1–7) discusses a series of biblical texts

ings in plant-like terms and is often employed to describe either the human life cycle (we "bloom" in youth, "mature" and "yield" throughout adulthood, and "wither" in old age) or the ephemeral nature of life itself (we are grass that springs up in the morning but withers by dusk). In Psalm 1, selections are made within the PLANTS domain so as to describe the quality of life in the PEO-PLE domain. The righteous are well-rooted, they are near a source of life (water), they yield fruit at the proper time, and they never wither. The wicked, by contrast, are that part of the harvest which has no redeeming value (chaff), they are withered instead of well-watered, and they disperse with the wind instead of being well-rooted.

When such choices are taken regarding the source domain (PLANTS), a particular structure is imposed upon the target domain (PEOPLE). Within the context of this conceptual metaphor, motion/change is not generally valued as a good thing: plants are not meant to move, they are meant to be firmly rooted in place. And when they do move, it is because they have become withered by-products that are separated from their life-giving roots and are blown away by the wind. Furthermore, plants cannot go seeking after their own sustenance: they either have their source of sustenance at hand, or it must be brought to them. Finally, a plant's health is measured solely by its fruitfulness: by the vitality of its foliage and the abundance of its produce.

Within Psalm 1, the PEOPLE ARE PLANTS conceptual metaphor's power of options is exercised in a particularly stark manner. The tree is either rooted by the stream or it is not. The metaphor makes no mention of a gardener who comes to tend the tree, a state of affairs which only emphasizes the reality that the tree *must* be rooted in a particular place or else it will die.[25] There is a definitive and permanent quality to the two options that have been specified in vv. 3–4 from among all of the possibilities within the PLANTS domain, and there is little allowance for change from one option to the other. Thus, chaff does not "reconstitute itself" so as to become a healthy plant, and a strong plant that is firmly rooted near water need not fear withering.

Note too that due to this exercise of the power of options, the metaphor's power of reason is also severely constrained. Within the scenario of Psalm 1, if a plant "notices" that it is withered, it has little choice but to endure the situa-

---

that employ this metaphor; for example Pss 37:2; 90:6; 92:8; 102:12; 129:6; Isa 37:27; 44:4; 51:12; Jer 17:8.

25 In this regard, Psalm 1 can be contrasted with other biblical PEOPLE ARE PLANTS metaphors that do mention the presence of gardeners who carefully tend their plants, not only keeping them healthy but actively working to restore them to fruitfulness after they have seemingly failed (see, e.g., Isa 5:1–7; Luke 13:6–9).

tion; there are basically no decisions to be made. The power of evaluation is similarly limited: there is no middle ground between the fruitful and the withered plant. One can immediately and accurately assess any plant's state of health.

If we now consider the manner in which the source domain structures the target domain, we find that the metaphor encourages thinking about people as being fairly stable in their moral character: they do not make radical life changes, and if change does come, it is not generally a positive occurrence. The assumption is that people will either cleave closely to the source of moral goodness or else wantonly disregard it. The quality of their moral state ought to be fully evident from the external quality of their lives. Thus, while a condition of moral stasis (i.e., that people do not fundamentally change their moral character) was inferred above from the psalm's underdeveloped portrayal of the LIFE IS A JOURNEY conceptual metaphor, that condition is made explicit in the more fully developed PEOPLE ARE PLANTS metaphor. Although one might initially expect these two disparate metaphors to convey different perspectives (i.e., the fluid motion of a journey versus the rooted stability of a plant), the psalmist has, in fact, employed them in such a way that they reinforce each other.

In the next section, I shall consider how the psalmist uses these metaphors to structure a worldview and will explore the resultant epistemology which that worldview engenders.

Worldview and Epistemology

Before analyzing how the conceptual metaphors of Psalm 1 contribute to its worldview, we should note that the psalm's theology reveals a good deal about its worldview as well. Many commentators have observed that the psalm presents a theology which is highly consonant with that of the Book of Deuteronomy and the Deuteronomistic History. Comparing the entire Psalter with Deuteronomy, P. D. Miller observes that: "One could make a fairly convincing case that the Psalter and Deuteronomy set before their readers a fundamental and shared claim, to wit, that following the law of the Lord is the way to blessing and life. The corollary to this is also often indicated: Disobedience to the law is the way to death."[26]

What Miller notes there about the entire Psalter is perhaps especially applicable to its opening poem. As many commentators have noted, the "two ways"

---

26 P. D. Miller, "Deuteronomy and the Psalms: Evoking a Biblical Conversation," *JBL* 118 (1999) 3–18.

and their attendant consequences (way of life/death) laid out in Deut 30:15–20 are echoed in the way of the righteous (דרך צדיקים) and the way of the wicked (דרך רשעים) in Psalm 1. Moses declares that the one who chooses life "walks in the way" (ללכת בדרכיו; Deut 30:16) of Yhwh, while the blessed man of Psalm 1 does not follow ("walk after") the counsel of the wicked (לא הלך בעצת רשעים). The expression "on his [Yhwh's] Torah day and night he meditates" (בתורתו יהגה יומם ולילה; Ps 1:2) is attested only one other time in the MT; namely, in Yhwh's exhortation to the people to meditate "day and night" (והגית בו יומם ולילה; Josh 1:8) on the law which Moses gave them.[27] Psalm 1 also resonates with the prescription from the law of the king in Deuteronomy (Deut 17:14–20) that the good king is one who sits on his throne and ponders Yhwh's torah for "all the days of his life."

Such a theology suggests a worldview in which the sole measure of value is the status of one's relationship with Yhwh, and the quality of that relationship is determined by the degree to which one is faithful to Yhwh's torah. This obviously holds not only for personal wellbeing, but also (and perhaps primarily) for the health of the people as a whole, as represented by their king.[28] Thus all conceivable human concerns, from those of the individual to the affairs of nations, are governed by the torah. As one discerns life's choices, or as a king discerns affairs of state, the only correct choice is the one which is most faithful to the torah. One need not fear ignorance of the torah's prescriptions, given the exhortation to ponder it unceasingly. The reward for doing so, or the consequence for refusing to do so, is immediately apparent: either life or death, respectively.

The conceptual metaphors in Psalm 1 strongly underscore this understanding of the ordering of the world. Here, the torah is presented as the life source near which the righteous are "rooted." Within the worldview that the PEOPLE ARE PLANTS conceptual metaphor helps to structure, one either focuses on

---

27 Ibid., 11. For further discussion of the Psalm 1 – Deuteronomy connection, see, e.g., B. S. Childs, *Introduction to the Old Testament as Scripture* (Philadelphia: Fortress, 1979) 513; J. L. Mays, "The Place of the Torah-Psalms in the Psalter," *JBL* 106 (1987) 4; W. Brueggemann, "Bounded by Obedience and Praise: The Psalms as Canon," *JSOT* 50 (1991) 65–66; Hossfeld and Zenger, *Die Psalmen: Psalm 1–50*, 47; R. G. Kratz, "Die Tora Davids : Psalm 1 und die Doxologische Fünfteilung des Psalters," *ZTK* 93 (1996) 7; E. Zenger, "Der Psalter als Buch: Beobachtungen zu seiner Entstehung, Komposition und Funktion," in *Der Psalter in Judentum und Christentum* (eds. Hans-Josef Klauck and Erich Zenger; Herders Biblische Studien 18; Freiburg: Herder, 1998) 36–38; J. A. Grant, *The King as Exemplar: The Function of Deuteronomy's Kingship Law in the Shaping of the Book of Psalms* (SBL Academia Biblica 17; Atlanta: Society of Biblical Literature, 2004) 43–55; Cole, *Psalms 1–2*, 46–78.
28 In the following section, I shall consider how the pairing of Psalm 1 with Psalm 2 invites an explicit consideration of the relationship between the king and torah.

the torah, and thus prospers, or one does not, and thus fails. To be close to the torah is an unfailing guarantee of one's prosperity and happiness. Conversely, if one's life displays prosperity and happiness, such qualities are taken to provide unfailing proof of one's meditation on the torah.

As we saw above, the psalm's conceptual metaphors seem to allow little opportunity for a foundational change in the orientation of one's life. Its structuring projects a worldview which is relatively static and fixed.[29] Such a worldview exerts a significant constraint upon its attendant social epistemology and the meanings of knowledge that are allowed by the society which is represented within the psalm.

Applying the diagnostic tool developed at the end of chap. 1, we can summarize the primary proposition of Psalm 1 as: "the righteous prosper and the wicked fail." This notion is portrayed with uncompromising conviction and there seems little doubt that it is firmly believed by those who embrace the worldview of the psalm.[30]

Leaving aside for the moment the question of the proposition's objective truth, we can address the method of its justification employed in the psalm. The starkly drawn depictions of the righteous and the wicked support a coherentist model for justification. There is no indication that the psalmist has drawn his conclusions from observing a range of good and evil people. Rather, he accepts as true the primary proposition, which he then applies to the conditions of people's lives to discern their moral characters. That is to say, the belief that a person is righteous (or wicked) can only be justified if that person appears to be prospering (or failing), for only such a conclusion coheres with the worldview depicted in the psalm. And as we saw above, that worldview is structured and supported by the psalm's conceptual metaphors.[31]

---

29 Note that, in this respect, Psalm 1 is more static than the theology represented by the Deuteronomistic History, which does allow for change of heart (with consequent change in fortunes). Consider, for example, the frequent refrain in the Book of Judges concerning the disobedient Israelites (who are suffering for their actions) crying out for salvation to Yhwh, who favorably responds: e. g., Judg 3:9; 4:3; 6:7.

30 I stress again that while the psalmist might subjectively disagree with the position he is portraying within the worldview of the psalm, we are here concerned solely with the portrayal itself. Note also that this portrayal is applicable whether the "good/wicked" persons in Psalm 1 refer to people in general, or (as Cole [*Psalms 1–2*] and others have argued) to the good and wicked kings represented in Psalm 2.

31 In the language of my chap.1, the structuring power of its conceptual metaphors helps to generate the objectivation and primary socialization of the social order represented within the psalm.

This raises the interesting question of how the psalmist might evaluate an apparently just man who was observed to be suffering (or an evil man observed to be prosperous). Such a scenario presents a strain on the overall coherency of the worldview scheme in Psalm 1. Kearney notes that a successful worldview requires two levels of consistency: internal and external: "The organization of world-view assumptions is shaped in two ways. The first of these is due to internal equilibrium dynamics among them. This means that some assumptions and the resultant ideas, beliefs, and actions predicated on them are *logically* and *structurally* more compatible than others, and that the entire world view will "strive" toward maximum logical and structural consistency. The second and main force giving coherence and shape to a worldview is the necessity of having to relate to the external environment."[32] Thus, the fundamental propositions upon which a worldview is based cannot be logically contradictory, nor can they be significantly at odds with the way the world actually is.[33]

The idea of a righteous person who suffers, or a wicked person who prospers, could never constitute "knowledge" within the society depicted by Psalm 1, for such a notion simply fails to cohere with its prevailing worldview. And yet, it is highly likely that in the actual life of the psalmist's social world (no less than in our own), people who were apparently righteous *did*, in fact, suffer. If the worldview of the psalm is to remain intact in the face of such apparent inconsistency, then some form of nihilation (cf. chap. 1) becomes necessary.

One form that such nihilation might take is the position adopted by Job's friends in the face of his suffering (see, e. g., Job 11:1–20): namely, the belief that the suffering of a person who is supposedly righteous only serves to expose the falsity of his purported righteousness. Thus, one means for addressing the anomaly of a righteous sufferer or a prosperous wicked man is to deny the veracity of their previous moral characterization: it is simply not possible that their supposed moral status is an accurate representation of who they really are.

What we find, therefore, is that the social epistemology represented within Psalm 1 severely limits the way in which one is permitted to think about life's sufferings and failures. If one believes he has seen a just man suffer, then he must somehow be mistaken—his supposition cannot constitute knowledge. The psalmist is hardly willing to entertain nuanced moral questions: one is simply good or wicked. Such a conclusion might seem obvious given the moral starkness of the psalm; nevertheless, our epistemological exercise regarding it

---

32 Kearney, *World View*, 52.
33 Note that each of these conditions supports the coherence justification for true beliefs (Kearney's "consistency" is a form of coherence).

will prove useful when we encounter the more complex scenarios presented in the remaining psalms to be analyzed in this study.

Epistemological Impact of the Canonical Placement of Psalm 1

Having seen how the social epistemology operative within the worldview of Psalm 1 places significant constraints upon the range of behaviors that one is permitted to reasonably comprehend (i. e., to consider as authentically true), we now consider how the canonical placement of such a worldview at the beginning of the Psalter yields a perspective that influences how all subsequent psalms are perceived.

A number of exegetes have suggested that Psalm 1 was a late (post-exilic) addition to a pre-existing collection (perhaps Psalms 2–72), primarily intended to transform the Psalter from a collection of liturgical hymns into a prayer book more suitable for personal prayer. Thus, R. Kratz argues that the psalm was deliberately composed as a proem for the Psalter to stress the importance of one's whole-hearted devotion to the torah of Yhwh. This focus, combined with the Psalter's frequent recalling of the action of Yhwh on Israel's behalf throughout her history (e. g., Psalm 78), could serve to unite the post-exilic community in the face of its fragility during the restoration period. He further notes that the use of such comprehensive language as not "walking," "standing," or "sitting" in the path of the wicked (Ps 1:1), but rather (by inference) completely abiding in the joy of the torah of Yhwh is evocative of the absolute commitment to the Lord that is called for by Deut 6:4–9.[34]

K. Seybold similarly notes that the late addition of Psalm 1 (and Psalm 119) to the Psalter, while rendering what had been a hymn book into a book for personal prayer, placed particular stress on the connection between one's actions and their attendant consequences (*Tun-Ergehen-Zusammenhang*). The stark contrast between the two paths described in Psalm 1 underscores the complete demise of the wicked (reminiscent of the fate of the wicked described in Ps 73:17).[35] Furthermore, when combined with the five-fold division of the Psalter resulting

---

34 Kratz, "Die Tora Davids," 3–5.
35 Seybold, *Die Psalmen*, 29. See also P. D. Miller ("The Beginning of the Psalter," in *The Shape and Shaping of the Psalter* [ed. J. Clinton McCann; JSOTSup 159; Sheffield: JSOT Press, 1993] 83–92), who argues that Psalm 1 sets the agenda for Book I of the Psalter (and strongly influences Books II–V) by clearly delineating the two categories of the wicked and the righteous and by placing strong emphasis upon the observance of torah

from the four doxologies (Ps 41:14; 72:18; 89:53; 106:48), the deuteronomistic perspective of Psalm 1 (discussed in the previous section) appears to shape the Psalter into a clear reflection of the Pentateuch. Indeed, Psalm 1 "reminds the reader of the way in which to use the Torah: 'Happy are those (whose) delight is in the law of the Lord, and on his law they meditate (Hebrew: murmur) day and night' (Ps. 1.1–2). This wise advice suggests that the whole Psalter is to be read as a wisdom text, in the same way."[36]

Other scholars who have made canonical study of the degree to which Psalm 1 relates to Deuteronomy, the deuteronomistic history, or other psalms with a strong torah emphasis include B. Childs (who notes parallels between Psalm 1, Deuteronomy 30, Joshua 1, and Psalms 19 and 119), F.-L. Hossfeld and E. Zenger (who, in addition to the parallels cited by Childs, highlight connections between Psalm 1, and Deuteronomy chapters 6 and 17), B. Sommer (who sees the addition of Psalm 1 as creating a "radically new vision" for the collection of psalms, rendering the Psalter into a "textbook" that one can turn to for guidance and instruction), and W. Brueggemann (who notes that Psalm 1 calls for a strict obedience to Yhwh's torah).[37]

On a somewhat different note, S. Gillingham suggests that Psalms 1 and 150 were intentionally added as "bookends" to the Psalter in order to highlight opposite ends of the spectrum of devotional prayer: while Psalm 1 sets a tone of reflective, personal piety and focuses on teaching the pray-er to observe Yhwh's torah, Psalm 150 is a universal (i.e., not limited to Israel or torah observance), festive, communal prayer addressed directly to God.[38] Furthermore, "Psalm 1 has clear dualistic concerns, focused on the different destinies of the righteous and the wicked; the means of finding God is by way of an obedient will, and the suppliant sees the life of faith defined by 'enemies' who are in fact within his own congregation. Psalm 150 has no such dualism....Far from

---

36 K. Seybold, "The Psalter as a Book," in *Jewish and Christian Approaches to the Psalms: Conflict and Convergence* (ed. Susan Gillingham; Oxford: Oxford University Press, 2013) 179. See also E. Ballhorn, "Der Torapsalter: Vom Gebetbuch zum Buch der Weisung," *BK* 65 (2010) 24–27.
37 B. Childs, *Introduction to the Old Testament*, 513; Hossfeld and Zenger, *Die Psalmen: Psalm 1–50*, 47; B. Sommer, "Psalm 1 and the Canonical Shaping of Jewish Scripture," in *Jewish Bible Theology: Perspectives and Case Studies* (ed. Isaac Kalimi; Winona Lake, IN: Eisenbrauns, 2013) 207; Brueggemann, *Bounded by Obedience*, 64–66.
38 See M. Leuenberger (*Konzeptionen des Königtums Gottes im Psalter. Untersuchungen zu Komposition und Redaktion der theokratischen Bücher IV-V innerhalb des Psalters* [ATANT 83; Zürich: Theologischer Verlag, 2004] 265–390) for a fuller discussion of this trend toward more universal worship of God at the end of the Psalter.

finding enemies within the congregation, those participating are bound together in their praise of their Creator."[39]

All of these observations about the significance of the placement of Psalm 1 draw upon the strict epistemological dualism that is engendered by its PEOPLE ARE PLANTS conceptual metaphor.

As noted above, although Psalm 1 stands at the head of the book, it has long been recognized that, in the Psalter's final redaction, Psalms 1 and 2 seem to have been deliberately joined via lexical, thematic, and even audial linkages.[40] If Psalms 1 and 2 are considered jointly as the introduction to the Psalter, then the Lord's "anointed king" in Psalm 2 can be understood explicitly as the "blessed man" of Psalm 1. Conversely, the evil nations and kings in Psalm 2 can be identified with the "wicked" of Psalm 1.[41] When the two psalms are considered to be intimately related in this way, they provide a perspective from which to view the entire Psalter that is even more deuteronomistically influenced than the perspective resulting from Psalm 1 alone. E. Zenger argues that a redac-

---

39 S. Gillingham, "Entering and Leaving the Psalter: Psalms 1 and 150 and the Two Polarities of Faith," in *Let Us Go Up to Zion: Essays in Honour of H. G. M. Williamson on the Occasion of his Sixty-Fifth Birthday* (eds. I. Provan and M. J. Boda; Leiden: Brill, 2012) 388–89.

40 Some of the more obvious connections are the presence of the beatitude formula (אשרי) that forms an *inclusio* between Ps 1:1 and 2:12; the fact that Psalms 1 and 2 are two of only four psalms in Book I of the Psalter without superscriptions; the dual appearance of הגה (1:2 and 2:1) and אבד (1:6 and 2:12). For extensive discussions of these and many more points of connection between the two psalms see G. T. Sheppard, *Wisdom as a Hermeneutical Construct: A Study in the Sapientializing of the Old Testament* (BZAW 151; Berlin: de Gruyter, 1980) 136–44; and Cole, *Psalms 1–2*, 46–141.

41 For a discussion of the implications of reading Psalms 1 and 2 as an integral unit (though not necessarily composed as a single text), see, for example: J. C. McCann, "Books I–III and the Editorial Purpose of the Hebrew Psalter," in *The Shape and Shaping of the Psalter* (ed. J. Clinton McCann; JSOTSup 159; Sheffield: JSOT Press, 1993) 103–104; idem, "The Shape of Book I of the Psalter and the Shape of Human Happiness," in *The Book of Psalms: Composition and Reception* (ed. P. W. Flint and P. D. Miller; VTSup 99; Leiden: Brill, 2005) 342; P. D. Miller, "The Beginning of the Psalter," in *The Shape and Shaping of the Psalter*, 87; idem, "Kingship, Torah Obedience, and Prayer: The Theology of Psalms 15—24," in *Neue Wege der Psalmenforschung: Für Walter Beyerlin* (eds. K. Seybold and E. Zenger; Herders Biblische Studien 1; Freiburg: Herder, 1994) 141; M. Millard, *Die Komposition des Psalters: Ein Formgeschichtlicher Ansatz* (FAT 9; Tübingen: Mohr, 1994) 21; Høgenhaven, "Opening of the Psalter," 169–73; R. Rendtorff, "The Psalms of David: David in the Psalms," in *The Book of Psalms: Composition and Reception*, 60; B. Janowski, "Ein Tempel aus Worten: Zur Theologischen Architektur des Psalters," in *The Composition of the Book of Psalms* (ed. Erich Zenger; BETL 238; Leuven: Uitgeverij Peeters, 2010) 280–88; Cole, *Psalms 1–2*, 1–45; D. M. Howard, "The Proto-MT Psalter, the King, and Psalms 1 and 2: A Response to Klaus Seybold," in *Jewish and Christian Approaches to the Psalms: Conflict and Convergence* (ed. S. Gillingham; Oxford: Oxford University Press, 2013) 187.

tor added Ps 2:10–12 to what had been a royal psalm in order to link it with Psalm 1 (via the beatitude saying in Ps 1:1), thus portraying the anointed king as exemplary monarch: not only because he has the Lord's favor, but also because he perfectly follows the instructions set out for him in Deut 17:16–20, meditating on Yhwh's torah day and night. The king therefore becomes a kind of "Torah-teacher" (*Tora-Lehrer*) for the people.[42]

The pairing of Psalms 1 and 2 thus situates all the subsequent psalms within a complex inter-connection of torah, divine kingship, and human kingship. J. L. Mays' observation of the consequences of this close relationship between the first two psalms is representative of many of the scholars cited in this chapter:

> One part [i.e., Psalm 1] addresses the question of the individual, the other [i.e. Psalm 2] of history. One is concerned with the problem of the wicked in society, the other with the nations of the world. There is a choice between two ways for the individual (one can scoff at torah or delight in it) and for the nations (one can rebel or one can serve the Lord). This intricate pairing as introduction says that all the psalms dealing with the living of life under the Lord must be understood and recited in the light of the reign of the Lord and that all psalms concerned with the kingship of the Lord are to be understood and recited with the torah in mind.[43]

F.-L. Hossfeld and E. Zenger echo the sentiment that the combination of Psalms 1 and 2 conveys a philosophy of life that is governed by a stark dichotomy of choices—in effect, there is no real choice at all, since one of the options leads not to a concrete goal but to a complete abyss. As Moses laid the option of life or death before the Israelites (Deut 30:19), so Psalms 1 and 2 present a similarly striking alternative.[44] And just as Joshua triumphed by faithfully adhering to Yhwh's torah (Josh 1:1–9), so must post-exilic Israel faithfully adhere to "David's torah," the Psalter.[45]

It is important to note that even when Psalm 1 is considered in conjunction with Psalm 2, there is no alteration of the structuring power of the former's conceptual metaphor. In Psalm 2 there is never any question of the wicked rulers or nations actually succeeding in their plotting against the Lord or his anointed king. Indeed, their demise is as certain and unquestionable as that of the wicked

---

42 Zenger, "Der Psalter als Buch," 36–37. See M. Leuenberger (*Konzeptionen des Königtums Gottes*, 94–95) for a discussion of the diachronic development of the relationship between Psalms 1 and 2.

43 Mays, "Place of the Torah-Psalms," 10.

44 Hossfeld and Zenger, *Die Psalmen: Psalm 1–50*, 45–7. On this point, Cole (*Psalms 1–2*, 37–38 et passim) adamantly argues that the "blessed man" of Psalm 1 refers singularly to Yhwh's favored king in Psalm 2 and does not refer to humanity in general.

45 Zenger, "Der Psalter als Buch." 37.

in Psalm 1. Similarly, the rule of the Lord and his anointed is never diminished or threatened.[46]

We find, therefore, that the canonical placement of Psalm 1 casts a shadow of deuteronomistic theology across the entire Psalter. It is nevertheless the case, however, that such a theology often appears in tension with the rest of the book. In the face of that tension, Brueggemann concludes that the opening psalm of the Psalter is meant to refute what follows: "Psalm 1 intends to insist on a certain reading of the psalter which seems against the grain of the poems themselves. When read unemcumbered by Psalm 1, many of the other Psalms assert that the wicked are not cut off from the community, and that even the righteous have doubts about these claims. Psalm 1 wants, however, as much as possible to preclude such an awareness."[47]

I suggest, however, that an alternative characterization of the relationship between Psalm 1 and the following poems is also possible. Namely, Psalm 1 may serve to deliberately provoke the question of whether the moral view of the world which it puts forth is actually true. We can imagine that, within the worldview presented by Psalm 1, such a challenging question might be posed by a social "deviant" (to employ the language of social epistemology presented in the first chapter of this study). We realize, of course, (as surely as would a pray-er of this psalm in antiquity) that such a question is firmly grounded in everyday experience. The worldview of Psalm 1 would not seem to be the worldview that most people inhabit. The psalms which follow could then be interpreted as attempting an answer to that fundamental question raised by the "deviant."

Conclusion

However the relationship between Psalm 1 and the rest of the Psalter is understood, the principal challenge to the epistemology of Psalm 1 (with its deuteronomistic conceptual metaphor) is the fact that the righteous often do seem to suffer and fail, while the wicked enjoy prosperity. A response to such a challenge along the lines taken by Job's friends is ultimately unsatisfactory in the face of lived experience (as Job himself affirms; cf. Job 27:1–6). The Psalter itself ac-

---

46 It should be noted, however, that—unlike in Psalm 1—the wicked party in Psalm 2 would seem to have recourse for redemption insofar as they are exhorted in Ps 2:12a to "kiss the son" (נשקו־בר), that is, to pay homage to the Lord and his king. There are, however, exegetical difficulties with this verse for which the reader is referred to the standard commentaries.
47 Brueggemann, "Bounded by Obedience and Praise," 66.

knowledges this challenge, insofar as the problem of the suffering just man is acknowledged in many subsequent psalms.

In the following chapter, I shall consider one such example: Psalm 73. After exploring the worldview (with its conceptual metaphors) represented within the psalm, I shall investigate its accompanying social epistemology. I shall then apply the results of this analysis to address the question of whether the speaker in Psalm 73 was able to *know* and to *understand* a claim which can only be classified as an untenable contradiction within the worldview of Psalm 1: namely, that a good man might suffer and a wicked man might prosper.

Chapter V.
Psalm 73: Mystical Knowledge

Psalm 73 opens Book III of the Psalter with a frank acknowledgement of the challenging fact that wicked people often thrive, in spite of the foundational belief that Yhwh blesses the just and punishes the wicked. As we saw in the previous chapter, this foundational belief is put forward at the very beginning of the Psalter. Now we shall explore how one psalmist addresses the questions and doubts which arise when that belief is threatened.

After a translation of Psalm 73 and a brief discussion of text-critical, structural, and dating issues, I present a discussion of the primary conceptual metaphor employed by the psalmist. Next I provide an exegetical study of v. 17, an interpretive crux for the poem. Finally, I discuss the psalm's epistemological implications in order to assess the psalmist's treatment of the challenging issues he raises.

Text and Translation

1   מִזְמוֹר לְאָסָף אַךְ טוֹב לְיִשְׂרָאֵל אֱלֹהִים לְבָרֵי לֵבָב׃

2   וַאֲנִי כִּמְעַט נָטוּי רַגְלָי כְּאַיִן שֻׁפְּכָה אֲשֻׁרָי׃

3   כִּי־קִנֵּאתִי בַּהוֹלְלִים שְׁלוֹם רְשָׁעִים אֶרְאֶה׃

4   כִּי אֵין חַרְצֻבּוֹת לְמוֹתָם וּבָרִיא אוּלָם׃

5   בַּעֲמַל אֱנוֹשׁ אֵינֵמוֹ וְעִם־אָדָם לֹא יְנֻגָּעוּ׃

6   לָכֵן עֲנָקַתְמוֹ גַאֲוָה יַעֲטָף־שִׁית חָמָס לָמוֹ׃

7   יָצָא מֵחֵלֶב עֵינֵמוֹ עָבְרוּ מַשְׂכִּיּוֹת לֵבָב׃

8   יָמִיקוּ וִידַבְּרוּ בְרָע עֹשֶׁק מִמָּרוֹם יְדַבֵּרוּ׃

9   שַׁתּוּ בַשָּׁמַיִם פִּיהֶם וּלְשׁוֹנָם תִּהֲלַךְ בָּאָרֶץ׃

10   לָכֵן יָשׁוּב¹ עַמּוֹ הֲלֹם וּמֵי מָלֵא יִמָּצוּ לָמוֹ׃

11   וְאָמְרוּ אֵיכָה יָדַע־אֵל וְיֵשׁ דֵּעָה בְעֶלְיוֹן׃

12   הִנֵּה־אֵלֶּה רְשָׁעִים וְשַׁלְוֵי עוֹלָם הִשְׂגּוּ־חָיִל׃

13   אַךְ־רִיק זִכִּיתִי לְבָבִי וָאֶרְחַץ בְּנִקָּיוֹן כַּפָּי׃

14   וָאֱהִי נָגוּעַ כָּל־הַיּוֹם וְתוֹכַחְתִּי לַבְּקָרִים׃

15   אִם־אָמַרְתִּי אֲסַפְּרָה כְמוֹ הִנֵּה דוֹר בָּנֶיךָ בָגָדְתִּי׃

16   וָאֲחַשְּׁבָה לָדַעַת זֹאת עָמָל הִיא בְעֵינָי׃

17   עַד־אָבוֹא אֶל־מִקְדְּשֵׁי־אֵל אָבִינָה לְאַחֲרִיתָם׃

18   אַךְ בַּחֲלָקוֹת תָּשִׁית לָמוֹ הִפַּלְתָּם לְמַשּׁוּאוֹת׃

19   אֵיךְ הָיוּ לְשַׁמָּה כְרָגַע סָפוּ תַמּוּ מִן־בַּלָּהוֹת׃

20   כַּחֲלוֹם מֵהָקִיץ אֲדֹנָי בָּעִיר צַלְמָם תִּבְזֶה׃

---

1 Here reading the *Qere* in place of the *Kethib* (ישיב).

21 כִּי יִתְחַמֵּץ לְבָבִי וְכִלְיוֹתַי אֶשְׁתּוֹנָן:

22 וַאֲנִי־בַעַר וְלֹא אֵדָע בְּהֵמוֹת הָיִיתִי עִמָּךְ:

23 וַאֲנִי תָמִיד עִמָּךְ אָחַזְתָּ בְּיַד־יְמִינִי:

24 בַּעֲצָתְךָ תַנְחֵנִי וְאַחַר כָּבוֹד תִּקָּחֵנִי:

25 מִי־לִי בַשָּׁמָיִם וְעִמְּךָ לֹא־חָפַצְתִּי בָאָרֶץ:

26 כָּלָה שְׁאֵרִי וּלְבָבִי צוּר־לְבָבִי וְחֶלְקִי אֱלֹהִים לְעוֹלָם:

27 כִּי־הִנֵּה רְחֵקֶיךָ יֹאבֵדוּ הִצְמַתָּה כָּל־זוֹנֶה מִמֶּךָּ:

28 וַאֲנִי קִרֲבַת אֱלֹהִים לִי־טוֹב שַׁתִּי בַּאדֹנָי יְהוִה מַחְסִי לְסַפֵּר כָּל־מַלְאֲכוֹתֶיךָ:

1 A psalm of Asaph.
Surely God is good to Israel, to the pure of heart.

2 But as for me, my feet almost slipped,
my steps almost stumbled.

3 For I envied the boastful,
the prosperity of the wicked I saw.

4 For they have no pangs concerning their deaths,
and their belly is fat.

5 They are not in the midst of the toil of humanity;
and they are not afflicted like (most) human beings.

6 Therefore, pride is a necklace for them,
and violence wraps them like a cloak.

7 Their eyes protrude out from fat,
delusions of their heart overflow.

8 They scoff and speak about evil;
from a lofty height they speak oppression.

9 They set their mouth in the heavens,
and their tongue travels on earth.

10 Thus his people turn back[2] hither,
and abundant waters are slurped by them.

11 And they say, "How can God know?
Is there knowledge in the Most High?"

12 Behold! These are the wicked,
forever at ease, they greatly increase in wealth.

13 Surely, in vain I have kept my heart pure,
and have washed my hands in innocence.

14 And I was stricken all the day,
and my reprimand came each morning.

---

2 Following the Qere (see n. 1 above).

15 If I had said, "I will speak thusly..."
Behold, with the generation of your children I would have dealt treacherously.

16 I considered how to understand this.
It was toilsome in my eyes,

17 until I entered into the sanctuary of God,
and I understood their end.

18 Surely, among slippery footing you set them,
and make them fall into deceptions.

19 How they become horrific in an instant –
terminated completely by terrors.

20 Like a dream – upon waking, O Lord,
upon waking you despise their shadowy form.

21 When my heart turned bitter,
and my kidneys felt pierced,

22 and I was stupid and did not understand,
I was a beast beside you.

23 Yet I am continually with you,
you hold fast my right hand.

24 With your counsel you lead me,
and afterward, with glory you will receive me.

25 Whom do I have in the heavens (beside you)?
And beside you, I do not desire (anything) on earth.

26 My flesh and my heart have come to an end,
but God is the rock of my heart and my portion forever.

27 For indeed, those who are far away from you will be destroyed.
You silence all who wantonly turn from you.

28 But as for me, the nearness of God is good for me,
I have made the Lord Yhwh my place of refuge,
to proclaim about all your works.

Text-Critical Issues[3]

Verse 4

חרצב is attested only one other time in the MT, i.e., Isa 58:6 (חרצב רשע "bonds of injustice"). Here it seems to be associated with the burdensome worry one feels in the face of mortality.

---

3 In addition to the commentaries cited in chap. 3 (n. 46), the following studies concerning Psalm 73 were consulted: N. H. Snaith, "The Prosperity of the Wicked: A Study of Psalm 73," *Religion in Life* 20 (1951) 519 – 29; H. Ringgren, "Einige Bemerkungen zum LXXII. Psalm," *VT* 3 (1953) 265 – 72; H. Birkeland, "The Chief Problems of Ps 73:17ff," *ZAW* 67 (1955) 99 – 103; S. Jellicoe, "The Interpretation of Psalm lxxiii. 24," *ExpTim* 67 (1956) 209 – 10; D. Macleod, "Faith Beyond the Forms of Faith: An Exposition of Psalm 73," *Int* 12 (1958) 418 – 21; M. Buber, "Das Herz Entscheidet: Psalm 73," in *Werke* (2 vols.; Munich/Heidelberg: Kösel, 1964) 2. 971 – 83; P. A. H. de Boer, "The Meaning of Psalm LXXIII 9," *VT* 18 (1968) 260 – 64; E. Würthwein, "Erwägungen zu Psalm 73," in *Wort und Existenz: Studien zum Alten Testament* (Göttingen: Vandenhoeck & Ruprecht, 1970) 161 – 78; M. Mannati, "Sur le quadruple *avec toi* de Ps. LXXIII 21 – 26," *VT* 21 (1971) 59 – 67; idem, "Les adorateurs de Môt dans le Psaume LXXIII," *VT* 22 (1972) 420 – 25; T. L. Smith, "A Crisis in Faith: An Exegesis of Psalm 73," *ResQ* 17 (1974) 162 – 84; R. Chester, "Faith on Trial: Psalm 73," *ResQ* 20 (1977) 88 – 92; L. G. Perdue, *Wisdom and Cult: A Critical Analysis of the Views of Cult in the Wisdom Literatures of Israel and the Ancient Near East* (SBLDS 30; Missoula, MT: Scholars, 1977) 287 – 91; J. F. Ross, "Psalm 73," in *Israelite Wisdom: Theological and Literary Essays in Honor Samuel Terrien* (eds. J. G. Gammie, W. A. Brueggemann, W. L. Humphreys, and J. M. Ward; New York: Union Theological Seminary, 1978) 161 – 75; B. Renaud, "Le psaume 73, méditation individuelle ou prière collective?" *RHPR* 59 (1979) 541 – 50; L. C. Allen, "Psalm 73: An Analysis," *TynBul* 33 (1982) 93 – 118; idem, "Psalm 73: Pilgrimage from Doubt to Faith," *Bulletin for Biblical Research* 7 (1997) 1 – 10; E. A. Martens, "Psalm 73: A Corrective to a Modern Misunderstanding," *Direction* 12 (1983) 15 – 26; F. Stolz, *Psalmen im nachkultischen Raum* (Theologische Studien 129; Zürich: Theologischer Verlag, 1983); J. L. Crenshaw, "Standing Near the Flame: Psalm 73," in *A Whirlpool of Torment: Israelite Traditions of God as an Oppressive Presence* (OBT 12; Philadelphia: Fortress, 1984) 93 – 109; H. Irsigler, *Psalm 73 – Monolog eines Weisen: Text, Programm, Struktur* (ATSAT 20; St. Ottilien: EOS, 1984); idem, "Die Suche nach Gerechtigkeit in den Psalmen 37, 49, und 73," in *Vom Adamssohn zum Immanuel: Gastvorträge Pretoria 1996* (ATSAT 58; St. Ottilien: EOS, 1997) 71 – 100; G. Rice, "An Exposition of Psalm 73," *JRT* 41 (1984) 79 – 86; R.-J. Tournay, "Le psaume LXXIII: Relectures et interprétation," *RB* 92 (1985) 187 – 99; J. C. McCann, "Psalm 73: A Microcosm of Old Testament Theology," in *The Listening Heart: Essays in Wisdom and the Psalms in Honor of Roland E. Murphy, O. Carm.* (eds. Kenneth G. Hoglund, E. F. Huwiler, J. T. Glass, and R. W. Lee; JSOTSup 58; Sheffield: JSOT Press, 1987) 247 – 57; D. Michel, "Ich aber bin immer bei dir: Von der Unsterblichkeit der Gottesbeziehung," in *Im Angesicht des Todes: Ein interdisziplinäres Kompendium* (2 vols.; eds. H. Becker, B. Einig, and P.-O. Ullrich; Pietas Liturgica 3; St. Ottilien: EOS, 1987) 1. 637 – 58; J. Luyten, "Psalm 73 and Wisdom," in *La Sagesse de l'Ancien Testament* (nouvelle édition mise à jour; ed. Maurice Gilbert; BETL 51; Leuven: Leuven University Press, 1990) 59 – 81; E. Nielsen, "Psalm 73: Scandinavian Contributions," in *Understanding Poets and Prophets; Essays in Honour of George*

Many modern commentators emend the MT למותם by splitting the conso-
nants such that v. 4a ends with למו and v. 4b begins with תם (thus rendering
v. 4: "For they have no pangs, their belly is full and fat"). These scholars generally note that the absence of concern by the wicked over their deaths would not
be in keeping with the dire prediction of their demise which vv. 17–19 describe.[4]
Such an argument fails to recognize, however, that in vv. 3–4 the psalmist deliberately highlights the fact that the wicked are rendered oblivious by their prosperity to any worries over hardships or even their own demise.

Wishart Anderson (ed. A. Graeme Auld; JSOTSup 152; Sheffield: JSOT Press, 1993) 273–83; P.
Auffret, "Et moi sans cesse avec toi: Etude structurelle du psaume 73," *SJOT* 9 (1995) 241–76; W.
Brueggemann and P. D. Miller, "Psalm 73 as a Canonical Marker," *JSOT* 72 (1996) 45–56; M. D.
Goulder, *The Psalms of Asaph and the Pentateuch. Studies in the Psalter, III* (JSOTSup 233;
Sheffield: Sheffield Academic Press, 1996); E. Wendland, "Introit 'into the Sanctuary of God'
(Psalm 73:17): Entering the Theological 'Heart' of the Psalm at the Centre of the Psalter," *Old
Testament Essays* 11 (1998) 128–53; R. L. Cole, *The Shape and Message of Book III (Psalms 73–
89)* (JSOTSup 307; Sheffield: Sheffield Academic Press, 2000) 15–27; C. Mihaila, "The Theolo-
gical and Canonical Place of Psalm 73," *Faith and Mission* 18 (2001) 52–59; L. D. Pettegrew, "'Is
There Knowledge in the Most High?' (Psalm 73:11)," *The Master's Seminary Journal* 12 (2001) 133–
48; J. P. Nordin, "'There is Nothing on Earth That I Desire': A Commentary on Psalm 73," *Currents
in Theology and Mission* 29 (2002) 258–64; M. Witte, "Auf dem Weg in ein Leben nach dem Tod:
Beobachtungen zur Traditions- und Redaktionsgeschichte von Psalm 73," in *Von Ewigkeit zu
Ewigkeit: Weisheit und Geschichte in den Psalmen* (BThSt 146; Neukirchen-Vluyn: Neukirchener
Verlag, 2014) 95–115; L. Boadt, "The Use of 'Panels' in the Structure of Psalms 73–78," *CBQ* 66
(2004) 533–50; B. Janowski and K. Liess, "Gerechtigkeit und Unsterblichkeit. Psalm 73 und die
Frage nach dem 'ewigen Leben'," in *Alles in allem: eschatologische Anstösse: J. Christine zum
60. Geburtstag* (eds. R. Heß and M. Leiner; Neukirchen-Vluyn: Neukirchener Verlag, 2005) 69–
92; C. Süssenbach, *Der elohistische Psalter: Untersuchungen zur Komposition und Theologie von
Ps 42–83* (FAT 2.7. Tübingen: Mohr, 2005); J. N. Clayton, "An Examination of Holy Space in Psalm
73: Is Wisdom's Path Infused with an Eschatologically Oriented Hope?" *Trinity Journal* 27 (2006)
117–42; J. S. Vassar, *Recalling a Story Once Told: An Intertextual Reading of the Psalter and the
Pentateuch* (Macon, GA: Mercer, 2007) 64–90; O. Nicolau, "'Ciertamente, es Bueno para Israel,
Dios': Estudio del Sal 73 en su Contexto," *RevistB* 71 (2009) 133–47; L. Schwienhorst-
Schönberger, "'Bis ich eintrat in die Heiligtümer Gottes' (Ps 73,17): Ps 73 im Horizont biblischer
und theologischer Hermeneutik," in *"Gerechtigkeit und Recht zu üben" (Gen 18,19): Studien zur
altorientalischen und biblischen Rechtsgeschichte, zur Religionsgeschichte Israels und zur Reli-
gionssoziologie. Festschrift für Eckart Otto zum 65. Geburtstag* (eds. R. Achenbach and M. Arneth;
Beihefte zur Zeitschrift für Altorientalische und Biblische Rechtsgeschichte 13; Wiesbaden: Harrassowitz, 2009) 387–402; K. Liess, "Von der Gottesferne zur Gottesnahe: Zur Todes-und-Lebensmetaphorik in den Psalmen," in *Metaphors in the Psalms* (eds. P. van Hecke, and A. Labahn;
BETL 231; Leuven: Uitgeverij Peeters, 2010) 167–95; A. M. Reisenauer, "The Goodness of God in
Psalm 73," *Anton* 86 (2011) 11–28.

4 See, e.g., Delitzsch; Duhm; Briggs and Briggs; Kraus; Dahood; Gunkel; Hossfeld and Zenger;
this emendation is also adopted by *NAB* and *NRSV*, and suggested by *BHS*.

Given that the ancient versions attest the MT reading "their deaths" (LXX: θανάτῳ αὐτῶν; Syr: ܡܘܬܗܘܢ), that there are no Hebrew manuscripts which attest the suggested emendation, and that the sense of the MT reading is consistent with the overall meaning of vv. 3–4, I see no need to emend the MT here.[5]

Verse 7

BHS (following LXX and Syr) suggests emending עינמו ("their eyes") to עונמו ("their iniquity"). A number of scholars adopt this change to the MT, as do *NJB* and *NAB*. Briggs and Briggs contend (without further comment) that "their eyes" is not "appropriate" in this context; Kraus finds the MT to be an "absurd conception"; and Hossfeld and Zenger reluctantly accept the emendation, citing the disagreement of the singular verb יצא with the dual עינמו.[6]

In support of the MT reading, Delitzsch notes that the image of the eyes of the wicked peering out from the folds of their fat (in line with v. 4), agrees with that of Job 15:27, in which the wicked are described as having faces "covered in their fat" (כסה פניו בחלבו).[7] I find that the MT reading coheres with the psalmist's overall portrayal of the wicked as corpulent, due to their prosperity, and I concur with Tate's observation that "we are dealing with an archaic metaphor here, and fair equivalence [in our translation] is all that is necessary."[8]

Verse 9

Dahood notes that the context for the unusual image portrayed in this verse is given by an Ugaritic text: "'a lip against the nether world, a lip against heaven, the tongue against the stars'.... The psalmist likens the prosperous unbelievers to

---

5 The MT is retained by Tate, Goldingay, and NJPSV. Irsigler (*Psalm 73*, 15), retains the MT but understands the ל in a temporal sense (cf. my understanding of ל as "concerning/in regard to"): "*Denn keine Schmerzen gibt es bis zu ihrem Tod*", i.e., the wicked are troubled by no pangs right up to the time of their deaths. Mannati ("Quadruple *avec toi*," 59–60) suggests that v. 4 refers to the Canaanite god of death, Môt, and that the "wicked" of v. 3 are those who worship this deity.
6 Briggs and Briggs, *Commentary*, 2. 143; Kraus, *Psalmen*, 2. 502; Hossfeld and Zenger, *Psalmen 51–100*, 333 (contra Hossfeld and Zenger, I note that there are other instances in the MT in which the dual "eyes" takes a singular verb [see, for example, 1 Sam 4:15; Mic 4:11]). See also Irsigler (*Psalm 73*, 18–20) for a detailed argument in favor of the emendation.
7 Delitzsch, *Kommentar*, 489. The MT reading "their eyes" is also followed by Duhm; Dahood; Gunkel; Tate; Goldingay; *NRSV*; and NJPSV.
8 Tate, *Psalms 51–100*, 228.

the monstrous voracious gods who devour everything in sight and yet are not sated."[9]

Verse 10

Whether one adopts the *Qere* reading יָשׁוּב עַמּוֹ ("his people turn back") or the *Ketib* יָשִׁיב עַמּוֹ ("he brings back his people") significantly alters the meaning of the verse as well as the focus of the whole psalm. The *Qere* implies that Yhwh's people are following the wicked, seduced by their abundant words and lavish lifestyle, which they "slurp up." By stark contrast, the *Ketib* suggests that Yhwh is saving his people by bringing them back to him, away from the seductive clutches of the wicked, and that the people drink deeply from Yhwh's abundant waters.

Both the LXX (ἐπιστρέψει) and Syr (ܢܦܢܐ) appear to be reading the *Qere*. While Briggs and Briggs reject the entire verse as a later gloss inserted as "a marginal note of consolation," many modern scholars concur with the ancient versions and accept the *Qere*.[10] I find the *Qere* to be entirely consistent with the overall sense of the first nine verses of the psalm. The psalmist laments that the prosperity of the wicked is seducing Yhwh's people and leading them to question whether God possesses any real knowledge of them (v. 11). If, at this relatively early point in the poem, Yhwh were already said to be leading his people away from the wicked and back to himself, the psalmist would seem to be preempting the divine salvific actions he describes in vv. 23–28. Furthermore, the psalmist's despair over the prosperity of the wicked and his own suffering in vv. 12–16 would be markedly out of place if v. 10 actually described Yhwh's rescue of his people from the influence of the wicked. I therefore adopt the *Qere* reading.

---

9 Dahood, *Psalms*, 2. 190. For further discussion of this verse, see also: Ringgren, "Einige Bemerkungen zum LXXIII. Psalm," 267; de Boer, "Meaning of Psalm LXXIII 9," 260–64.
10 Briggs and Briggs (*Commentary*, 2. 144) read both the *Ketib* and the *Qere* as a promise of Israel's restoration: i.e., either that Yhwh will bring his people back to him, or that his people will return themselves; all of the remaining commentators considered in this study read the *Qere* (as do *NAB*, *NRSV*, *NJB*) with the exception of Dahood (*Psalms* 2. 190) who – drawing upon several Ugaritic mythological motifs – renders v. 10a as "And so they quickly gorged themselves."

Verse 17

Here I follow many modern commentators and translations in rendering the plural מקדשי אל as "sanctuary of God."[11] Both the LXX (ἁγιαστήριον) and Syr (ܡܩܕܫܐ) also attest singular nouns. Briggs and Briggs suggest that the psalmist employs the "plural of intensity" to emphasize the holiness of the sanctuary, while Dahood sees the use of the plural here as conforming to the Canaanite practice of employing plural forms for the names of dwelling places.[12] I shall argue below that the psalmist is employing the word "sanctuary" in a metaphorical sense (rather than in reference to particular shrines or temples) and hence that the issue of whether it is properly plural or singular is not significant.

Verse 18

משואה is attested only one other time in the MT (Ps 74:3). *HALOT* suggests that it derives from II נשא ("to deceive"), in which case its meaning is something like "falsehoods/deceptions." Dahood understands the word as a poetic name for the netherworld and translates it "Desolation." Given that the word is employed here in parallel with חלקות ("slippery places/footing"), the overall sense is that the ways of the wicked eventually cause them to fall, exposing the falsehood of their apparent blessing (suggested by their previous prosperity [cf. vv. 3–4]) by Yhwh.

Verse 20

In v. 20b, the LXX reads κύριε, ἐν τῇ πόλει σου τὴν εἰκόνα αὐτῶν ἐξουδενώσεις ("O Lord, in your city you will despise their image"), leading *BHS* to suggest that the LXX translator had before him בעורך (instead of MT בעיר). Syr (ܒܩܪܝܬܐ "at cockcrow"), however, concurs with the MT. Dahood renders בעיר צלמם as "in the city of phantoms," by which he understands the City of Death (i.e., that place to which Yhwh condemns the wicked).[13] With the exception of Dahood,

---

11 See, for example, Briggs and Briggs; Kraus; Dahood; Tate; Goldingay; *NRSV*; NJPSV; *NAB*. The plural ("sanctuaries") is retained by, for example, Delitzsch; Duhm; Gunkel; Hossfeld and Zenger; *NJB*. See Ps 68:36, "in your sanctuary" (ממקדשיך), for another use of the plural form of מקדש with a likely singular meaning.
12 Briggs and Briggs, *Commentary*, 2. 146; Dahood, *Psalms*, 2. 192.
13 Dahood, *Psalms*, 2. 193–94.

the modern commentators and translations consulted for this study adopt the MT reading. While somewhat awkward (to our sensibility, not necessarily to an ancient Israelite's), the MT imagery in this verse is understandable: the apparent prosperity and blessing, which the wicked seem to enjoy (and which the psalmist laments in the first half of the poem), are actually no more real than a dream, which is dispelled upon waking.

Verse 24

It is not obvious how the syntactic status of כבוד should be understood in v. 24b. I follow LXX (μετὰ δόξης) and translate adverbially, i.e., "*with* glory [you will receive me]."[14] While not text-critically difficult, this verse has been the subject of extensive scholarly debate (see references listed above in n. 3) as to whether or not the psalmist is referring to an afterlife, and what, precisely, the intended meaning of "glory" is in this context. For the purposes of our epistemological analysis of the psalm, however, we need not concern ourselves with this particular discussion.

Structure, Unity, and Dating

Psalm 73 is a carefully structured poem which leads the reader/hearer along a spiritual journey marked by both linguistic and theological cues.[15] Verses 1 and 28 (both containing טוב) form an *inclusio* that frames the entire psalm: while v. 1 offers a general confession about the goodness of Yhwh, v. 28 is a more personal statement by the psalmist about the goodness of Yhwh's nearness to him.[16] The particle אך ("surely") occurs three times (vv. 1, 13, 18), dividing the poem into three distinct segments. The first segment (vv. 1–12) describes the psalmist's personal crisis over the prosperity of the wicked; the second segment (vv. 13–17) relates the psalmist's (mostly futile) attempts to resolve the crisis on

---

14 A similar reading is adopted by, e.g., Delitzsch; Dahood; Tate; Hossfeld and Zenger. Alternatively, some scholars understand "glory" as the destination toward which God is taking the psalmist: thus, Goldingay, "you will take me to honor" (see also Briggs and Briggs; NJPSV).
15 My discussion of the psalm's structure is largely based upon Crenshaw ("Standing Near the Flame," 93–94) and Tate (*Psalms 51–100*, 232–34). For highly detailed discussions of the structure, see Allen ("Psalm 73," 93–107), Irsigler (*Psalm 73*, 140–334), and Auffret ("Et moi sans cesse avec toi," 246–76).
16 See, e.g., Hossfeld and Zenger, *Psalmen 51–100*, 337.

his own; and the third segment (vv. 18–28) articulates the final resolution of the crisis at Yhwh's hands.

Within this broad demarcation, however, there is a finer structure that can be outlined as follows:

v. 1   Yhwh's goodness to Israel
    vv. 2–3   the plight of the psalmist
        vv. 4–12   prosperity and arrogance of the wicked
        vv. 13–16   psalmist's lament over the apparent futility of being righteous
            v. 17   revelation in the sanctuary of Yhwh
            vv. 18–20   realization that the prosperity of the wicked is fleeting
        vv. 21–26   Yhwh's comfort and guidance of the psalmist
    vv. 27   the plight of the wicked
v. 28   Yhwh's goodness to the psalmist

Verse 17 clearly represents a turning point in the psalmist's understanding of the meaning of the suffering and prosperity he perceives within his worldview. The epistemological significance of this verse will be extensively explored later in this chapter.

None of the scholars referenced in this study seriously questions the original unity of the poem. I agree with this position, noting that the psalm's coherent structure, use of *inclusio*, and repetition of key words all suggest an originally unitary composition.

As is common with attempts to date the psalms, there is no clear consensus among scholars on the possible date of composition for Psalm 73. For example: Briggs and Briggs argue for a date from the beginning of the Greek period, claiming that vv. 10, 27–28 are glosses from Maccabean times (looking toward the future restoration of Israel); Kraus notes the similarity between the tenor of the psalm and Jer 12:1–4 (which he suggests may be a *terminus a quo* for the psalm); Irsigler dates the psalm to the Persian period (fifth-fourth centuries); Gerstenberger, citing similarities between Psalm 73 and the Book of Job, describes the *Sitz im Leben* as a community gathering of the early Jewish period under Persian rule.[17] We would do well to note, however, that there is a timeless quality to the lament of anyone (at any place, in any era) who perceives himself to be suffering more than a prosperous neighbor, whom he holds to be morally inferior to himself.

---

17 Briggs and Briggs, *Commentary*, 142; Kraus, *Psalmen*, 2. 504; Irsigler, *Psalm 73*, 371; Gerstenberger, *Psalms: Part 2*, 74.

Psalm 73: Metaphor Analysis

Like many psalms, Psalm 73 is rich with metaphorical imagery, much of which is conveyed in no more than a single verse. For example, the prosperity of the wicked is described in terms of corpulence (fat belly, v. 4; fat face, v. 7); their wickedness adorns them like jewelry or a garment (v. 6); their prosperous existence is ephemeral, like a dream (v. 20); while God is a rock (v. 26) and a place of refuge (v. 28).

The primary metaphor of the poem, however, is the LIFE IS A JOURNEY conceptual metaphor. As in Psalm 1, the psalmist only weakly exercises the metaphor's power of options (see chap. 1 for the definition of a metaphor's powers of options, reason, and evaluation) and offers relatively few descriptive details. The characters mentioned are the psalmist, the wicked, and God. The psalmist portrays himself as walking (cf. v. 2) along on a journey. But at the psalm's opening, no starting or ending point for this journey is mentioned, nor is there any indication of a clearly marked path or direction of travel. While the psalmist does allude to an impediment along the way that nearly causes him to stumble (v. 2), he does not directly attribute the obstacle to either God or the wicked. Rather, he is impeded by his own envy of the prosperity of the wicked (v. 3) as well as by the seeming futility of his righteousness (vv. 13–14, 16). Although the source of the psalmist's difficulties may be external (the situation of the wicked), his actual struggle results from the way in which he internalizes and evaluates his perceptions of others. It is not inevitable that his observations of the wicked should pose an obstacle to his journey.

At v. 17, the psalmist makes an important stop along the journey when he enters God's "sanctuary." There is no indication within the journey metaphor that this was either an intended destination or even an expected resting place for the traveler to refresh himself. Rather, he seems almost to have stumbled upon it haphazardly.[18]

As I stated above in my structural analysis of the poem, v. 17 marks a turning point in the psalmist's understanding of prosperity, suffering, and divine justice. This transition is reflected in the conceptual metaphor as well. Whereas, in the first half of the psalm, the wicked are portrayed as fairly static and content in their opulence, in the second half they, too, are travelers. Now it is their turn

---

[18] To be sure, the fact that the word "sanctuary' is used may well imply that this was a normal – and intentional – temple visit. However, within the journey metaphor itself, the traveler describes himself as "slipping" (v. 2), "stumbling" (v. 2), "envious" (v. 3), feeling "futile" (v. 13), "stricken" (v. 14), and "weary" (v. 16) – terms which hardly suggest someone moving with clear determination and direction.

to slip and fall (v. 18). Significantly, however, while the psalmist slipped due to his own feelings and perceptions, the wicked are *made* to slip by Yhwh himself. In their journey, they turn away from God and travel far from him (v. 27).

The psalmist, by contrast, after v. 17 no longer wanders aimlessly. On his journey, he now always has Yhwh as a near companion, even when he is a "stupid and ignorant beast" (v. 22). Indeed, Yhwh holds him by the hand (v. 23) and leads him (v. 24). The psalmist now has a point of destination, though this is not a particular place. Rather, the destination of the journey is simply to be with Yhwh (v. 28), who "receives" the psalmist (v. 24). To be near Yhwh is to be grounded on solid rock (v. 26) and protected in a place of refuge (v. 28). Compared to such a rock-solid divine presence, the wicked are as unstable as a dream in Yhwh's sleep that dissipates upon his waking.

Given the psalmist's particular realization (i.e., the "linguistic metaphor" – see chap. 1) of the LIFE IS A JOURNEY conceptual metaphor, he is limited by the metaphor's power of reason in terms of his possible responses to the jealousy and debilitating frustration he feels over the perceived prosperity of the wicked. Within the source domain of the metaphor, the stumbling and wayward traveler can only be helped along his journey by a revelatory insight from God. The implication for the metaphor's target domain (i.e., the reader/hearer of the psalm) is that no amount of rational thought about the moral state of the wicked, nor extended observation of their lifestyle, will bring satisfaction to the suffering righteous person. And yet, once Yhwh's insight about the true status of the wicked is communicated, one need never fear feeling without direction in life or feeling distant from Yhwh.

Given the linguistic metaphor's power of evaluation, a righteous person who is frustrated by the apparent prosperity of the wicked might be comforted insofar as he can rest assured that his frustration or anxiety need not be attributed to his own faults or shortcomings. Indeed, unless and until he receives insight from Yhwh, he has no reason to expect to understand his situation in life in such a way that he can feel at peace. Furthermore, should he be so fortunate as to receive such a divine insight, he can be confident that he need never fear feeling aloof from Yhwh (and Yhwh's ultimate justice toward the wicked) again.

The obvious question that the metaphor raises for any reader/hearer is: "what/where is 'God's sanctuary' and how do I access the revelation it can provide?" It is thus necessary to turn now to a consideration of the meaning of Ps 73:17.

Exegesis of Ps 73:17

Hossfeld and Zenger rightly note that most of the vast scholarship on this verse tends to adopt one of two positions: either the psalmist is describing the prayer experience of an actual temple visit, or he is using the language of a temple visit as a metaphor for a personal insight he has gained (perhaps from a wisdom teaching).[19] Of course, these views need not be mutually exclusive. Ross, for example, notes that the psalmist could be reflecting upon not only what he prayed in the temple, but also lessons that he was taught in the wisdom schools.[20] Perdue also sees in this verse evidence of influence from both the wisdom and cultic traditions.[21] Similarly, in a recent literary analysis of this text, Schwienhorst-Schönberger observes that the ambiguity regarding the literal and the metaphorical understanding of the sanctuary visit leads the audience from a literal to a spiritual understanding of v. 17.[22]

For the purposes of this study, we need not overly concern ourselves with whether or not v. 17 alludes to an actual temple visit.[23] Rather, I shall focus on the matter of what changed for the psalmist as a result of his experience in the "sanctuary of God." The primary shift is in regard to the psalmist's *perspective* on the world. In the moment represented by v. 17, nothing overtly changes around him: the wicked are still prosperous and his material lot in life (i.e., the level of his own prosperity) has not improved. What has changed, as the sec-

---

19 Hossfeld and Zenger, *Psalmen 51–100*, 343. Among those commentators who interpret v. 17 in terms of an actual temple visit are Delitzsch; Briggs and Briggs; Kraus; Gerstenberger; as well as Birkeland ("Chief Problems of Ps 73:17," 100); Würthwein ("Erwägungen zu Psalm 73," 177); Crenshaw ("Standing Near the Flame," 104); Irsigler (*Psalm 73*, 369); Luyten ("Psalm 73 and Wisdom," 72); Allen ("Psalm 73: Pilgrimage," 6); Clayton ("Examination of Holy Space," 131). Among those commentators who interpret v. 17 metaphorically are Dahood; Hossfeld and Zenger; as well as Buber ("Das Herz Entscheidet," 977); Michel ("Ich aber bin immer bei dir," 646); Wendland ("Introit 'into the sanctuary of God,'" 139).
20 Ross, "Psalm 73," 165–69. See also Allen ("Psalm 73," 107–118), for an extensive review of the scholarly arguments put forth for either a cultic or a wisdom setting of this verse.
21 Perdue, *Wisdom and Cult*, 290–91.
22 Schwienhorst-Schönberger, "'Bis ich eintrat in die Heiligtümer Gottes," 395–400. The psalmist invites a similar shift in interpretation of the word "good" which appears in vv. 1 and 28. While the word initially implies material wellbeing, it comes to mean "nearness of God" (idem, 391–95).
23 I do, however, understand the insight which the psalmist gains to be the result of some form of direct communication from God (whether in formal cultic prayer or in personal meditation). I do not find evidence in the text to support the idea that the psalmist is representing a lesson that he was taught, say, only by a parent or only by a teacher in a wisdom school.

ond half of the psalm makes clear, is the psalmist's understanding of the wicked, of himself, and of God.[24]

As a result of his sanctuary experience, the psalmist perceives the wicked in a new light. He gains a broader overview of the course of their entire lifetimes, as opposed to the myopic view offered by a single snapshot in the present moment.[25] Now when he looks at the wicked, he sees not only their current prosperity but also "their end" (אחריתם), which entails downfall (v. 18) and destruction (vv. 19 – 20). Here, "end" need not only be taken in a temporal sense, but also in the sense of a moral orientation, that is, the "primary direction" of one's moral life.[26] Such an understanding is suggested by the LIFE IS A JOURNEY metaphor. By choosing to employ such a metaphor, the psalmist challenges (at least implicitly) his audience to ascertain the destination of the life path of each of the characters depicted within the source domain. Thus the wicked in Psalm 73, with "their end" now clearly in focus, are seen as they truly are. While they once seemed invulnerable, they now appear frail; while they once seemed to be blessed by God (as indicated by their prosperity), now God is seen as the agent of their downfall (v. 18).

In addition to his new viewpoint on the wicked, the psalmist also gains a new self-awareness. In his essay on Psalm 73, Buber notes that the interpretative key to this poem is the condition of the psalmist's heart.[27] God is good only to those who are "pure of heart" (ברי לבב). Only the one whose heart is in such a state can appreciate that God's goodness does not inhere in material prosperity (and, conversely, that suffering does not necessarily imply that one is divorced from God's goodness).[28] And yet, although the psalmist professes that he has kept his heart pure (v. 13), he was driven by envy of the prosperity of the wicked (v. 3) and feared that his own virtuous living has been in vain (v. 13).

---

24 See Tate, *Psalms 51 – 100*, 238 – 39, for this threefold analysis. Similar analyses are offered by Brueggemann ("Bounded By Obedience and Praise," 85) and Wendland ("Introit 'into the sanctuary of God'," 139 – 40). See Stolz (*Psalmen im nachkultischen Raum*, esp. 46 – 50) for a discussion of Psalm 73 with respect to the disorientation and reorientation that accompanies one's passage through a crisis that challenges the prevailing worldview.

25 On this point, see Crenshaw, "Standing Near the Flame," 104.

26 The extensive scholarly literature considering the question of whether the "end" of the wicked (as well as the "glory" with which those who are pure in heart will be received [v. 24]) has soteriological implications is beyond the scope of this study and is not relevant to my epistemological focus. The interested reader is referred to Clayton, "An Examination of Holy Space in Psalm 73," 117 – 42, and references therein.

27 Buber, "Das Herz Entscheidet," 973. "Heart" (לבב) occurs six times in the psalm (vv. 1, 7, 13, 21, 26 [*bis*]).

28 See Hossfeld and Zenger, *Psalmen 51 – 100*, 346 – 47.

The psalmist's dismal evaluation of his path in life changes markedly upon his entering into God's sanctuary. His heart remains as pure as it ever was, but now he perceives the true meaning of God's goodness which can come only to the pure of heart: God's goodness is God's nearness, i.e., God's presence (vv. 23, 28). In that divine presence, the psalmist no longer understands himself to be aimlessly stumbling (v. 2), but rather to have safely arrived at his rock and refuge (vv. 26, 28).

This change in the psalmist's self-awareness is only possible because he now also perceives God in a new way. As a result of his sanctuary experience, the psalmist knows that the truism "God is good to Israel" (v. 1) – which can seem hollow in the face of the prosperity of the wicked or the suffering of the righteous – is manifested in the counsel and guidance (v. 23–24) which God provides to the pure of heart.[29] While such counsel might always have been available to the psalmist, he was unable to "take it to heart" until he had been made aware of God's intimate presence. Throughout his entire transformative experience in the sanctuary, God never changed, but the psalmist's perception of God changed significantly.

While nearly all commentators and scholars agree that v. 17 marks a turning point in the psalm by means of which the psalmist's perspective is significantly broadened, they also concede that there is no explicit indication of *how* the shift in perspective occurred.[30] Crenshaw notes that "the decisive thing concerns a relationship that blossoms in that holy environment. We can only guess how the psalmist became convinced of divine presence and counsel. Was it by means of a priestly oracle of salvation? Did a prophetic mediator utter a word of the Lord? Or did the assurance come directly to the worshiper?"[31] Kraus suggests that vv. 18–20 describe a divine revelation (*Gottesspruch*) or a theophany (as in Job 40) that removes the psalmist's illusion about the prosperity of the wicked; this information is imparted via a "new dimension" that supplies what cannot be obtained from empirical evidence alone.[32]

---

29 Buber, "Das Herz Entscheidet," 979–80.

30 For an alternative to the conventional scholarly view that v. 17 represents the turning point of the psalm, see McCann, "Psalm 73," 250–51. He argues that the turning point is actually v. 15, for here the psalmist resolves not to betray his fidelity to the community of God's people. Once that decision is made, "the stage is set for the reversal of perspective that is represented in vv. 18–28" (ibid., 250).

31 Crenshaw, "Standing Near the Flame," 105.

32 Kraus, *Psalmen*, 508. Würthwein ("Erwägungen zu Psalm 73," 177) also views the psalmist's experience as a prophetic revelation; Perdue (*Wisdom and Cult*, 290) describes the psalmist's insight as a "revelatory message" which may have been part of a "theophanic experience."

Yet even if the psalmist were the recipient of direct divine revelation, it is important to note that he arrived at that point only after a strenuous intellectual quest. From empirical observation, he knew about the prosperity of the wicked and he struggled to make sense of their good fortune. His intellectual struggle was so great, in fact, that it exhausted him (v. 16). Thus, while he may well have entered the sanctuary looking for divine help, he did so seeking an aid to his human reason (not a replacement for it). Tate astutely observes that "the sanctuary experience came after strenuous intellectual effort. Worship is no substitute for rigorous mental pondering. The efforts to understand are supplemented by the disclosures of worship. The sanctuary is no place for a pious fool who thinks that piety can take the place of reflection and the quest for knowledge."[33]

Nevertheless, the psalmist makes clear that reason alone is not adequate to resolve the apparent contradiction between the wicked who prosper and the righteous who do not. The broader perspective that is required to properly contextualize this state of affairs can come only from God. Perdue notes that "it is only in the cultic experience of God that one is able to transcend the intellectual incongruities between wisdom teaching concerning retribution [i.e., that the wicked will be destroyed] and one's own sapiential experience."[34]

Given this rich and complex relationship in Psalm 73 between human understanding and divine presence, I shall now explore the extent to which the information that the psalmist receives within God's sanctuary properly constitutes "knowledge," in the formal epistemological sense. In order to adequately assess that information, we must first consider the process whereby the information is conveyed by God and received by the psalmist (i.e., the pedagogy underlying the experience described in v. 17).

Epistemological Analysis

Our discussion above of v. 17 revealed that epistemological issues lie at the heart of the psalm. Words related to knowledge (or the lack of it) and reason figure prominently throughout the poem. When God's intimate presence is either not recognized (as in the case of the psalmist) or pridefully ignored (as in the case of the wicked), human reason is found wanting. Before his experience in

---

33 Tate, *Psalms 51–100*, 238.
34 Perdue, *Wisdom and Cult*, 291; cf. Luyten's comment: "[w]here reason halts, faith continues" ("Psalm 73 and Wisdom," 77).

God's sanctuary, the psalmist is wearied from considering (חשב) how to understand (ידע) the prosperity of the wicked (v. 16). And in referring to the days when he futilely tried to make sense out of the apparent inequity that he observed around him (v. 22), he describes himself as stupid (בער) and unable to understand (לא ידע). Luyten observes that vv. 16 and 22 reveal "the limitation of human knowledge especially in relation to God's wisdom, works, and management."[35] The wicked, for their part, display their ignorance by denying that God has the capacity to know (ידע) anything (v. 11), or that he possesses knowledge (דעה). Significantly, once the psalmist enters God's sanctuary (v. 17), he does not obtain wealth or power, but rather the ability to *discern* (בין) the true state of affairs, whereas he had previously known only frustration in his intellectual quest.

It seems clear that the psalmist's new-found insight is not the result of empirical observation (for example, tracking the lives of many wicked people over the course of their lifetimes and so determining their ultimate fates). How, then, is the critical lesson alluded to in v. 17 both taught and learned?

Pedagogy[36]

In his study of ancient Israelite pedagogy, Crenshaw identifies three fundamental ways of acquiring knowledge, all of which are relevant to Psalm 73: (1) empirical observation; (2) analogy (comparing received "creeds" with observed reality); and (3) direct encounter with the divine.[37] Of these three, empirical observation is by far the one most commonly cited in Israel's literature. It was up to the careful observer to draw lessons from the natural realm and apply them to the human realm. Teachings arrived at in this way often took the form of a gnomic saying, with a brief observation about a natural phenomenon or a human behavior immediately followed by an application to daily life, but without any detailed discussion of the connection between the two parts. Many proverbs illustrate this sort of formulation; for example: "The crucible for silver, and the furnace for

---

35 Luyten, "Psalm 73 and Wisdom," 72. On this point see also Clayton, "An Examination of Holy Space in Psalm 73," 132–33.

36 The material in this section is largely based upon the writings of J. L. Crenshaw, especially: *Education in Ancient Israel: Across the Deadening Silence* (ABRL; New York: Doubleday, 1998) and "Wisdom and Authority: Sapiential Rhetoric and Its Warrants," in idem, *Urgent Advice and Probing Questions: Collected Writings on Old Testament Wisdom* (Macon, GA: Mercer, 1995) 326–43.

37 Crenshaw, *Education*, 120–30.

gold, but the tester of hearts is the Lord" (Prov 17:3); "For as the crackling of thorns under a pot, so is the fool's laughter" (Qoh 7:6).

Crenshaw notes that simple observation occasionally developed into "instruction," or explicit advice about how one should act. While there are no such gnomic sayings or ethical instructions directly conveyed in Psalm 73, the psalmist clearly assumes a certain standard of ethical behavior that any righteous person would be expected to follow. "Wicked behavior" is associated with pride and violence (v. 6), oppression (v. 8), and scorning God (v. 11); "righteous behavior" involves maintaining innocence and a pure heart (v. 13), as well as trusting in God that the wicked will ultimately be punished and the righteous rewarded. It is not difficult to imagine such ethical standards to be the product of the type of education Crenshaw describes as "empirical observation."[38]

In learning by analogy, Crenshaw's second pedagogical method, the student relied upon a received tradition of wisdom, handed down from previous generations. These "creedal statements" carried with them a certain level of authority, but they were not to be accepted uncritically. Each new generation of students had to ask: do these hold true for me? Crenshaw notes that the danger of received knowledge is that it can easily petrify into dogma, with each new generation assuming that it is unqualified to challenge the masters of the past. When such dogma is confronted by present challenges that do not seem consonant with it, great personal crisis can result.

This is especially true concerning the matter of human suffering. The traditional wisdom that the evil are punished while the good prosper is constantly challenged by the reality of daily life. Crenshaw cites Job's experience of suffering versus the traditional wisdom offered by his friends as an example of such a crisis: "Canonical wisdom bears impressive witness to the difficulty encountered by those who tested faith reports in the light of their own experience of reality. The unknown author of Job examines this dilemma with immense pathos, finally declaring the bankruptcy of secondhand faith."[39]

Crenshaw's analysis of Psalm 73 is particularly interesting in this connection. He identifies this text as embodying a struggle between creed and reality. As we have seen, after an opening confession of faith in God's goodness to those who are pure in heart (v. 1), the psalmist bitterly notes that the experience

---

38 Consider, for example, an admonition such as "Let not kindness and fidelity leave you; bind them around your neck [cf. Ps 73:6 in which the wicked wear pride like a "necklace"]; then will you win favor and good esteem before God and man. Trust in the Lord with all your heart, on your own intelligence rely not; in all your ways be mindful of him, and he will make straight your paths" (Prov 3:3–6; *NAB*).

39 Crenshaw, *Education*, 125.

of life does not support such a claim. The evil often prosper and the good often suffer (vv. 3–16). But then he enters God's sanctuary (v. 17) and realizes that he has always been led by Yhwh's counsel (v. 24). "Suddenly, a redefinition of divine goodness overwhelms the psalmist, who realizes for the first time that God's goodness has absolutely nothing to do with things that can be seen and touched, such as material prosperity. Instead, the goodness which comes to decent persons is a feeling of divine presence that bestows confidence regardless of the circumstances. Then at long last the psalmist is able to subscribe to the ancient confession, now that its real meaning has become clear."[40]

Crenshaw's observations suggest that the tension between traditional wisdom and lived experience can be resolved by an intimate awareness of Yhwh's presence, and this, in turn, leads to Crenshaw's third pedagogical category for describing the acquisition of knowledge: direct encounter with the divine. Job's final response to Yhwh (Job 42:1–6) reflects this kind of intimate awareness: "I had heard of you by word of mouth, but now my eye has seen you" (Job 42:5; *NAB*). Crenshaw notes that such insight as the psalmist claims to acquire in God's sanctuary seems to lack verifiability insofar as it entails an unmediated interaction between the human being and God. "How can others test the truth of claims about encountering the deity?"[41]

The ending of Psalm 73 is subject to this criticism: who but the psalmist (and anyone else who has been favored with such privileged insight from God) could claim to know or grasp such new insights into God's goodness? Nevertheless, we must not confuse the issue of verifiability with the question of whether or not the psalmist's new insight constitutes genuine knowledge *for him*. That is the epistemological question to which we now turn.

Epistemic Knowledge and Realization-Discovery

Applying the epistemological tool developed at the end of chap. 1, I note that the primary proposition of Psalm 73 is quite similar to that of Psalm 1: "God is good to the pure of heart but he makes the wicked fail." There are, however, two important corollaries to this proposition that are lacking in Psalm 1: (1) "momentary observations to the contrary notwithstanding"; and (2) "God's goodness = God's nearness."

---

40 Ibid., 126.
41 Ibid., 127.

The significant epistemological advance of Psalm 73 over Psalm 1 is that the psalmist does at least acknowledge that the wicked sometimes prosper and the pure of heart sometimes lack material prosperity. Such a possibility is not even contemplated by the psalmist in Psalm 1.[42] But just because the primary proposition of Psalm 73 appears to be more faithful to empirical observation of genuine life experience, that does not necessarily mean it is "knowledge" in the epistemological sense (i.e., a true, justified belief).

Insofar as the psalmist's unqualified acceptance of the primary proposition only comes after his experience in God's sanctuary, I classify the justificatory scheme of his belief in the proposition as foundationalist (see chap. 1 above). At the opening of the psalm, he likely holds to the proposition with something like the coherentist justification followed in Psalm 1. Upon receiving direct communication from God, however, the proposition for him is no longer a core statement with which other propositions might or might not cohere. Rather, it takes the form of a fundamental basic belief. And because this belief comes directly from God, its truth value is not questioned. Thus, the primary proposition of Psalm 73 does constitute genuine knowledge for the psalmist.

Given the centrality of divine revelation within the epistemological justification scheme of Psalm 73, we note that this psalm provides a prime example of Kellenberger's "realization-discovery" (see the discussion of this epistemic process in chap. 3). Recall that this type of knowing depends not primarily upon reason but on feeling, on not merely observing but "beholding." What allows or prevents one from beholding what is always before one is the condition of one's heart. Because of the disposition of their hearts, the fool in Ps 14:1 and the wicked person in Ps 10:4 do not find God's presence in their lives. Their blind disposition is characterized by pride and self-centeredness. Realization-discovery requires both that one is able to transcend total self-focus (by, for example, undergoing a personal crisis that turns one's focus toward God) and that one receives a heightened awareness of God's presence. Such an awareness is pure gift from God (Kellenberger calls it a "grace").

This process, as Kellenberger outlines it, is precisely what unfolds in Psalm 73. The wicked lack pure hearts because of their pride and arrogant self-absorption. Like the "fool" who says in his heart that there is no God (Ps 14:1), they deny that God is aware of the moral state of the world (Ps 73:11). The psalmist, whose heart is pure, breaks out of his self-focused despair (and, perhaps, self-pity)

---

42 Recall that within the worldview of Psalm 1, an apparently righteous person who suffered misfortune was necessarily proven to be only apparently righteous, and his outward appearance fraudulent.

when he faces the crisis of potentially turning his back on his own people ("God's children"; v. 15). But he still must experience the gift of God's revelation to him in the sanctuary before he can fully understand that God is near to him always, and that this nearness is actually the "goodness" that God has to share with the pure of heart (vv. 1, 28).

Social Epistemology

The worldview of Psalm 73 is one which acknowledges that the wicked do occasionally prosper and the pure of heart do occasionally suffer. Nevertheless, God's justice ultimately prevails. Given the psalm's particular realization (i.e., the linguistic metaphor) of the LIFE IS A JOURNEY conceptual metaphor, it is clear that God directly enforces his justice by making the wicked fall (vv. 18–20) and leading the pure of heart by the hand (vv. 23–24).

We find, therefore, that Psalm 73 – much more than Psalm 1 – addresses the social epistemological issues of objectivation and internalization (see the discussion of these terms in chap. 1). The formulaic slogan "God is good to Israel, to the pure of heart" opens the poem and basically conveys the theme of Psalm 1. This is the message that the society within the worldview of the psalm wishes to propagate from generation to generation (objectivation).

Almost immediately, however, the psalmist takes up the challenge posed by the prosperity of the wicked (internalization). If not addressed, such a challenge could threaten the very structure of the society by undermining its central proposition. The prosperous wicked must not be allowed to persist in their positions of wealth and power. The first step in removing this threat to society is to clearly identify who the wicked are. Gerstenberger notes that portrayals of the wicked (as in vv. 4–12) "are necessary in any process of socialization and education to make clear that socially unjust behavior does not work out and must be ostracized. The profile of 'bad man' or 'bad woman' has to be delineated clearly. The main points of emphasis in such a presentation of the godless would be their misconduct and due fate."[43] In this instance, "nihilation" (the society's means of removing incorrigible obstacles to the successful propagation of its worldview to future generations) is quite literally the "annihilation" of the wicked at the hands of God.

In addition to nihilation, there is a kind of "therapy" (see the discussion of this term in chap. 1) for the pure of heart insofar as they are enabled to reinter-

---

43 Gerstenberger, *Psalms: Part 2*, 71.

pret the meaning of God's "goodness." They no longer understand it in terms of material wellbeing but rather as an awareness of God's intimate presence.

Conclusion

Viewed from a social-epistemological perspective, therefore, Psalm 73 describes a fairly successful process of defining, preserving, and passing on a particular worldview. Given the psalmist's choice of conceptual metaphor and our analysis of the psalm's underlying epistemology, we find that Psalm 73 is able to preserve the central tenet of Psalm 1 while dealing with the apparent moral injustices of life in a more satisfying (because more realistic) manner.

It must be noted, however, that the solution afforded to the psalmist in Psalm 73 is highly individualistic in nature. The psalmist enters into the sanctuary of God alone, and he does not communicate how he came to his new insight about the ultimate fate of the wicked. One wonders how much solace the psalmist's message would bring to a person who was also pure of heart but who had not been fortunate enough to enjoy such an encounter with the divine.

In the following chapter, I shall make an epistemological analysis of Psalm 90. There, too, the psalmist confronts the challenges posed by the struggles of life which affect both the wicked and the righteous. We shall see, however, that this psalm approaches the matter from a much more communal perspective than does Psalm 73.

Chapter VI.
Psalm 90: Seeking for Knowledge

Psalm 90, the opening psalm of Book IV of the Psalter, presents a fairly stark perspective on the nature of human life. Like the lifetime of a plant that blooms in the morning and withers at nightfall, so too all people pass through life in a relatively brief amount of time, and many of their years are stricken with toil and hardship. Furthermore, there is no distinction between the righteous and the wicked in regard to how life is experienced: it is the same lot for all. To be sure, Yhwh can be appealed to for relief, but his response is by no means certain, whereas the toil of life is unavoidable. Even so, from within the midst of this worldview, the psalmist boldly calls out to Yhwh in search of new knowledge about the human condition. The nature of this epistemological request, and the manner in which it is posed, constitute the focus of this chapter.

I begin with a translation of the psalm and a discussion of text-critical and interpretative issues, followed by an analysis of the structure of the psalm, its original unity, and possible dates of composition. I next offer a detailed study of the psalm's principal metaphors and the worldview they help to structure. Finally, I present a consideration of the psalm's primary epistemological features. An appendix provides a detailed study of a key lexical distinction which is relevant to the interpretation of the psalm text.

Psalm 90 Translation and Text-Critical Issues[1]

תְּפִלָּה ֿלְמֹשֶׁה אִישׁ־הָאֱלֹהִים אֲדֹנָי מָעוֹן אַתָּה הָיִיתָ לָּנוּ בְּדֹר וָדֹר: 1

---

[1] In addition to the commentaries cited in chap. 3 (n. 46), the following studies concerning Psalm 90 were consulted: D. W. Thomas, "A Note on זרמתם שנה יהיו in Psalm XC 5," *VT* 18 (1968) 267–68; A. Macintosh, "The Spider in the Septuagint Version of Psalm XC.9," *JTS* 23 (1972) 113–17; G. v. Rad, "Der 90. Psalm," in *Gottes Wirken in Israel: Vorträge zum Alten Testament* (Neukirchen-Vluyn: Neukirchener Verlag, 1974) 268–83; W. J. Urbrock, "Mortal and Miserable Man: A Form-Critical Investigation of Psalm 90," *SBLSP 1974* (2 vols.; Atlanta: Scholars, 1974) 1. 1–34; B. Vawter, "Postexilic Prayer and Hope," *CBQ* 37 (1975) 460–70; P. Auffret, "Essai sur la structure littéraire du Psaume 90," *Bib* 61 (1980) 262–76; C. Whitley, "The Text of Psalm 90,5," *Bib* 63 (1982) 555–57; H.-P. Müller, "Der 90. Psalm: Ein Paradigma exegetischer Aufgaben," *ZTK* 81 (1984) 265–85; M. Tsevat, "Psalm XC 5–6," *VT* 35 (1985) 115–17; Th. Booij, "Psalm 90,5–6: Junction of Two Traditional Motifs," *Bib* 68 (1987) 393–96; J. Schnocks, "Ehe die Berge geboren wurden, bist du," *BK* 54 (1999) 163–69; idem, *Vergänglichkeit und Gottesherrschaft: Studien zu Psalm 90 und dem vierten Psalmenbuch* (BBB 140; Berlin/Vienna: Philo Verlagsgesellschaft,

בְּטֶ֤רֶם ׀ הָ֘רִ֤ים יֻלָּ֗דוּ וַתְּח֣וֹלֵֽל אֶ֣רֶץ וְתֵבֵ֑ל וּֽמֵעוֹלָ֥ם עַד־עוֹלָ֗ם אַתָּ֥ה אֵֽל׃ 2

תָּשֵׁ֣ב אֱ֭נוֹשׁ עַד־דַּכָּ֑א וַ֝תֹּ֗אמֶר שׁ֣וּבוּ בְנֵי־אָדָֽם׃ 3

כִּ֤י אֶ֪לֶף שָׁנִ֡ים בְּֽעֵינֶ֗יךָ כְּי֣וֹם אֶ֭תְמוֹל כִּ֣י יַעֲבֹ֑ר וְאַשְׁמוּרָ֥ה בַלָּֽיְלָה׃ 4

זְ֭רַמְתָּם שֵׁנָ֣ה יִהְי֑וּ בַּ֝בֹּ֗קֶר כֶּחָצִ֥יר יַחֲלֹֽף׃ 5

בַּ֭בֹּקֶר יָצִ֣יץ וְחָלָ֑ף לָ֝עֶ֗רֶב יְמוֹלֵ֥ל וְיָבֵֽשׁ׃ 6

כִּֽי־כָלִ֥ינוּ בְאַפֶּ֑ךָ וּֽבַחֲמָתְךָ֥ נִבְהָֽלְנוּ׃ 7

שַׁתָּ֣² עֲוֺנֹתֵ֣ינוּ לְנֶגְדֶּ֑ךָ עֲ֝לֻמֵ֗נוּ לִמְא֥וֹר פָּנֶֽיךָ׃ 8

כִּ֣י כָל־יָ֭מֵינוּ פָּנ֣וּ בְעֶבְרָתֶ֑ךָ כִּלִּ֖ינוּ שָׁנֵ֣ינוּ כְמוֹ־הֶֽגֶה׃ 9

יְמֵֽי־שְׁנוֹתֵ֨ינוּ בָהֶ֥ם שִׁבְעִ֪ים שָׁנָ֡ה וְאִ֤ם בִּגְבוּרֹ֨ת ׀ שְׁמ֘וֹנִ֤ים שָׁנָ֗ה וְ֭רָהְבָּם עָמָ֣ל וָאָ֑וֶן כִּי־גָ֥ז חִ֝֗ישׁ וַנָּעֻֽפָה׃ 10

מִֽי־י֭וֹדֵעַ עֹ֣ז אַפֶּ֑ךָ וּ֝כְיִרְאָתְךָ֗ עֶבְרָתֶֽךָ׃ 11

לִמְנ֣וֹת יָ֭מֵינוּ כֵּ֣ן הוֹדַ֑ע וְ֝נָבִ֗א לְבַ֣ב חָכְמָֽה׃ 12

שׁוּבָ֣ה יְ֭הוָה עַד־מָתָ֑י וְ֝הִנָּחֵ֗ם עַל־עֲבָדֶֽיךָ׃ 13

שַׂבְּעֵ֣נוּ בַבֹּ֣קֶר חַסְדֶּ֑ךָ וּֽנְרַנְּנָ֥ה וְ֝נִשְׂמְחָ֗ה בְּכָל־יָמֵֽינוּ׃ 14

שַׂ֭מְּחֵנוּ כִּימ֣וֹת עִנִּיתָ֑נוּ שְׁ֝נ֗וֹת רָאִ֥ינוּ רָעָֽה׃ 15

יֵרָאֶ֣ה אֶל־עֲבָדֶ֣יךָ פָעֳלֶ֑ךָ וַ֝הֲדָרְךָ֗ עַל־בְּנֵיהֶֽם׃ 16

וִיהִ֤י ׀ נֹ֤עַם אֲדֹנָ֥י אֱלֹהֵ֗ינוּ עָ֫לֵ֥ינוּ וּמַעֲשֵׂ֣ה יָ֭דֵינוּ כּוֹנְנָ֥ה עָלֵ֑ינוּ וּֽמַעֲשֵׂ֥ה יָ֝דֵ֗ינוּ כּוֹנְנֵֽהוּ׃ 17

1 A prayer of Moses, the man of God.
Lord, a safe dwelling you have been for us from generation to generation.

2 Before the mountains were born, and you brought to birth the land and the world, from eternity to eternity, you are El.

3 You return people to dust, and say "Return, sons of men."

4 For a thousand years in your eyes are like a former day that passes, and a watch in the night.

5 You overwhelm them; they become sleep. In the morning, like grass, they are fleeting.

6 In the morning it blooms but it is fleeting, toward evening it withers and dries up.

2002); R. J. Clifford, "What Does the Psalmist Ask for in Psalms 39:5 and 90:12?" *JBL* 119 (2000) 59–66; idem, "Psalm 90: Wisdom Meditation or Communal Lament?" in *The Book of Psalms: Composition and Reception* (ed. P. W. Flint and P. D. Miller, Jr.; VTSup 99; Leiden: Brill, 2005) 190–205; R. Brandscheidt, "'Unsere Tage zu zählen, so lehre du' (Psalm 90,12): Literarische Gestalt, theologische Aussage und Stellung des 90. Psalms im vierten Psalmenbuch," *TTZ* 113 (2004) 1–33; J. Schnocks, "Mose im Psalter," in *Moses in Biblical and Extra-Biblical Traditions* (eds. A. Graupner and M. Wolter; BZAW 372; Berlin: de Gruyter, 2007) 79–88; J. S. Vassar, *Recalling a Story Once Told: An Intertextual Reading of the Psalter and the Pentateuch* (Macon, GA: Mercer, 2007) 108–23; Z. Zięba, "The Meaning of the Expression לבב חכמה 'The Heart of Wisdom' (Ps 90:12) in the Context of the Transitory and Frail Life of Human Beings in Psalm 90," *Polish Journal of Biblical Research* 7 (2008) 113–24; K. Seybold, "Psalm 90 und die Theologie der Zeit (Zeiten)," in *Studien zu Sprache und Stil der Psalmen* (idem; BZAW 415; Berlin: de Gruyter, 2010) 129–43.
2 The *Ketib* reads שֵׁת, but the proper pointing for a 3 m.s. verb would be שָׁת. The context of the verse calls for a 2 m.s. verb.

7   For we fade away by your anger, and by your rage we are dismayed.

8   You[3] have set our sins before you, hidden from us is the light of your face.

9   For all our days dwindle away in your rage, we finish our years like a sigh.

10 The days of our years, concerning them, seventy years, or if in strength, eighty years. And their hurrying, a trouble and distress. For they pass by in haste, and we fly away.

11 Who knows the strength of your wrath, and, in accordance with fear of you, your rage?

12 To number our days rightly teach us, so that we might gain a heart of wisdom.

13 Turn back, Yhwh; how long? And change your mind about your servants.

14 Satisfy us in the morning with your loving-kindness, so that we might shout with joy and we might rejoice all our days.

15 Make us glad as many days as when you oppressed us, as many years when we saw evil.

16 Let your work appear to your servants, and your splendor over their children.

17 And may the kindness of the Lord our God be upon us. And the work of our hands, promote it on our behalf, and the work of our hands, promote it.

In his commentary on Psalm 90, Dahood notes that: "The psalmist's terse style often makes the sense elusive and causes the text to bristle with grammatical and stylistic difficulties."[4] In the following analysis I shall only treat the more significant such issues that have direct bearing on the focus of this study. For a more complete discussion, the interested reader is referred to the sources listed in the notes.

Verse 1

A few Hebrew manuscripts read מְעוֹז ("mountain stronghold, place of refuge") in place of MT's מָעוֹן, a state of affairs which has provoked a substantial scholarly debate over the intended divine attribute that is being referred to at the opening of the poem.[5] However, insofar as the overall connotation of both מָעוֹן and מְעוֹז is a place of safety and protection, and given that מָעוֹן is clearly used to describe God himself in Ps 70:3, I find no compelling reason for reading מְעוֹז in v. 1.

---

3 Following the *Qere* (see n. 2 above).
4 Dahood, *Psalms*, 2. 322.
5 For an extensive review of the literature on this matter, see Schnocks, *Vergänglichkeit*, 43.

Verse 5

The diverse renderings of this line in the ancient versions have made it the focus of several modern scholarly treatments.[6] Those versions read:

τὰ ἐξουδενώματα αὐτῶν ἔτη ἔσονται. τὸ πρωὶ ὡσεὶ χλόη παρέλθοι

Years will be their undoings. In the morning may it pass by like a first shoot.

ܩܢܝ̈ܢܗܘܢ ܫܢܬܐ ܗܘܘ ܘܒܨܦܪܐ ܐܝܟ ܥܘܦܝܐ ܐܫܠܡ

Their generations will become a year, and in the morning like a bloom it will change/sprout.[7]

quae pro nihilo habentur eorum anni erunt (Vg)

Things that are considered as nothing will their years be.

percutiente te eos somnium erunt (Jerome's *iuxta Hebraicum*)

By you [God] striking them, they will become a dream.

It would seem that the LXX, Vg, and *iuxta Hebraicum* read זרם in light of the same semantic field as meaning either to deal with something violently ("to strike") or as the result of such violent treatment ("nothingness," "contemptible"); Syr possibly read זרע ("seed"). With respect to MT שֵׁנָה ("sleep"), the LXX, Vg, and Syr apparently read שָׁנָה ("year"). All three non-Semitic versions render חלף with some term for "to pass by/through": παρέρχομαι (LXX), *transeo* (Vg), *pertranseo* (*iuxta Hebraicum*).

In light of the substantial editorial changes proposed for this verse during the twentieth century, it is interesting that Delitzsch, in 1894, saw no need to emend the MT at all. He reads זרם as "to wash away, as in a flood," and then notes that there is no contradiction between this image and the imagery of שנה יהיו (becoming "sleep"), arguing that to be washed away in a flood is to be effectively delivered into the "sleep" of death (cf. Ps 76:6; Jer 51:39, 57).[8] While I agree that the MT is both self-consistent and intelligible in this verse, I do not regard "sleep" here as necessarily the sleep of death. The focus of vv. 5–6 is not upon new grass that represents "life" in opposition to "death,"

---

6 See, e. g., G. R. Driver, "Old Problems Re-examined," *ZAW* 80 (1968) 174–83; Thomas, "A Note on שנה יהיו זרמתם," 267–68; Whitley, "Text of Psalm 90,5," 555–57; Tsevat, "Psalm XC 5–6," 115–17; Booij, "Psalm 90,5–6," 393–96.

7 ܐܫܠܡ can either be Pael ("to change") or Aphel ("to sprout").

8 Delitzsch, *Kommentar*, 588. Of all the other commentators cited in this study, only Hossfeld and Zenger (*Psalmen 51–100*, 604), writing at the end of the twentieth century, agree with Delitzsch that the MT need not be emended.

but rather upon the beginning of a new cycle which is timeless: new shoots replace old ones, which will themselves be supplanted. It is the cycle itself, always
in motion, that the psalmist highlights. As morning passes into day, which passes into night, so also does waking pass into sleep, just as grass passes from
blooming to withering (cf. the use of חלף in Job 9:26, to describe the passing
of boats before one's eyes).

Verse 8

The second half of this verse has given rise to numerous divergent understandings, beginning with those of the ancient versions. The MT points עֲלֻמֵנוּ as the
singular Qal passive participle of עלם (the root's only attestation in the Qal in
the MT): "what is hidden; what is secret." Many modern exegetes accept this
MT reading and understand עֲלֻמֵנוּ as a parallel to עֲוֺנֹתֵינוּ.[9] That this verb caused
confusion among early translators is suggested by the LXX rendering: αἰών
("age, lifetime"), perhaps indicating that the translator read עוֹלָמֵנוּ. This reading
is further reflected in Syr (ܠܥܠܡ) and the Vg (*saeculum*). *Iuxta Hebraicum* attests
neglegentia ("carelessness, heedlessness, negligence"), which is closer to the
concept of "hidden sin" but is hardly synonymous with it (as *BHS* suggests).

To better understand the meaning of עלם in our verse, it is helpful to consider its use throughout the MT. It occurs in the Nifal stem twelve times.[10] It is generally construed with the preposition מן to mean "concealed from (someone)" or
"to be unaware." In this sense, it often indicates an inculpable lack of awareness
about a sin or transgression (Lev 4:13; 5:2, 3, 4; Num 5:13). In 1 Kgs 10:3//2 Chr 9:2,
none of the answers to the Queen of Sheba's questions is concealed from Solomon's wisdom. In Job 28:21, wisdom is described as being concealed from the
eyes of human beings.[11] Only two of the twelve Nifal attestations imply a deliberate act of concealment so as to deceive others: God will call everyone to account for all actions that have been concealed, both good *and evil* (Qoh 12:14);
the righteous man does not sit with hypocrites (literally, "those who are concealed," Ps 26:4).

---

9 Thus: "*Geheimstes*" (Delitzsch), "*Verborgenes*" (Duhm; Hossfeld and Zenger; Schnocks),
"*geheimen Fehler*" (Gunkel), "*verborgenen Fehler*" (Kraus), "*verborgene Schuld*" (Westermann),
"hidden (sins)" (Tate).
10 Lev 4:13; 5:2, 3, 4; Num 5:13; 1 Kgs 10:3; 2 Chr 9:2; Job 28:21; Ps 26:4; Qoh 12:14; Sir 11:4; Nah 3:1.
11 A similar idea is expressed in Sir 11:4 (the deeds of God are hidden [עלם] from human
beings).

The verb is attested in the Hiphil stem six times (Lev 20:4; 2 Kgs 4:27; Isa 1:15; Ezek 22:26; Prov 28:27; Lam 3:56), usually combined with מִן as part of the idiom "to conceal one's eyes from...," meaning "to ignore, to disregard." In these uses, it never means to conceal one's sins. Finally, the verb is attested four times in the Hithpael stem (Deut 22:1, 3; Isa 58:6; Ps 55:2), always in association with מִן, meaning "to hide oneself from," in the sense of "to ignore."

The nominal form תַּעֲלֻמָה ("secret, hidden thing") is attested three times in the MT (Job 11:6; 28:11; Ps 44:22). The first two occurrences (Job) refer to something which is hidden *from* human beings (these will be discussed below); the third occurrence (Psalm 44) alludes to a quality *within* human beings that is (supposedly) hidden from God: God seeks out the "secrets of the heart" (תעלמות לב) of human beings who are worshipping idols. To be sure, these secrets are sinful, but there is no reason to assume that תַּעֲלֻמָה, taken out of this particular context (and not paired with לב), carries the generic meaning "hidden sins."

What this survey reveals is that עלם is most often employed to indicate one's disregard for, or unawareness of, another's plight or need, rather than a covering up of one's own sins (an action expressed, for example, by סתר).[12] If then the Qal stem usage in v. 8 is understood as synonymous with either the Niphal or the Hiphil meaning, a possible translation of עלמנו might be "what has been hidden from us," or "what we disregard."[13]

The expression מאור פניך is a *hapax* in the MT.[14] Most often, מאור refers to the source of light, rather than to light itself.[15] Many exegetes understand the expres-

---

[12] The distinction between the two meanings is well illustrated in Num 5:12b-13 (NJPSV): "If any man's wife has gone astray and broken faith with him in that a man has had carnal relations with her unbeknown to her husband (נעלם מעיני אישה), and she keeps secret (ונסתרה) the fact that she has defiled herself...."

[13] In Hebrew poetry it is possible to dispense with the preposition usually associated with a participle. See, for example, קמי, "those who rise up [against] me," Ps 18:40. Such a use of עלם (i.e., without מן), while uncommon, is nevertheless attested elsewhere in the MT. Thus: "the one who shuts his eyes (רב מארו מעלים עיניו) will be roundly cursed" (Prov 28:27b, NJSPV); "Hear my plea, do not shut your ear (שמעת אל־תעלם אזנך קולי) to my groan" (Lam 3:56, NJPSV). See B. K. Waltke and M. O'Connor, *An Introduction to Biblical Hebrew Syntax* (Winona Lake, IN: Eisenbrauns, 1990) §37.3d.

[14] But see Prov 15:30, "What brightens the eye (מאור־עינים) gladdens the heart" (NJPSV). In this translation, מאור in understood to refer to the agent generating the light. Another way to interpret the expression is as a reference to the light itself which comes through the eyes ("cheerful glance" [*NAB*]; "light of the eyes" [RSV]).

[15] The word is used to describe two distinct sources of light: heavenly bodies (Gen 1:14, 15, 16; Ps 74:16; Ezek 32:8) and oil lamps (Exod 25:6; 27:20; 35:8, 14, 28; 39:37; Lev 24:2; Num 4:9, 16). As seen in the previous note, there is ambiguity concerning its usage in Prov 15:30.

sion as a simple reference to the light of God's face.[16] But whereas the expression "light of God's face" (אור פני יהוה) consistently refers to a benevolent light, bringing blessing to those upon whom it shines and alluding to a comprehensive display of God's favor (see, e. g., Num 6:25; Pss 4:7; 31:17; 44:4; 67:2; 80:4, 8, 20; 89:16; 119:135; Qoh 8:1), with the possible exception of Ps 90:8, the light of God's face is never used in reference to the exposure of hidden sins.[17]

Given the above discussion, I understand the entire phrase עלמנו למאור פניך to mean "hidden from us is the light of your face" (i. e., the blessing of your face's presence is denied us).[18] I shall further explore this understanding in my discussion of the epistemology of the psalm below.

Verse 9

The verb in v. 9a, פנה, attested 116 times in the Qal stem throughout the MT, generally means "to turn." *HALOT*, however, lists no fewer than seven definitions that represent various nuances of this basic meaning. In Ps 90:9, the suggested meaning is "to come to an end, to change" (perhaps related to the Arabic *faniya:* "to pass by, to dwindle away"). *HALOT* cites six other attestations of this usage: Gen 24:63; Deut 23:12; Jer 6:4 (each of these referring to day passing into night); Exod 14:27; Judg 19:26; Ps 46:6 (referring to night passing into morning). This meaning is particularly fitting in our text given the images in Ps 90:4 – 6 of a day passing from morning into evening, or a passing watch in the night. The sense is one of gradual, rather than abrupt, change—in this respect the term forms a close parallel to the use of כלה in v. 7 ("to fade away").

---

16 Thus: "*an die Lichthelle deines Angesichts*" (Delitzsch), "in the sunlight of thy face" (Briggs and Briggs), "*vor deines Antlitzes Licht*" (Gunkel, Kraus), "*in das Licht deines Angesichts*" (Westermann, Hossfeld and Zenger), "in the light of your face" (Tate), "*in das Licht deines Gesichtes*" (Schnocks).

17 It is important to note that in Psalm 44, while God does seek out the "secrets of the heart" of human beings who are worshipping idols (Ps 44:22), that seeking is not done via the "light of his face." Indeed, the very expression אור פניך *does* occur in Psalm 44 (v. 4), but as an indication of God's favor (וזרועם לא הושיעה למו כי ימינך וזרועך ואור פניך כי רציתם, "nor did their own arms bring victory; it was your right hand, your own arm, the light of your face, for you favored them" [*NAB*]).

18 Here, ל governs the subject of a passive verb (see Waltke and O'Connor, *Syntax*, §11.2.10g).

Verse 10

The nominal derivative רֹהַב, from the root רהב, is a MT *hapax*. *TDOT* notes that this root is attested in several Semitic languages with a range of meanings: "to tremble, rage" (Akkadian, Neo-Babylonian), "to be afraid, to fear" (Arabic), "to make proud" (middle Hebrew, Aramaic), "to hasten, be excited, flow swiftly" (Syriac). The sense of violent surging is preserved in the name of the sea monster רַהַב (Isa 51:9; Ps 89:11; Job 9:13). *HALOT* offers "pushing, surging" as the meaning of רֹהַב, while noting that the precise meaning is obscure. The issue is complicated insofar as the ancient versions apparently read some variant of רבב.[19] But given that the sense of "their hurrying," as a translation of רהבם, is consonant with the image of passing time developed in vv. 4–6, 9–10, there is no compelling need to emend the MT.[20]

Verse 12

The finite verb in v. 12a, הודע, can be understood as הודיענו ("teach us"), with the suffix of ימינו serving "double duty."[21] I understand כן to be stronger than simply "thus" or "so" here. As Gunkel notes, the force of כן in conjunction with ידע is illustrated by 1 Sam 23:17 in which Jonathan tells David that he need not fear Saul, for even his father knows it is true (גם שאול אבי ידע כן) that David will be king. In Ps 90:12a, כן conveys the idea of numbering one's days "truly" or "rightly."[22]

---

19 In place of רהבם ("their hurrying"), the versions read: πλεῖον αὐτῶν, *amplius eorum*, ܣܘܓܐܐ "many/more of them." On this evidence, some exegetes argue that the MT ought to be emended to רבם ("many of them") – see, for example, Briggs and Briggs, Westermann, *BHS*, Tate.
20 Without emending the MT, a number of exegetes understand the root meaning of רהב as "to bluster, to boast" and thus render רהבם as "their boasting," "their pridefulness" (thus, Delitzsch, Duhm, Gunkel, Kraus, Dahood).
21 See Müller, "Der 90. Psalm," 276.
22 Gunkel, *Psalmen*, 401. HALOT similarly interprets כן in this verse, as does Delitzsch ("*recht*"). All of the remaining exegetes considered in this study, however, either opt for the weaker force ("thus," "so") or else do not include the word in their translation at all (curiously, given his observation noted above, Gunkel drops the word in his translation).

Verse 13

The Niphal imperative of נחם, when combined with על, generally means "to change one's mind about something one had planned to do" (cf. Exod 32:12, 14; Jer 18:8, 10; Amos 7:3, 6; Joel 2:13; Jonah 3:10; 4:2; Job 42:6).[23] Thus, the psalmist is not necessarily telling God to "regret" or "to be sorry" about his treatment of his servants, but rather to change his mind with respect to them.

Structure, Unity, and Dating

Structure

In Psalm 90, there is a decided shift from the more somber mood in vv. 3–10 to the more hopeful tone in vv. 13–16. That transition is reflected in a chiastic pattern that shapes the entire psalm.[24]

```
vv. 1b-2     God's eternal protection of humanity
    vv. 3–6      complaint over brevity of generations
        vv. 7–10      complaint over God's wrath
            vv. 11–12     petition for wisdom
        vv. 13–14     petition for God's mercy
    vv. 15–16    petition for continuity of following generations
v. 17      prayer for God's blessing upon work of humanity
```

In this scheme, vv. 11–12 have a unique function insofar as they constitute a "pivot point" between the two halves of the poem, transitioning from the somber complaints to the hopeful petitions. These verses form a lexical hinge as well: the keywords אף and עברה link v. 11 to vv. 7 and 9, while יום connects v. 12 to vv. 9, 10, 14, and 15.

Unity

A number of early twentieth-century exegetes question the psalm's original unity. Duhm, for example, cites both the apparently self-contained character

---

23 D. Patrick, "The Translation of Job XLII 6," *VT* 26 (1976) 369–71.
24 I primarily base my discussion of the psalm's structure upon Auffret, "Essai sur la structure littéraire du Psaume 90," 262–76; Schnocks, "Ehe die Berge geboren wurden," 164–67; Hossfeld and Zenger, *Psalmen 51–100*, 605–7.

of vv. 1–12 and the sharp shift in tone between the mournful reflection on the brevity of life in these verses and the hopeful petitions of vv. 13–17. Briggs and Briggs accept the unity of vv. 1–15, but understand vv. 16–17 as the work of a later redactor. Gunkel is perhaps the most influential proponent of the idea that the psalm was composed in multiple stages. He suggests a two-stage developmental model in which an original core comprising vv. 1–12 (dealing with the relationship between divinity and humanity) was later supplemented by vv. 13–17 (concerning the relationship between Yhwh and Israel (perhaps inspired by a national crisis or disaster).[25]

Most later exegetes cautiously avoid definitive claims concerning the (dis) unity of the original psalm, in the absence of strong textual evidence on the matter. A notable exception to this trend, however, is represented by Hossfeld and Zenger. While not necessarily endorsing Gunkel's model of its expansion over time (driven, for example, by national events that broadened the psalm's focus from an original reflection on the individual human condition), they identify an original core comprising vv. 1b-12, that was later expanded by the addition of vv. 13–17 in order to extend the theological scope of the poem at the time of its inclusion in the final canonical ordering of the Psalter.

In support of this argument, they note that vv. 13–17 appear to have been composed as an appeal for joy *after* some (unnamed) affliction had already been endured. Thus, while the first half of the psalm is a reflection on the entire human condition, from birth until death, the second half seems to address a temporary crisis. If this were not so, then the appeal for Yhwh to "turn back," "change his mind," "make us glad," etc., would essentially be a plea for him to reverse human mortality (at least, as mortality is described in vv. 1b-12) – an obvious impossibility. Therefore, according to this argument, the joy appealed for in the second half of the psalm is not to be found in the midst of the unavoidable suffering that comes with human mortality, but rather after a temporary hardship has passed.[26]

While these points are well taken, Westermann, who acknowledges the same distinctions between the two halves of the psalm, nonetheless concludes that they do not represent evidence for multiple redactors, but rather the intentional technique of a careful stylist.[27] For example, by repeating the motif of "days and years" in v. 15, the psalmist links the petitions of vv. 13–16 with the earlier com-

---

25 Gunkel, *Psalmen*, 399.

26 Hossfeld and Zenger, *Psalmen 51–100*, 608. A similar argument is put forward by Clifford, "What Does the Psalmist Ask For?" 59–66; idem, "Psalm 90: Wisdom Meditation or Communal Lament?" 190–205.

27 Westermann, *Psalmen*, 115–20.

plaint over the transitory nature of life found in vv. 4 (continued in vv. 5–6) and 9. In this way, a time of trial and distress for the nation serves as a particular example of the affliction caused by the brevity of individual life.

Furthermore, the juxtaposition of the somber note struck in the first half of the psalm and the more hopeful note in the second half is not necessarily incoherent. In this connection, Westermann observes that the psalmist, like Qoheleth (Qoh 3:4), recognizes that there is a time for weeping and for joy. Praise of God is possible even when confronting the brevity of life, with all its suffering, so long as one can remain confident in God's eternal trustworthiness (as celebrated in vv. 1b-2). In this reading, the petition for a wise heart in v. 12 is not a plea that goes unanswered, but is rather the fitting response to the double question posed in v. 11: only by honestly facing the mortality (i.e., "counting one's days") that is so vividly depicted in vv. 3–10, is one able to accept that God, in his eternal refuge, can be known (taking "fear" in v. 11 in the sense of "awe") even in the face of death.

While a definitive resolution of the question concerning the psalm's original unity is not likely to be attained, I do not find the arguments put forward by Hossfeld and Zenger for the multiple-stage composition of the psalm compelling. Insofar as their evidence is grounded primarily upon apparent inconsistencies in content and meaning between the two halves of the poem (rather than in textual discrepancies), I find that Westermann's analysis provides a reasonable response to these concerns, affirming as it does that a single author could have skillfully drawn together the various themes represented in the psalm. To be sure, the resultant work has a unique character that makes it difficult to classify using traditional categories. At the same time, however, it is this very character that can provide clues regarding the psalm's possible date of composition.

Dating

The majority of scholars considered in this study identify Psalm 90 as a fairly late (late exilic or postexilic) composition. Briggs and Briggs, for example, argue for a late exilic date, citing the overall tone of the psalm as a prayer for the restoration of divine favor, the image of God as a dwelling place for his people (as in Ezek 11:16–20), the expectation for a comparable length of time for both affliction and gladness (cf. Isa 40:2), and the juxtaposition of לב and חכמה (as in Job 9:4; 1 Kgs 3:12; Prov 16:23; Qoh 7:4; 8:5; 10:2). Similarly late dates are proposed by Kraus (postexilic), Vawter (postexilic), and Müller (exilic/postexilic). Tate, for his part, notes that use of the term עבדים ("servants") in Psalm 90 (vv. 13 and 16) for the faithful of Israel is similar to that of Trito-

Isaiah (Isa 56:6; 65:8 – 9, 13 – 15; 66:14). Hossfeld and Zenger, who argue for a two-stage composition of the psalm (see above), date the original text, vv. 1b-12, to the late fifth or early fourth century.[28] They contend that the psalm took its final form only when the sequence of Psalms 90 – 92 was inserted into the canonical Psalter, sometime during the middle or late fourth century.

Without attempting to distinguish between late exilic and postexilic dates for the psalm, I accept a generally late date of composition. Such dating is consistent with the psalm's blending of genres, which suggests an author who was familiar with a well-developed psalmody tradition.[29] It is also consistent with the apparent intertextual similarities between the psalm and certain themes from the wisdom tradition. I shall further explore that relationship later in this chapter.

Psalm 90: Metaphor and Worldview

With its evocation of the brevity of life and the hardships that all people endure, Psalm 90 is particularly rich in metaphorical imagery. The psalm is governed by the primary conceptual metaphor A LIFETIME IS A DAY. It is supported by two secondary conceptual metaphors: TIME MOVES and PEOPLE ARE PLANTS (we shall see that the latter of these is employed rather differently here than in Psalm 1).[30]

The A LIFETIME IS A DAY conceptual metaphor maps the entire span of a human life onto the passage of a single day. Thus, some point in the day represents the moment of birth, and some point represents death. The intervening hours represent all the events of a lifetime: from childhood, through adulthood, to old age. In Psalm 90, the psalmist alludes to this basic metaphor by his overall representation of time throughout the poem. Thus, in the eyes of Yhwh, a thousand years are "like a former day" or a single night's watch (v. 4). Our life begins in the morning (vv. 5 – 6, 14) and by evening it has ended (v. 6), we become as sleep (v. 5), and we end our years like a sigh (v. 9).

---

28 Hossfeld and Zenger, *Psalmen 51–100*, 608. In light of the wisdom themes and language represented in these verses, they consider the original psalm to be somewhat older than Qoheleth.
29 Westermann observes that Psalm 90 could be considered a psalm of trust, given the emphatic opening declaration of confidence in God's eternal protection of humanity (vv. 1b-2). But he also notes that the overall structure of the psalm is reminiscent of a communal lament, given the 1pl. speech (vv. 1, 7–10, 12, 14, 15, 17), and the petitions of vv. 13, 15, and 16 (*Psalmen*, 115).
30 For extensive discussion of these conceptual metaphors, based upon examples drawn from English literature, see G. Lakoff and M. Turner, *More than Cool Reason: A Field Guide to Poetic Metaphor* (Chicago: University of Chicago Press, 1989) 1– 56.

The psalmist structures his portrayal of the nature of life by the PEOPLE ARE PLANTS conceptual metaphor. Here, contrary to Psalm 1, the metaphor is not used to focus on the contrast between healthy, well-rooted plants and dry, withered chaff (that part of the plant which is undesirable). Rather, the focus is on the transition that grass undergoes every day from healthy and blooming in the morning to withered and dry in the evening (vv. 5–6). There is no question of some grass faring better or worse than other grass: every plant shares the same fate, both in its glory and in its demise.

The psalmist also employs the TIME MOVES conceptual metaphor, in which time is portrayed as a vehicle that either approaches or recedes from the present moment. A thousand years are like a day that "passes by" (v. 4). The days of one's life "hurry" and "pass by in haste" (v. 10). Indeed, the entire span of one's life is represented by the passage of time from sunrise to sunset.

As the psalmist develops his conceptual metaphors within the source domain, he exercises the metaphors' power of options (see the discussion of a metaphor's powers of options, reason, and evaluation in chap. 1) in such a way that there is little room for independent choice or variation. For example, only one type of plant is discussed (grass). Every plant begins the day healthy and ends the day withered. There is no mention of how these plants are maintained (e. g., by a gardener or by a nearby stream as a source of water, etc.); thus, there is no suggestion that a given plant might avoid this inevitable fate. The fact that the plant begins its life strong and blooming does not assure it any protection against the ravages of time. Similarly, the time span represented by the day flies by quickly. There is no sense that there is any moment during which it slows or lingers, or that its pace is (or could be) contingent upon any external conditions.

As a result of the psalmist's structuring of the source domain, he presents a worldview for the target domain (humanity) that is fairly stark and devoid of freedom of choice. Every person is guaranteed some prosperity (during their "morning bloom"), but every person is also assured of progressively greater hardship such that each life will ultimately fade into dissolution. While the psalmist does acknowledge that Yhwh's rage (presumably in response to human sin [see v. 8]) is a cause for some of life's struggles (vv. 7, 9, 11), there is also a resignation to the fact that life is difficult and relatively brief for all people, regardless of their moral standing (vv. 5–6, 9–10).

In the worldview represented by the psalm, it is impossible to judge one's moral character based upon the state of his prosperity. No one is spared suffering: both the righteous and the wicked must endure hardship and the former enjoy no more longevity than the latter.

While the psalmist acknowledges every person to be a sinner in v. 8, there is no recognition of a disparity among the population in the degree to which people sin. Obviously, the psalmist is aware that some people are more wicked than others. However, insofar as he chooses not to highlight that reality (which, by contrast, the psalmist in Psalm 1 does highlight), he places all the more emphasis on the fact that suffering is part of the universal human condition. That good people suffer is simply an unavoidable part of life.

To be sure, the psalmist does point to a possible source of relief: a prayerful appeal to Yhwh's mercy (vv. 1, 13 – 17). In the worldview of Psalm 90, as throughout most of the Psalter, Yhwh is a faithful protector of Israel (this is underscored by the metaphorical designation of Yhwh as an eternal "safe dwelling" [מעון] in v. 1). But even that designation does not guarantee the outcome of one's personal appeal to Yhwh for the amelioration of human suffering. In crying out to Yhwh, the psalmist is attempting to transcend the limitations of the worldview of his psalm. Only Yhwh—if he chooses—can slow the otherwise inexorable pace of the decline of the quality of life. Only Yhwh can bring joy into the midst of sorrow (v. 14).

In the following section we shall see that the psalmist does not only seek to break free from the limitations of his worldview by appealing for relief from suffering. In addition, he appeals to Yhwh to be taught a *new type of knowledge:* a knowledge that he could never hope to attain from within the worldview we have just described.

Social Epistemology

If we view Psalm 90 from an epistemological perspective and apply the diagnostic tool developed at the end of chap. 1, then we might summarize the primary proposition of the psalm as: "Despite momentary joys, human life is mostly difficult and relatively brief." Within the worldview of the psalm, belief in the proposition is supported by a coherentist justification scheme. The psalmist is not attempting to provide new information or a novel perspective. Indeed, he does not relate any particular events or experiences at all, but instead conveys an overarching observation on the nature of human existence. Each individual hearer of the psalm is invited to compare her or his own perceptions of life to determine whether or not they cohere with the psalmist's proposition.

The proposition can only count as actual knowledge if (1) belief in the proposition is justified, and (2) if the proposition is true. Given the nature of the primary proposition in Psalm 90, it is clear that any attempt to satisfy these two conditions will be highly subjective. Nevertheless, every human life contains both joys and hardships, and every person has some sense of the pace at which their life passes by. Thus, one's acceptance of the proposition as knowledge will always be at least partially warranted to a greater or lesser degree, depending upon one's judgment of the quality of his or her life. This situation of the partial acceptance of a proposition varies markedly from the strict dichotomy posed between the righteous and the wicked in the primary proposition of Psalm 1 (in that case, it is conceivable that one could firmly deny the existence of such a stark distinction and thus unequivocally reject the proposition).

While the "knowledge status" of the primary proposition of Psalm 90 will always be subject to the lack of certitude which characterizes any coherentist scheme, there is a point in the poem at which the psalmist goes beyond what the primary proposition can establish. At Ps 90:12, the psalmist asks for Yhwh himself to impart knowledge that can be acquired from no other source.[31] But in asking Yhwh to teach him "to number his days rightly," what precisely is the psalmist requesting?

I argued above that Ps 90:8b could be translated: "hidden from us [Qal passive participle of עלם] is the light of your face." Two of the three attestations in the MT of the nominal form תַּעֲלָמָה ("secret, hidden thing") appear in wisdom literature: Job 11:6 and 28:11 (the third, Ps 44:22, was discussed above). In Job 11:6 the form refers to the "secrets of wisdom" (תעלמות חכמה) which only God can reveal to human beings. In Job 28:11, human beings' futile attempt to discover wisdom on their own (without God) brings many "hidden things" to light, but does not disclose wisdom, which remains "hidden" (Job 28:21, Niphal stem of עלם) from the eyes of human beings.

Given this language, I contend that the concept of concealed wisdom is operative in the psalmist's lament in Ps 90:8b which anticipates his ardent petition in v. 12. That petition itself constitutes the primary instance of a wisdom motif in Psalm 90: the psalmist's request to be "taught" (Hiphil imperative of ידע) by God "to number his days rightly," so that he might gain a "heart of wisdom" (לבב חכמה).[32] We must ask, therefore, in what sense the wisdom to correctly number one's days constitutes hidden knowledge, which only Yhwh can impart.

---

31 Insofar as the information, if actually conveyed, would come directly from Yhwh, it is reasonable to characterize such information as both justifiably believable and objectively true, i.e., as actual knowledge.

32 The heart as the seat of wisdom is a common motif in Proverbs (e. g., Prov 10:8; 14:33; 15:14; 16:23; 23:15; cf. also Job 37:24), as is the concept of "fear (יראה) of the Lord," which occurs in Ps 90:11. In fact, every occurrence of "fear" (יראה) in Proverbs has יהוה as the object (Prov 1:7, 29; 2:5; 8:13; 9:10; 10:27; 14:26, 27; 15:16, 33; 16:6; 19:23; 22:4; 23:17) – note especially Prov 1:7 (יראת יהוה ראשית דעת; "The fear of the Lord is the beginning of knowledge"; cf. Ps 111:10).

Review of Exegesis of Ps 90:12

The petition in v. 12 ("to number our days rightly teach us") has traditionally been understood by exegetes to express the psalmist's desire to know more fully the limitations of human mortality. Thus, while vv. 3–10 vividly depict the brevity and harshness of life, if only one could gain the wisdom to completely accept the finitude of his days, then there would be a kind of calm in the face of inevitable limitations—one would no longer resist the irresistible end to life. Hence, Delitzsch understands the "heart of wisdom" of v. 12 to denote the state of one who has learned to continually remind himself of his ultimate end (by counting each day as it passes).[33]

Von Rad, by contrast, understands the appeal of the psalmist in v. 12 as an attempt to ground humanity's relationship with God.[34] Given the suffering and brevity of life, human beings are left wondering how God is a part of their existence – other than as a fierce punisher of sins (vv. 7–9). In the face of such perplexity, what humanity needs above all else is a heart of wisdom, and that can come only from God. Once one has been so educated by God, the suffering of life at least becomes more bearable because now the sufferer knows that God is a part of his life. Kraus sees the request for a heart of wisdom as rooted in the desire of the psalmist to approach God in prayer. A foolish heart lacks the ability to express genuine repentance or to earnestly seek forgiveness for the sins that have been causing such misery.[35] Only wisdom can bring one to experience the salvation of God's mercy, but that wisdom can only come from God. Such readings of the psalm still do not directly explain *how* one might acquire a heart of wisdom (other than to acknowledge that it will come directly from God).

Dahood reads the psalm in a manner similar to Delitzsch: "A meditation on the brevity and misery of human life…. [T]he essence of Wisdom lies in recognizing the transience of human life."[36] Urbrock develops this perspective further by arguing that the heart of wisdom is one that grasps that *all* humanity—the good as well as the evil, the rich as well as the poor—experience the same finitude and suffering at the hand of God.[37] This, he contends, is a view that the psalmist shares with the authors of Job and Qoheleth. Once again, these scholars do not concern themselves with the question of how one comes to acquire a deeper appreciation for the "transience of life." If it were simply a question of honestly

33 Delitzsch, *Kommentar*, 591.
34 Von Rad, "Der 90. Psalm," 275–76.
35 Kraus, *Psalmen*, 631.
36 Dahood, *Psalms*, 2. 322.
37 Urbrock, "Mortal and Miserable Man," 12.

accepting finitude, no special wisdom would seem to be required other than basic human experience. And while the poor (or the righteous) might derive some personal satisfaction from seeing the rich (or the evil) suffering from the same limitations as themselves, that too would hardly seem to be the lofty goal of divinely inspired wisdom.

Hossfeld and Zenger, while basically following in the tradition of an "existential" reading of the psalm (i. e., that the psalmist is addressing fundamental questions about the nature of humanity), are nevertheless more optimistic about the consolation that could be afforded one by the wisdom which is sought in v. 12. In particular, they note that in v. 12, the psalmist transforms his perception of God: no longer is he a God of wrathful judgment, condemning human beings for their sins; now he is appealed to as the "teacher of life" ("*Lehrer des Lebens*").[38] The psalmist does not try to escape from his mortality, but rather seeks to gain a proper perspective – a perspective from which suffering is not understood to be divine punishment, but rather, one in which every moment of life (every "counted day") is recognized as divine gift. Insofar as wisdom is meant to be the "art of living" ("*Lebenskunst*"), this heart of wisdom enables one to accept the challenges of each day (which truly do limit us) with a sense of hope and purpose.

Much of the scholarship on Ps 90:12 has been surveyed by H.-M. Wahl, who concludes that the psalmist is here seeking a share in divine wisdom by enhancing the awareness of his own finitude. God knows our limits perfectly, and by seeking to know them as well, we seek knowledge like God's own knowledge. Wahl thus paraphrases v. 12, stressing that the goal of our seeking wisdom is to know that our humanity must yield to mortality: "Do teach us to understand that humanity is subjected to finitude!"[39]

Contrary to the above tradition of interpretation of Ps 90:12, R. J. Clifford has recently argued that vv. 11–12 only make sense within the overall context of the poem if the psalmist is speaking about a *particular event*, under which he is suffering and from which he seeks relief.[40] He suggests that the psalmist is asking to know the duration of the divine anger that is causing his community a current period of struggle; he is not seeking to know the finitude of human life in general. The specific nature of the struggle with which the psalmist's community is engaged, however, is not named (possibilities are war, famine, plague, etc.). On

---

38 Hossfeld and Zenger, *Psalmen 51–100*, 611.
39 "*Zu begreifen, daß der Mensch der Endlichkeit verfallen ist, lehre doch!*" H.-M. Wahl, "Psalm 90,12: Text, Tradition und Interpretation," *ZAW* 106 (1994) 116–23, here 122. Zięba ("The Meaning of the Expression לבב חכמה," 121) offers a similar understanding.
40 Clifford, "Psalm 90," 202–3.

this interpretation, the expression למנות ימינו כן ("to number our days rightly") "does not mean 'let us know the brevity of human life'.... [but] refers to an accurate knowledge of the time period of the divine wrath behind the distress."[41]

Clifford arrives at this suggestion by arguing that מנה ימים ("to number days") is equivalent in meaning to ספר ימים. While the former expression is a *hapax*, the latter occurs four times in the MT: Lev 15:13, 28; 23:16; and Ezek 44:26. In each of these other instances, the phrase refers to the measuring of a specific period of time (time required for purification, or time needed for a sacrificial offering).[42]

"To number our days rightly teach us" (למנות ימינו כן הודע)

What all of the exegetical discussions considered thus far seem to lack is an explicit awareness of the fact that the psalmist does not simply ask for wisdom in v. 12, but also states the *means by which he can acquire it*: למנות ימינו כן הודע ("to number our days rightly teach us"). This expression is a *hapax* in the MT. While there is nothing unusual about the request for wisdom, the idea that one can acquire it by the numbering of days is unique in the MT. Several of the exegetical treatments we have reviewed simply assume that to carefully count one's days can bring a calming resignation vis-à-vis the finitude of life. I contend, however, that the psalmist has much higher expectations for the wisdom he is seeking.

In Ps 90:12, the psalmist does not seem to be imploring Yhwh to teach him the simple act of enumerating his days, but rather of rightly ordering them in such a way as to understand their nature and meaning. Such an act of ordering would be properly reserved to Yhwh alone, and so only he would be capable of teaching it to humanity. As to what such a "proper ordering" entails, we can only speculate, but the context of Psalm 90 itself provides important clues. It seems clear that the psalmist is not simply seeking the capacity to count each day as it succeeds its predecessor. Indeed, given the stress upon the brevity of life (vv. 4–10), such a simple tabulation would not be particularly challenging, nor would it need to be done "rightly."[43]

---

41 Clifford, "What Does the Psalmist Ask For?" 65.

42 Note that Clifford's argument hinges on the assumption that מנה and ספר are simple synonyms. In the appendix to this chapter, I shall explore the validity of that assumption.

43 To this extent, I agree with Clifford ("What Does the Psalmist Ask For?" 65) in his rejection of such a simplistic understanding of "counting one's days." I do not, however, share his contention that the psalmist is seeking knowledge of the duration of some specific period of affliction that has beset Israel.

Furthermore, it is interesting to note that, elsewhere in the MT, the syntactic usage of מנה (as opposed to other counting verbs such as ספר and פקד) can connote a type of counting that Yhwh alone undertakes. For example, when Yhwh compares Abraham's descendants to the number of dust grains on the ground (Gen 13:16), the implication is that human beings could never make such a count – only Yhwh can enumerate (מנה) the innumerable grains.[44]

I suggest, therefore, that in Ps 90:12 the psalmist is seeking an understanding of life that only Yhwh's wisdom can supply. The need for such knowledge is emphasized by the harshness and brevity of life, and the awareness that both the righteous and the wicked alike suffer equally. The desire for such knowledge is inflamed by the hope that, with a proper reckoning of time, Yhwh's work and splendor might be revealed (v. 16), and that the proper ordering of a day might reveal that it begins with Yhwh's eternal חסד (v. 14) rather than with a rapidly fading bloom (vv. 5–6). Significantly, the psalmist is seeking this knowledge directly from Yhwh; he is not attempting to acquire it on his own. It is only by virtue of Yhwh's willingness to teach (הודע) this ability to order (מנה) that human beings can enjoy the knowledge which such ordering procures.

Conclusion

We thus find in Psalm 90 a direct epistemological appeal for an extraordinary kind of knowledge: a "divine knowledge" which transcends the knowledge represented by the primary proposition of the psalm itself. Were such knowledge to be granted, the recipient would certainly be justified in believing it, given that its source is Yhwh himself. Within the worldview of Psalm 1, it is inconceivable that the righteous could suffer. But from within the worldview of Psalm 90, the psalmist is hopeful enough to directly ask Yhwh to impart the requisite knowledge for human beings to understand meaning and purpose in a world in which *every* life is subject to harsh limitations.

---

44 See the appendix to this chapter for a more detailed exploration of the relevant occurrences of מנה in the MT.

Appendix

In this appendix, I explore the usage of מנה ("to count") throughout the MT in an attempt to better understand the force of this verb in Ps 90:12a, as it applies to Yhwh's counting.

The basic meaning of מנה is "to count." But the word further implies a deliberate calculating or ordering, rather than a neutral enumeration (which is generally conveyed by the more common verbs ספר and, in the case of counting populations, פקד).[45] The distinction between מנה and ספר can be partially discerned by comparing their nominal forms מָנָה ("part, portion"; e.g., Exod 29:26; Lev 7:33) and מִסְפָּר ("number"; e.g., Judg 7:6; 21:23). That the two verbs are not exact synonyms is suggested by the fact that they are sometimes used together in the same verse to measure the same objects (e.g., "a people too vast to count [מנה] or number [ספר]," 1 Kgs 3:8; oxen and sheep "too many to number [ספר] or count [מנה]," 1 Kgs 8:5 // 2 Chr 5:6).

As a verb, מנה is attested twenty-eight times in the MT (ten of which are in the Piel and Pual stems, meaning "to appoint;" I shall not consider these further in this appendix). The remaining attestations are in the Qal and Niphal stems, as listed in the following table:

Qal and Niphal Attestations of מנה Within the MT

Object Ordered/ Counted	Context	Citation
I. money	temple funds to be paid for wages	2 Kgs 12:11
II. livestock	sacrificial animals too many to count	1 Kgs 8:5; 2 Chr 5:6
	after return from the Exile, shepherds will count their flocks	Jer 33:13
III. wisdom	missing wisdom cannot be counted (supplied)	Qoh 1:15
IV. stars	Yhwh can count the stars	Ps 147:4
V. people	"uncountable" descendants of Abraham	Gen 13:16 (bis); Num 23:10; 1 Kgs 3:8
	David's census	2 Sam 24:1; 1 Chr 21:1; 21:17; 27:24
	king of Aram counts out men for a new army	1 Kgs 20:25
	Suffering Servant counted among the wicked	Isa 53:12
	those who forsake the Lord are designated for slaughter	Isa 65:12
VI. days	request that Yhwh teach us to order our days	Ps 90:12

---

45 *TDOT*, "מנה," 8. 397.

In several of these occurrences, objects or persons are counted, not to determine an absolute number, but so that they can be reordered for another purpose or because they are being invested with a symbolic significance. Thus, temple funds are counted so that they can be redistributed as wages to the workers who are repairing the temple (2 Kgs 12:11). The king of Aram counts out men to replace the army he has lost in battle against Israel (1 Kgs 20:25); the exact size of this army is not specified, only that it was very large (1 Kgs 20:13, 27). In Deutero-Isaiah, one of the special qualities of the suffering servant is that, though innocent, he was "counted" among the wicked (Isa 53:12). Furthermore, those who forsake the Lord will be counted out for slaughter (Isa 65:12). And Jeremiah envisions a restored Jerusalem in which, as a sign of its revived fortunes, shepherds will once again be able to count their sheep (Jer 33:13).

A second category in which מנה is used concerns people or things that cannot be counted or ordered. Thus, Qoheleth laments that the wisdom he seeks cannot be found (חסרון לא יוכל להמנות, "a deficiency that cannot be counted," Qoh 1:15). In other instances, things cannot be counted because they are too numerous for our human mental capacity. For example, at the dedication of the temple, Solomon sacrifices sheep and oxen with an abundance that cannot be counted (1 Kgs 8:5 // 2 Chr 5:6).

At the very heart of Yhwh's covenant with Abraham lies the promise of descendants too numerous to count. Yhwh foretells that Abraham's offspring shall be as uncountable as the dust (עפר) of the earth (Gen 13:16). When Balaam relates Yhwh's oracle against the king of Moab, he uses this same metaphor for Jacob's descendants being as uncountable as dust particles (Num 23:10). And when Solomon prays for wisdom, he notes that he rules a people too vast to count (1 Kgs 3:8). Although not explicitly stated, the presumption in these texts seems to be that Yhwh alone is capable of counting or ordering such things. Thus, in Ps 147:4 the psalmist declares that Yhwh can count the stars (which are presumably as uncountable for humans as is the dust of the earth).

Finally, there is a third category of attestations of מנה which refer to David's attempt to take a census of the Israelites. As related in 2 Samuel, Yhwh is angry with Israel and so incites David to attempt to number the people (2 Sam 24:1). In the Chronicler's redaction of this account, it is (a) "satan" who incites David to make the count (1 Chr 21:1). When Yhwh is about to punish Israel for this act, the king pleads for mercy for his people, insisting that it was he alone who ordered that the people be counted (1 Chr 21:1). Later in Chronicles we find that David's general, Joab, was prevented from completing his count of the people because of Yhwh's wrath (1 Chr 27:24).

In light of the foregoing simple cataloging and classification of the usage of the verb מנה throughout the MT, we can now more deeply analyze its meaning by comparing its use with those of ספר and פקד. Like מנה, these words are also employed in contexts addressing both Yhwh's promise of descendants to Abraham and the incident of David's ill-fated census.

Within the MT, there are three images that are consistently used to illustrate the great size of the people of Israel. Their number is compared to "dust" (עפר), "sand" (חול), or "stars" (כוכב).[46] In a small subset of the pericopes that contain these metaphors, the given image is used in conjunction with one of the counting verbs, מנה or ספר. In these instances, מנה is always paired with עפר (Gen 13:16 [*bis*]; Num 23:10), while ספר is always paired with חול or כוכב (the image of sand occurs in Gen 32:13; Hos 2:1, the image of stars in Gen 15:5; 1 Chr 27:23).

The prevailing usage of עפר in the MT is simply in reference to physical dust or earth, without any metaphorical implications. Indeed, out of 110 attestations in the MT, עפר implies "a huge number" in only four verses (Gen 13:16; 28:14; Num 23:10; 2 Chr 1:9). In all of these cases it refers to the people of Israel, and in all but one instance it alludes to Yhwh's promise of future descendants (i.e., not to an already established population). Only in 2 Chr 1:9, does the term refer to the presently-existing population of Israel, and even here Solomon employs the metaphor within the context of Yhwh's promise to David of an ever-lasting kingdom.

By contrast, חול is employed in a wide variety of contexts to simply refer to a very large number. Along with the instances noted above in which it does refer to the people of Israel, it is also used to describe quantities of grain (Gen 41:49), the size of armies opposing Israel (Josh 11:4; 1 Sam 13:5), a number of days (Job 29:18), the number of Yhwh's thoughts (Ps 139:18), the number of future widows in Israel (Jer 15:8), and the number of prisoners taken by the Chaldeans (Hab 1:9).

Next considering כוכב, we find as with עפר, that whenever it is used to imply a large number, it always refers to the population of Israel. However, unlike עפר, it often refers to the presently-existing population (i.e., to a state of affairs that actually exists) rather than to Yhwh's promise of future progeny (see, e.g., Deut 1:10; 10:22; 28:62; Neh 9:23; 1 Chr 27:23).

That מנה is used exclusively with עפר, while ספר is used exclusively with חול and כוכב, suggests at least one possible distinction between these verbs: מנה may imply an ordering or reckoning that is properly the work of Yhwh alone (such as numbering a population which, by Yhwh's own promise, is innumerable for

---

46 For עפר see Gen 13:16; 28:14; Num 23:10; 2 Chr 1:9. For חול see Gen 22:17; 32:13; 2 Sam 17:11; 1 Kgs 4:20; Isa 10:22; Jer 33:22; Hos 2:1. For כוכב see Gen 15:5; 22:17; 26:4; Exod 32:13; Deut 1:10; 10:22; 28:62; Neh 9:23; 1 Chr 27:23.

human beings) or of the people whom Yhwh has designated to perform this task (such as the scribes and priests who are to count the temple funds, or the shepherds who will manifest Yhwh's restored favor by counting their sheep after the return from the Exile).

The counting, or enumerating, that is most commonly the task of human beings seems to be ספר. This form of counting is "first and foremost an expression of power, of having something or someone at one's disposal. A foreign ruler demonstrates his power over a subjected people by counting and weighing their tribute (Isa 33:18). Solomon orders a census to provide labor for the temple construction (2 Chr 2:1, 16).... [C]ounting the number of defensive towers is supposed to demonstrate the invulnerability and power of Jerusalem (Ps 48:13)."[47] Thus, Joseph stores grain in such quantity that it cannot be counted (Gen 41:49), thereby manifesting his power in Egypt.

To be sure, Yhwh is also occasionally the subject of ספר. The Book of Job, in particular, celebrates his ability to measure every aspect of creation: the footsteps of a man's life (Job 14:16; 31:4), the clouds (Job 38:37), or the length of the gestation periods of animals (Job 39:2). In each of these cases, Yhwh's superior power with respect to human beings is highlighted.

Turning to the two accounts of Yhwh's promise to Abraham that he will be the father of "uncountable" generations (Genesis 13 and 15), it might seem that ספר in Gen 15:5 is used in exact equivalence with the usage of מנה in Gen 13:16. But the fact that ספר is used here in conjunction with כוכב (as opposed to עפר), when taken in connection with the other uses of ספר throughout the MT, suggests that what is being underscored in Gen 15:5 is Yhwh's unmatched power to count the uncountable. This is fundamentally the same act of counting that human beings are capable of, only now with an infinitely higher capacity. By contrast, מנה in Gen 13:16 suggests the exercise of a uniquely divine power of reckoning that human beings can partially possess only if Yhwh bestows that ability upon them.

Within the context of Genesis, the difference between עפר and כוכב is further emphasized by the fact that עפר is intimately related to the very nature of being human. In Gen 2:7, Yhwh forms the man out of the dust (עפר) of the earth (אדמה). Thus, while both עפר and כוכב can serve as effective metaphors for large numbers, to order or reckon עפר is in some sense to mirror the very act of Yhwh's creation of humanity.

The incident of David's attempt to take a census of the people (2 Samuel 24 // 1 Chronicles 21), yields an illustrative comparison between the uses of מנה and

---

47 J. Conrad, "ספר," *TDOT*, 10. 309–10.

ספר. Throughout the MT, a number of census takings are attested and there is nothing problematic *per se* in the activity. Indeed, in Exod 30:11–16, it is Yhwh himself who orders Moses to count the Israelites ("take a head count," נשא את ראש). This order is carried out to completion and a number is cited for all men over the age of twenty (Exod 38:26). Again, in Num 1:2, Yhwh orders Moses to count (נשא את ראש) the Israelites. The verb describing Moses' actual registry of the various tribes is פקד (this verb is attested 81 times in Numbers 1–4). As before, the command is followed completely and an actual head count is listed (Num 1:43). After Moses and the Israelites defeat the Midianites, Yhwh orders Moses to take yet another census (נשא את ראש, Num 26:2), which is carried out and completed (26:51).[48]

The census that David undertakes is clearly different from these other instances, for it incurs Yhwh's wrath upon the king and his people. As with the counts that Moses takes, it is Yhwh who instigates the census, but he does so because his anger has flared up against Israel (2 Sam 24:1).[49] He uses David as the instrument of his anger and incites the king against the people by commanding him to "number" (מנה) the men of Judah and Israel. In the MT, this is the only context in which מנה is used to refer to a general census.[50] When David, in turn, actually gives the command for the census to Joab, he does not use מנה, but rather פקד (2 Sam 24:2, 4). Joab completes the count and produces a number (24:9). After the act is done, David reproaches himself and laments having counted (ספר) the people (24:10), which he adjudges to be a great sin.

We find, therefore, that when Yhwh wishes to incite David to undertake an act that will be harmful to himself and to Israel, he orders the king to do the act designated by the verb מנה. But David himself gives the order not with מנה but with a more common verb (regularly used to describe the actions of human be-

---

48 Other head counts (listed without an accompanying counting verb) are attested in Ezra 2:2– 64; 1 Chr 7:40. In 2 Chr 2:16, Solomon takes a census (ספר) of aliens to be used for labor. In 2 Chr 25:5, Amaziah takes a count (פקד) of men fit for battle. Each of these latter two censuses are successfully completed and a number is recorded.

49 The interested reader is referred to the commentaries for speculation over why Yhwh was angry. The text offers no explicit reason.

50 Given that David's commander, Joab, and his officers are the ones who make the count (2 Sam 24:4), and that the numbers reported are of battle-ready men (24:9), it might be argued that this census is like the mustering of troops by the king of Aram (1 Kgs 20:25) which is also described by the verb מנה. However, David is the only *Israelite* whose census is described in this way. Furthermore, unlike the king of Aram, who was actually calling up troops to prepare for a specific battle, David is making a general head count without acting under the threat of imminent conflict.

ings throughout the MT), i.e., פקד. Once again, after the task has been completed, the term used for what has been carried out is not מנה but ספר.

When this incident is recounted in 1 Chronicles 21, it is (a) "satan" rather than Yhwh who incites David to take a census. Still, as in 2 Samuel, the verb used to describe the instruction given to the king is מנה (1 Chr 21:1). David, for his part, uses ספר in commanding Joab to take the census (21:2). Joab undertakes the task and produces a count (21:5), but we are later told that he was prevented from finishing the count because of Yhwh's anger (1 Chr 27:24). When, in the face of Yhwh's wrath, David accepts responsibility for his sinful act (21:17), he acknowledges that he intended the people to be numbered (מנה): הלא אני אמרתי למנות בעם. Unlike 2 Sam 24:10, David is not referring here to the completed act (ספר), but rather to his intended action (מנה).

What the comparison of these two accounts suggests is that the forbidden act is not the counting itself (ספר or פקד), but rather the ordering or reckoning denoted by מנה. This point is underscored in that when we are told of Joab's failed attempt to complete the census, the term used for counting is מנה (1 Chr 27:24). Indeed, in the entire account of David's census, no human being is ever described as actually having completed the act of מנה.

The text itself is not explicit about why מנה should be offensive to Yhwh. Perhaps the reason is that this action is one that is properly a function of Yhwh alone and that, in pursuing it, David encroaches upon Yhwh's authority. The suggested distinction between מנה and ספר (or פקד) in the story of David's census appears to be consistent with the above discussion of Yhwh's promise to Abraham that he would have numberless descendants.

This survey of the usage of מנה in the MT, while not conclusive, suggests that this verb entails not the simple act of counting, but rather an ordering – and thus an understanding – of the nature of things (primarily human beings) that only Yhwh may rightfully engage in, and that only he is fully capable of performing. Thus, when the psalmist asks to be taught to "number" (מנה) his days (Ps 90:12), he may well be boldly asking for a type of knowledge that is proper to Yhwh himself.

Chapter VII.
Psalm 107: The Epistemology of Salvation

Psalm 107, the opening psalm of Book IV of the Psalter, presents a series of four scenarios in four strophes, each strophe describing an anonymous group of people suffering from a different hardship. In every instance, they cry out to Yhwh for help, and in every instance he provides assistance for them. To that degree, Psalm 107 could rightfully be considered a psalm of thanksgiving (as it is generally classified) in which the psalmist thanks Yhwh for his merciful חסד (vv. 1, 8, 15, 21, 31).

The final verse of the psalm, however, suggests that there may be more to this poem than the above summary indicates. In v. 43, the psalmist exhorts "whoever is wise (חכם)" to carefully observe all that has been recounted, and to not simply thank Yhwh for his חסד, but to "consider it closely (בין)."

The fundamental question I address in this chapter is: what is it that the wise person should learn from Psalm 107? While it is not considered a "wisdom psalm" by the usual standards used to define that classification, I consider Psalm 107 to contain "wisdom qualities," particularly in its final exhortation to the wise person. After a translation of the psalm and brief discussion of text-critical and interpretative issues, I present a detailed analysis of Psalm 107, focusing on the manner in which its metaphors structure the worldview represented within the text and how these affect the text's epistemology. Finally, I apply the results of this analysis to suggest an answer to the question raised by v. 43.

Psalm 107 Translation and Text-Critical Issues[1]

1 הֹדוּ לַיהוה כִּי־טוֹב כִּי לְעוֹלָם חַסְדּוֹ:

2 יֹאמְרוּ גְּאוּלֵי יהוה אֲשֶׁר גְּאָלָם מִיַּד־צָר:

3 וּמֵאֲרָצוֹת קִבְּצָם מִמִּזְרָח וּמִמַּעֲרָב מִצָּפוֹן וּמִיָּם:

---

1 In addition to the commentaries cited in chap. 3 (n. 46), the following studies were consulted: J. Mejía, "Some Observations on Psalm 107," *BTB* 5 (1975) 56–66; W. Beyerlin, *Werden und Wesen des 107. Psalms* (BZAW 153; Berlin: de Gruyter, 1979); P. Auffret, "Ses merveilles pour les fils d'Adam: Étude structurelle du Psaume 107," in *Merveilles à nos yeux: Etude structurelle de vingt psaumes dont celui de 1Ch 16,8–36* (BZAW 235; Berlin: de Gruyter, 1995) 105–29; J. Jarick, "The Four Corners of Psalm 107," *CBQ* 59 (1997) 270–87; J. W. Roffey, "Beyond Reality: Poetic Discourse and Psalm 107," in *A Biblical Itinerary: In Search of Method, Form and Content. Essays in Honor of George W. Coats* (ed. E. E. Carpenter; JSOTSup 240; Sheffield: Sheffield Academic Press,

4 תָּעוּ בַמִּדְבָּר בִּישִׁימוֹן דָּרֶךְ עִיר מוֹשָׁב לֹא מָצָאוּ׃
5 רְעֵבִים גַּם־צְמֵאִים נַפְשָׁם בָּהֶם תִּתְעַטָּף׃
6 וַיִּצְעֲקוּ אֶל־יהוה בַּצַּר לָהֶם מִמְּצוּקוֹתֵיהֶם יַצִּילֵם׃
7 וַיַּדְרִיכֵם בְּדֶרֶךְ יְשָׁרָה לָלֶכֶת אֶל־עִיר מוֹשָׁב׃
8 יוֹדוּ לַיהוה חַסְדּוֹ וְנִפְלְאוֹתָיו לִבְנֵי אָדָם׃
9 כִּי־הִשְׂבִּיעַ נֶפֶשׁ שֹׁקֵקָה וְנֶפֶשׁ רְעֵבָה מִלֵּא־טוֹב׃
10 יֹשְׁבֵי חֹשֶׁךְ וְצַלְמָוֶת אֲסִירֵי עֳנִי וּבַרְזֶל׃
11 כִּי־הִמְרוּ אִמְרֵי־אֵל וַעֲצַת עֶלְיוֹן נָאָצוּ׃
12 וַיַּכְנַע בֶּעָמָל לִבָּם כָּשְׁלוּ וְאֵין עֹזֵר׃
13 וַיִּזְעֲקוּ אֶל־יהוה בַּצַּר לָהֶם מִמְּצֻקוֹתֵיהֶם יוֹשִׁיעֵם׃
14 יוֹצִיאֵם מֵחֹשֶׁךְ וְצַלְמָוֶת וּמוֹסְרוֹתֵיהֶם יְנַתֵּק׃
15 יוֹדוּ לַיהוה חַסְדּוֹ וְנִפְלְאוֹתָיו לִבְנֵי אָדָם׃
16 כִּי־שִׁבַּר דַּלְתוֹת נְחֹשֶׁת וּבְרִיחֵי בַרְזֶל גִּדֵּעַ׃
17 אֱוִלִים מִדֶּרֶךְ פִּשְׁעָם וּמֵעֲוֺנֹתֵיהֶם יִתְעַנּוּ׃
18 כָּל־אֹכֶל תְּתַעֵב נַפְשָׁם וַיַּגִּיעוּ עַד־שַׁעֲרֵי מָוֶת׃
19 וַיִּזְעֲקוּ אֶל־יהוה בַּצַּר לָהֶם מִמְּצֻקוֹתֵיהֶם יוֹשִׁיעֵם׃
20 יִשְׁלַח דְּבָרוֹ וְיִרְפָּאֵם וִימַלֵּט מִשְּׁחִיתוֹתָם׃
21 יוֹדוּ לַיהוה חַסְדּוֹ וְנִפְלְאוֹתָיו לִבְנֵי אָדָם׃
22 וְיִזְבְּחוּ זִבְחֵי תוֹדָה וִיסַפְּרוּ מַעֲשָׂיו בְּרִנָּה׃
23 יוֹרְדֵי הַיָּם בָּאֳנִיּוֹת עֹשֵׂי מְלָאכָה בְּמַיִם רַבִּים׃
24 הֵמָּה רָאוּ מַעֲשֵׂי יהוה וְנִפְלְאוֹתָיו בִּמְצוּלָה׃
25 וַיֹּאמֶר וַיַּעֲמֵד רוּחַ סְעָרָה וַתְּרוֹמֵם גַּלָּיו׃
26 יַעֲלוּ שָׁמַיִם יֵרְדוּ תְהוֹמוֹת נַפְשָׁם בְּרָעָה תִתְמוֹגָג׃
27 יָחוֹגּוּ וְיָנוּעוּ כַּשִּׁכּוֹר וְכָל־חָכְמָתָם תִּתְבַּלָּע׃
28 וַיִּצְעֲקוּ אֶל־יהוה בַּצַּר לָהֶם וּמִמְּצוּקֹתֵיהֶם יוֹצִיאֵם׃
29 יָקֵם סְעָרָה לִדְמָמָה וַיֶּחֱשׁוּ גַּלֵּיהֶם׃
30 וַיִּשְׂמְחוּ כִי־יִשְׁתֹּקוּ וַיַּנְחֵם אֶל־מְחוֹז חֶפְצָם׃
31 יוֹדוּ לַיהוה חַסְדּוֹ וְנִפְלְאוֹתָיו לִבְנֵי אָדָם׃
32 וִירֹמְמוּהוּ בִּקְהַל־עָם וּבְמוֹשַׁב זְקֵנִים יְהַלְלוּהוּ׃
33 יָשֵׂם נְהָרוֹת לְמִדְבָּר וּמֹצָאֵי מַיִם לְצִמָּאוֹן׃
34 אֶרֶץ פְּרִי לִמְלֵחָה מֵרָעַת יֹשְׁבֵי בָהּ׃
35 יָשֵׂם מִדְבָּר לַאֲגַם־מַיִם וְאֶרֶץ צִיָּה לְמֹצָאֵי מָיִם׃
36 וַיּוֹשֶׁב שָׁם רְעֵבִים וַיְכוֹנְנוּ עִיר מוֹשָׁב׃
37 וַיִּזְרְעוּ שָׂדוֹת וַיִּטְּעוּ כְרָמִים וַיַּעֲשׂוּ פְּרִי תְבוּאָה׃
38 וַיְבָרְכֵם וַיִּרְבּוּ מְאֹד וּבְהֶמְתָּם לֹא יַמְעִיט׃
39 וַיִּמְעֲטוּ וַיָּשֹׁחוּ מֵעֹצֶר רָעָה וְיָגוֹן׃
4 שֹׁפֵךְ בּוּז עַל־נְדִיבִים וַיַּתְעֵם בְּתֹהוּ לֹא־דָרֶךְ׃ס
41 וַיְשַׂגֵּב אֶבְיוֹן מֵעוֹנִי וַיָּשֶׂם כַּצֹּאן מִשְׁפָּחוֹת׃

1997) 60 – 76; I. Carbajosa, "Salmo 107: Unidad, Organización y Teología," *EstBib* 59 (2001) 451–85; M. Leuenberger, *Konzeptionen des Königtums Gottes im Psalter. Untersuchungen zu Komposition und Redaktion der theokratischen Bücher IV-V innerhalb des Psalters* (ATANT 83. Zürich: Theologischer Verlag, 2004); D. Tucker, Jr., "Empires and Enemies in Book V of the Psalter," in *The Composition of the Book of Psalms* (ed. Erich Zenger; BETL 238; Leuven: Uitgeverij Peeters, 2010) 723 – 31.

יִרְאוּ יְשָׁרִים וְיִשְׂמָחוּ וְכָל־עַוְלָה קָפְצָה פִּיהָ׃ 42

מִי־חָכָם וְיִשְׁמָר־אֵלֶּה וְיִתְבּוֹנְנוּ חַסְדֵי יהוה׃ 43

1 Give thanks to Yhwh, for he is good,
for his loving-kindness is forever,

2 may the redeemed of Yhwh say (thus);
those whom he redeemed from the hand of the enemy,

3 and gathered them together from the lands,
from the east, and from the west, and from the north, and from the sea.

4 They wandered in the desert, in a wilderness,
a way (to) a city for dwelling they did not find.

5 Hungry, and thirsty,
their soul within them was faint.

6 They cried to Yhwh in their distress,
and he rescued them from their affliction.

7 He led them in a straight path,
to come to a city for dwelling.

8 Let them give thanks to Yhwh (for) his loving-kindness,
and his marvelous works for the children of man.

9 For he satisfied the parched body,
and the hungry body he filled (with) good (things).

10 Those sitting in darkness and deathly shadow,
prisoners of misery and iron,

11 for they had been obstinate (against) the words of God,
and the counsel of the Most High they had disdained,

12 he humbled their heart with toil,
they stumbled, and there was no help.

13 They cried to Yhwh in their distress,
and he saved them from their affliction.

14 He brought them out of darkness and deep shadow,
and their fetters he pulled off.

15 Let them give thanks to Yhwh (for) his loving-kindness,
and his marvelous works for the children of man.

16 For he shattered the doors of bronze,
and he broke the crossbars of iron.

17 Fools, because of the way of their rebellion,
and because of their offenses, they were humbled.

18 Their body loathed all food,
and they arrived at the gates of death.

19 They cried to Yhwh in their distress,
and he saved them from their affliction.

20 He sent forth his word, and he healed them,
and he saved them from their pit.

21 Let them give thanks to Yhwh (for) his loving-kindness,
and his marvelous works for the children of man.

22 And let them offer sacrifices of praise,
and let them tell of his works with a shout of joy.

23 Those going down to the sea in ships,
doing work on the great seas,

24 they themselves saw the works of Yhwh,
his marvelous works in the deep.

25 He spoke and he roused a windstorm,
and it raised up its waves.

26 They went up to the heavens, they went down to the depths,
their bodies melted in distress.

27 They reeled and staggered, like a drunkard,
and all their skill was confused.

28 They cried to Yhwh in their distress,
and he brought them out from their affliction.

29 He made the storm be hushed,
and their waves were calm.

30 And they rejoiced, for they grew calm,
for he led them to the harbor they desired.

31 Let them give thanks to Yhwh (for) his loving-kindness,
and his marvelous works for the children of mankind.

32 Let them exalt him, in the assembly of the people,
and in the council of the elders, let them praise him.

33 He makes rivers into a desert,
springs of water into parched ground,

34 fertile land into a salt plain,
because of the evil of those dwelling there.

35 He makes a desert into a pool of water,
and a waterless land into springs of water.

36 He settles there the hungry,
and they establish a city for dwelling.

37 They sow fields and they plant vineyards,
and they produce fruit at harvest.

38 He blesses them and they greatly increase,
    and their cattle he does not diminish.

39 They diminish and are bent over,
    because of oppression, trouble, and sorrow.

40 He pours contempt upon nobles,
    and makes them wander in a wasteland with no path.

41 He raises the poor high out of misery,
    and he makes clans like a flock.

42 The righteous see and rejoice,
    but all wickedness shuts its mouth.

43 Let whoever is wise observe these things,
    and let them consider closely the loving-kindnesses of Yhwh.

Psalm 107 presents few text-critical or translational difficulties, the more significant of which I shall discuss here. I refer the interested reader to the sources listed above for a more complete treatment.

Verses 1–3

In v. 2, I translate צר by "enemy," given its pairing with יד "hand" (see, for example Gen 14:20).[2] Such a reading is consistent with that of the LXX (ἐχθρός). Elsewhere in the psalm (vv. 6, 13, 19, 28), I translate צר by the more common "distress."

In v. 3b, the expression ומים ("and from the sea") has generated considerable
scholarly discussion. A number of commentaries and translations emend this to
ומימין ("and from the south"), thus supplying the fourth of the cardinal directions, three of which (east, west, north) are mentioned earlier in the verse.[3]
Both the LXX and the Peshitta attest "sea," while the Targum reads "from the
sea in the south," suggesting that the targumic translator may have had before
him the MT reading "sea," which he then tried to reconcile with the desired symmetry of the four cardinal directions. There are no known Hebrew manuscripts
with the reading "south." Furthermore, the exact expression מצפן ומים is also attested in Isa 49:12 (one of several similarities between Deutero-Isaiah and Psalm
107, as we shall see), indicating that the phrase need not necessarily be under-

---

2 Beyerlin, *Werden und Wesen*, 69.
3 Thus, for example, Gunkel (*Psalmen*), Kraus (*Psalmen*), *JB*, *NRSV*, and *NAB*. *BHS* suggests this
emendation as well. Delitzsch (*Kommentar*) and Duhm (*Psalmen*), however, retain ומים.

stood as a scribal error. The desire for symmetry aside, there is no reason for emending the MT. Indeed, as J. Jarick has argued, the reference to the sea in v. 3b anticipates vv. 23–32 in which the plight of seafarers is addressed.[4] Insofar as the psalmist's treatment of the seafarers is the most developed and elaborate of the four scenarios considered in this psalm, it is fitting that, at the opening of the poem, the psalmist draws the reader's attention to this scenario by employing the literary technique of a broken symmetry.[5]

Verses 4–9

In v. 4, I follow the LXX (as well as *BHS*) in reading דרך ("way") as the beginning of the second colon. The MT reads it as the end of the first colon.

Verses 10–16

In v. 12a, the LXX reads "their hearts were brought low (ἐταπεινώθη) by exertion," thus suggesting that ויכנע be repointed from a Hiphil to a Niphal "[their heart] was humbled" (cf. *BHS*). I reject this possibility due to the lack of any known Hebrew attestations of such a variant, as well as by the inference to be drawn from v. 17 that Yhwh can indeed be the agent of suffering for the parties mentioned in the various strophes.

Verses 17–22

A number of scholars question the authenticity of the MT reading אולים ("fools") in v. 17. Briggs and Briggs, for example, argue that "foolishness" does not fit the context of the stanza, which describes people tormented by starvation because of their rebellious ways.[6] Instead, they amend the MT to חולים ("sick people"; from חלה, "to become ill"). This emendation is also adopted by Duhm, Snaith, Beyer-

---

4 See Jarick, "Four Corners," 272–73. On this point, see also: Beyerlin, *Werden und Wesen*, 68; Gerstenberger, *Psalms: Part 2*, 249.

5 The use of broken symmetry is all the more striking in that it presents a mixed metaphor: two images for gathering many peoples are blended, i.e., the metaphor of "all directions" (north, south, east, west) is combined with that of "all environments" (e.g., land, sea, and air). I shall further discuss the role of metaphor later in this chapter.

6 Briggs and Briggs, *Commentary*, 2. 360.

lin, Auffret, Jarrick, Roffey, *NAB*, *NRSV*, and is suggested by *BHS*. Kraus provides an alternative emendation, i.e., אמללים ("the weak"; from אמל, "to languish, wither"). This reading is also adopted by Gunkel and Dahood, and is suggested by *BHS*.

The LXX appears to be reading an entirely different Hebrew text for v. 17a: ἀντελάβετο αὐτῶν ἐξ ὁδοῦ ἀνομίας αὐτῶν ("he helped them from out of their lawless way").[7] Allen conjectures that the LXX translator may have read a variant of איל ("help"; cf. *HALOT*, 40).[8]

The most straightforward reading, however, and the one which I adopt, is to simply accept MT's אולים ("fools").[9] Delitzsch observes that the term אויל has a broader application than to the purely intellectual sphere: "One should not change אוילים into חלים; אויל is (cf., e.g., Job 5:3), like נבל (cf. Ps 14:1), *not merely a onesidedly intellectual but also an ethical term*. Such a person lives mindlessly for the day, destroying health, reputation, and household – in short, his very self – in every possible way."[10] Fox too underscores the ethical shortcoming involved, noting that the אויל is one who "vacates his mind from choosing good and rejecting evil.... אולת [foolishness] is the willful refusal to make moral choices. אולת *is moral corruption from the standpoint of its impact on judgment and reason*. Though the אויל may be shrewd and expert in some ways, he is rendered stupid in important regards by his warped values and distorted vision."[11] Such moral corruption is entirely consistent with the behavior of the persons described in v. 17, who rebel against Yhwh and are humbled for their offenses.

Another reason for retaining אולים in v. 17 is that this term – prevalent in Wisdom literature – is consistent with the psalmist's exhortation in v. 43 to the wise person (חכם) that he carefully observe the lessons of the preceding stanzas.[12] Avoiding the errors of the אולים would then constitute one such lesson.

---

7 Syr also attests "helped" (حبَ).

8 Allen, *Psalms 101–150*, 59.

9 Many modern scholars concur with this reading (e.g., Meija; Allen; Goldingay; Hossfeld and Zenger; see also *NJB*).

10 Delitzsch, *Kommentar*, 666 ("*Man hat* אוילים *nicht in* חלים... *zu ändern;* אויל *ist (vgl. z.B. Iob 5,3) wie* נבל *(s. 14,1) nicht ein nur einseitig intellektueller, sondern ein ethischer Begriff: ein solcher, der unsinnig in den Tag hineinlebt und Gesundheit, Ruf, Hauswesen, kurz sich selbst nach allen Seiten zu Grunde richtet*"; emphasis added).

11 Fox, *Proverbs*, 40 (original emphasis). Cf. Isa 35:8 where it is stated that the אויל will not walk along the "sacred way" (דרך הקדש).

12 While אויל is attested only here in the Psalter, it occurs 19 times in the book of Proverbs; similarly, while אולים is attested only twice in the Psalter (Pss 38:5 and 69:5), it occurs 23 times in Proverbs. Hossfeld and Zenger argue that amending אולים to חולים would remove the psalmist's

In v. 20b, I supply a 3pl. suffix for the MT מלט,"he saved." LXX ἐρρύσατο αὐτούς, "he saved them," suggests such a reading (thus, *BHS*). Alternatively, Dahood argues that the 3pl. suffix on וירפאם in v. 20a should be understood as applying to both verbs.[13]

Verses 33–43

BHS and a number of commentators suggest reversing the sequence of vv. 39 and 40.[14] They do so arguing that if the group alluded to in v. 39 were the "hungry" who are blessed in v. 38, then their subsequent oppression in v. 39 would seem to be contradictory (whereas the oppression of the nobles mentioned in v. 40 would be more expected). However, as Goldingay rightly notes, such a transposition is unnecessary if vv. 39–41 are understood as reprising the sequence presented in vv. 33–48.[15] I shall discuss this matter more extensively below.

Structure, Unity, and Dating

Structure

In its structure, Psalm 107 comprises four distinct sections, with the core of the poem (vv 4–32) further divided into four scenarios (strophes I-IV) describing the tribulations and salvation of several unnamed groups of people. Most commentators agree upon this basic structure. I present here a slightly modified version of Gerstenberger's outline.[16]

vv. 1–3	introduction and purpose	
vv. 4–32	crisis, salvation, thanksgiving	
vv. 4–9	lost in the desert	strophe I

---

intended reference to the "wisdom-theology framework" (*weisheitstheologischen Rahmen*) of vv. 42–43 (*Psalmen*, 142).

13 Dahood, *Psalms* 3. 85–86.

14 See, for example, Allen, *Psalms 101–150*, 60, and references therein.

15 Goldingay, *Psalms*, 3. 258.

16 Gerstenberger, *Psalms: Part 2*, 246. Similar outlines can be found in Kraus (*Psalmen*, 736), Gunkel (*Psalmen*, 470), Beyerlin (*Werden und Wesen*, 72–82), Allen (*Psalms 101–150*, 63), Jarick ("Four Corners," 274), Roffey ("Beyond Reality," 66–67), Carbajosa ("Salmo 107," 455–58), Goldingay (*Psalms*, 3. 246–48), Hossfeld and Zenger (*Psalmen 101–150*, 146–47). For an extensive structural analysis of the psalm, see Auffret, "Merveilles," 106–27.

vv. 10–16	imprisoned	strophe II
vv. 17–22	tormented for rebellion	strophe III
vv. 23–32	lost at sea	strophe IV
vv. 33–42	meditation on Yhwh's justice	
vv. 43	challenge to the wise	

Unity

Psalm 107 presents considerable variation in the form and tone of the different sections outlined above. For example, while the four narrative strophes each describe the trials of a group of sufferers, strophe IV is almost twice the length of the others. Furthermore, in contrast to the straightforward narrative style of the four strophes, vv. 33–42 offer a timeless reflection upon Yhwh's חסד. Turning to the opening verses of the psalm, v. 1 – with its open call to praise – presages the repeated exhortation to proclaim Yhwh's praise in vv. 8, 15, 21, and 31. In vv. 2–3, however, there is a shift in focus (not echoed in the later strophes) to those whom Yhwh has redeemed from enemies and recalled from distant lands.

It is perhaps not surprising, therefore, that there has been extensive debate over the psalm's original unity. Among those exegetes who consider the poem to consist of multiple independent units that were later joined, Beyerlin's analysis is representative.[17] He argues that the original core of the psalm is vv. 1, 4–22 – a psalm of thanksgiving (possibly preexilic). To this were later added vv. 23–32, followed by vv. 33–43.[18] Finally, vv. 2–3 were prefaced so as to turn the poem into a post-exilic communal hymn of praise commemorating the return from exile.[19]

---

17 Beyerlin, *Werden und Wesen*, 83–112.

18 Ibid., 53–59. Beyerlin argues that these verses could not be from the same author as vv. 4–22 given the greater length and subject development in strophe IV, compared to strophes I-III. He also notes that vv. 23–32 reflect the mythic triumph of Yhwh over the sea, rather than the common concerns of the Israelites depicted in vv. 4–22. Furthermore, he finds the psalmist's heightened concern with the natural elements in vv. 23–32 to be representative of "Wisdom influences" (pp. 56–57) that are lacking in the earlier strophes. Aside from the difference in length, it remains unclear to me how strophe IV is distinguished from the previous strophes on any of these counts.

19 Kraus (*Psalmen*, 737) presents a similar analysis of the psalm's layers of composition. He understands vv. 1, 4–32 to constitute the original core of the poem (perhaps a priestly summons to thanksgiving), to which vv. 2–3 would be a postexilic addition, followed still later by vv. 33–43 (Duhm [*Psalmen*, 392] refers to these latter verses as a "*Zusatzdichtung*"). For a summary of the positions taken by a number of recent commentators, see Allen, *Psalms 101–150*, 63.

Alternatively, a number of exegetes argue for the psalm's original unity of composition. They usually predicate their argument upon the psalmist's repeated use of certain key words or ideas throughout the entire poem. For example, Dahood notes that the use of רעבים ("the hungry") and עיר מושב ("city for dwelling") in v. 36 echoes the usage of those same words in vv. 4–5.[20] Hossfeld and Zenger argue for the original unity of the poem by noting repeated inter-textual references to Deutero and Trito Isaiah and Job throughout the entire psalm.[21] For example, the expression "the redeemed of Yhwh" (גאולי יהוה) in v. 2 is attested only one other time in the MT, at Isa 62:12 (which resumes the theme of Isaiah 42, in which Yhwh is presented as Israel's redeemer). Yhwh's leading of the lost travelers in the desert (Ps 107:4–9) may reflect the image in Deutero-Isaiah of Yhwh returning the exiles from Mesopotamia (cf. Isa 42:16; 49:10–12). Similarly, the image in Ps 107:10–16 of prisoners being freed and led out of darkness evokes comparable imagery used to describe release from Babylonian exile in such passages as Isa 42:7; 45:13; 49:9. The effective power of Yhwh's word in Ps 107:20 calls to mind Isa 55:11, while Yhwh's capacity to transform wasteland into fertile ground (Ps 107:33–38) recalls Isa 41:18; 43:19; 50:2. Finally, there are similarities between: Ps 107:42a and Job 22:19; Ps 107:42b and Job 5:16; Ps 107:43a and Hos 14:10.

Gerstenberger argues for the original unity of Psalm 107 on form-critical grounds. He notes that vv. 1–3 form a consistent whole insofar as they constitute a summons to the community to offer thanksgiving to Yhwh. Such a summons is often followed by a direct instruction concerning what the assembly should say in response (see, e.g., Pss 66:1b-3; 96:10; 118:1–4; 124:1b-5; 129:1b-3; 145:6–7, 10–11). Because Psalm 107 lacks an explicit instruction of this nature, Gerstenberger conjectures that the psalmist may have intended the assembly to recite all of the remaining psalm (i.e., vv. 4–42).[22] Commenting upon the four strophes, he notes that while each presents a different scenario (and that strophe IV differs considerably in length from the other strophes), they all present deep insight into the human condition, rather than simply representing specific instances of peril: "the mode of fashioning a poetic and theological unit is very homogeneous."[23]

---

20 Dahood, *Psalms* 3. 89.

21 Hossfeld and Zenger, *Psalmen 101–150*, 145–57. They also argue for the psalm's original unity of composition by noting that throughout the entirety of Psalm 107, there are inter-textual connections with Psalm 106.

22 Gerstenberger, *Psalms: Part 2*, 247.

23 Ibid., 251.

Finally, he reads vv. 33–43 as an intended "meditation" upon the scenarios of the strophes rather than as a separate composition.[24]

After considering the positions of numerous exegetes, Goldingay wryly observes: "As usual, the variety of theories about the possible redactional history of the psalm suggests that if it had a redactional history, we cannot determine what it was."[25] In this study I shall treat the received MT of Psalm 107 as a unified whole. I shall employ the differences among the various sections of the psalm noted above in order to explore the ways in which the psalmist exploits those differences in developing the theological perspective he presents in the text.[26]

Dating

As noted above, there are numerous similarities in both vocabulary and theme among Psalm 107, Deutero-Isaiah, and Job. As is often the case when such comparisons are made, one faces the question of whether similarity constitutes deliberate allusion, and, if so, who is alluding to whom? For example, is the psalmist integrating words and themes of the prophet? Or is the prophet borrowing powerful images from the (earlier) poem? Or are each simply integrating images and language commonly employed in their culture to describe peril and salvation? Nearly all the exegetes considered in this study (with the exception of Dahood, who argues that the supposed inter-textual references cited above are, in fact, explicit references to the exodus) take such inter-textual similarities as evidence for a late (exilic/postexilic) date for Psalm 107 – whether they mean by that the composition of a single (post)exilic psalmist or a (post)exilic redactor combining older texts. In any case, I find the considerable number of inter-textual similarities persuasive enough to warrant a late dating for Psalm 107.

---

24 On a similar note, Goldingay (*Psalms*, 3. 246) observes that the different format of vv. 33–43 (compared to that of the strophes) may simply reflect a "liking for variety within a framework of similarity" rather than an independent composition.

25 Ibid., 248.

26 In support of treating the text as a unified whole, Auffret's observation ("Merveilles," 105) is well worth heeding: "Evidemment composite, fruit d'une genèse assez complexe, le Ps 107 a retenu à tel point, sous cet angle, l'attention des commentateurs, qu'ils ne pensent guère y trouver une composition unifiée, négligeant plus ou moins de considérer comme un texte l'oeuvre du rédacteur final de ce psaume."

Psalm 107: Metaphor Analysis

Insofar as Psalm 107 contains no specific references to *particular* peoples and their plights (exilic or otherwise), it behooves us to at least explore the metaphors within the poem *as metaphors*, without immediately attempting to decipher which historical situations or personages they may be representing. My assumption throughout this analysis is that the scenarios in the psalm are purely metaphorical. To be sure, real people at particular times and places have traveled through deserts, languished in prisons, fallen ill, and sailed the seas. But I do not hold that the psalm explicitly refers to (or is limited by the experiences of) desert nomads, prisoners, sailors, etc. I take their plights and situations in life to be symbolic.[27]

While he does not address the importance of the metaphorical structure of the psalm, J. W. Roffey provides an insightful discussion of the value of treating Psalm 107 from the perspective of poetic discourse, free of any attempt to anchor it in a particular historical event. He argues that by doing so, the biblical exegete is actually in a better position to address questions about the *diachronic* structure of the text. Insofar as one has attained a thorough understanding of how the poem "works" internally, one is less prone to pursue improbable historical leads or to force historical facts to match literary constructions that will not support such identifications.[28]

Each of the four strophes in Psalm 107 contains the same conceptual metaphor: LIFE IS A JOURNEY; it is the predominant metaphor in strophes I and IV, and is implied in strophes II and III. Such a metaphor structures the perception of life as a process: it has a beginning and a destination, it is not a random series of events; people are travelers, and they live their lives with intentionality, moving toward a desired goal; people progress through life with a mode of "transportation" (education, careers, marriage, etc.) that is more or less suited to the journey they follow; life proceeds along (or strays from, or blazes new) determined paths that ought to help people reach their desired ends.

Unlike the weak development of the LIFE IS A JOURNEY metaphor in Psalm 1 (see chap. 4 of this study), here the psalmist elucidates the metaphor in considerable detail, choosing numerous options from within the source domain (JOURNEY). There are obvious similarities among the strophes: each contains a group of sufferers undergoing some form of hardship, who then cry out for help to

---

27 For an argument against any tendency to prefer abstraction over realism in biblical metaphor, see D. H. Aaron, *Biblical Ambiguities: Metaphor, Semantics and Divine Imagery* (Brill Reference Library of Ancient Judaism 4; Leiden: Brill, 2001).
28 Roffey, "Beyond Reality," 72.

Yhwh, whereupon they receive assistance. And yet, there are significant distinctions in the way the source domain is specified in each strophe. These distinctions allow the reader/pray-er of the psalm to gain unique insights into the relationship between human beings and Yhwh (the participants in the target domain). I shall argue that the insights derived from the metaphors of Psalm 107 provide a direct response to the deuteronomistic worldview of Psalm 1 (which I described in chap. 4). Furthermore, the metaphors of Ps 107:4–32 help to structure the "wise person's" (Ps 107:43) perception of his worldview, enabling him to learn something new that he had not known before.

Strophe I (vv. 4–9): Desert Wanderings

The participants in the source domain are desert travelers (whose identity remains unknown) and Yhwh. The travelling environment is inherently hostile (i.e., desert and wilderness are not temporary conditions of a landscape that might otherwise be benign). There may be a marked path through the desert, but if so, the travelers have strayed from it (they "wander"). Their desired destination is a city in which they may safely dwell. In addition to the harsh environment, the travelers face two impediments: one external and one internal. Externally, they are lost; internally, they are hungry and thirsty (conditions that could easily lead to death in a desert). Even a healthy traveler will be impeded on his journey if he is lost, while a starving traveler will be slowed down by his weakness even if he is following the proper course. Note that there is no culpability attributed to the travelers: we know neither why they are in the desert nor why they are lost.[29]

From their distress, the travelers cry out (צעק) to Yhwh, who rescues (נצל) them. Via their cry, the travelers transcend the metaphor of which they are a part. By "transcending" the metaphor, I mean that their cry is not limited to their role within the metaphor itself. Thus, they do not cry for a guide to lead them, or for someone to feed them, they simply cry out to Yhwh – anyone could utter such a cry, not only someone whose role is defined by the choices made in the source domain (the significance of this point will become clear

---

29 Most commentators simply acknowledge that desert travel is fraught with potential danger. Jarick's proposal ("Four Corners," 284–85) that the sinful nature of the persons featured in strophes II and III somehow implies (apparently, by association) the sinfulness of the desert travelers as well seems unwarranted.

once the remaining strophes have been discussed).[30] The assistance Yhwh offers is, however, firmly grounded within the source domain: he serves as a guide and he provides sustenance. Beyond that, he leads them to a desired destination (a city which they can inhabit).

In this instance, the metaphor's power of options (see the discussion of a metaphor's powers of options, reason, and evaluation in chap. 1) is exercised through the specific choice of wanderers in the desert. Because of that choice, the metaphor's power of reason creates the possibility that the travelers' plight might be alleviated. If one is lost, there is the hope of regaining direction – either by recovering proper orientation on one's own, or by the guidance of another. If one is hungry in the desert, there is hope of being fed, but only if food is provided from an outside source (the desert cannot provide food). The power of reason presented in strophe I differs markedly from the stark "chaff-vs.-fruit" dichotomy in the PEOPLE ARE PLANTS conceptual metaphor of Psalm 1, in which changing one's state in life is not an option (i.e., chaff is not fruit that has "lost its way" and can be reconstituted; it is fundamentally without value).

With his selection of the linguistic metaphor "travelers in the desert" from among all of the possibilities offered by the conceptual metaphor LIFE IS A JOURNEY, the psalmist exploits the metaphor's power of evaluation in such a way that the correlation between ethical culpability and the circumstances of one's life is far more complex than is the case with the metaphor of Psalm 1. The psalmist specifies the source domain in terms of travelers who have no moral failings ascribed to them. Nevertheless, they are blocked from their desired destination (inhabitable city) by a clearly defined problem (lost and hungry). It follows, therefore, that the participants in the target domain (i.e., the audience of the psalm) are free to understand their own life impediments (which keep them from their desired goals), and the impediments of their neighbors, as possibly something other than the consequences of personal wickedness. Just as a hostile environment might cause harm to a traveler through no fault of his own, so might the vagaries of life bring distress to the righteous as well as the wicked. The psalmist implies that in order to receive help, an appropriate response is to cry out to Yhwh, who can be expected to provide guidance and strength.

---

30 An example may clarify this point. An overworked clerk might metaphorically exclaim: "I'm swamped by this project! Could someone at least toss me a life preserver?" Here, both his plight and his plea for help are voiced from within the source domain (being overcome by water). If his plea for help were, instead, "Can somebody help me?" he would be speaking in a general way that transcends the metaphor and would make sense in any situation of duress.

Strophe II (vv. 10–16) Imprisonment

Here, the participants in the source domain are an unspecified group of prisoners and Yhwh. The concept of "prison" can only be understood by comparison with freedom of movement. Thus, although there is no explicit travel in this strophe, the conceptual metaphor is still LIFE IS A JOURNEY; in this instance, a journey that is arrested. Thus, within this conceptual metaphor, the psalmist exercises the power of options to formulate the linguistic metaphor of imprisonment. The psalmist's development of this metaphor reveals important details about the nature of Yhwh's interaction with the lives of human beings.

There are several impediments to the life journey of the prisoners. Their prison is fashioned metaphorically of both iron and their own "misery" (עני). Furthermore, Yhwh directly adds to their impediment, "humbling" the prisoners with toil and causing them to "stumble" (elements which reinforce the JOURNEY metaphor). Unlike the previous strophe, the cause of their impediment is directly ascribed to their own actions: they were obstinate (מרה) against Yhwh's words and disdained (נאץ) his counsel.

Given this situation, the metaphor's power of reason offers two options to the prisoners: they will either remain in prison or they will be freed. If the latter, then they will either free themselves or they will be set free by another. It is highly improbable that the prisoners will break free under their own power, given that they are near death (v. 10) and without anyone to help them (v. 12). As the lost travelers did in strophe I, the imprisoned travelers cry out (זעק) to Yhwh – also transcending the boundaries of the source domain – and he saves (ישע) them. However, in this instance Yhwh's salvific action differs markedly from his treatment of the desert wanderers. He removes the source of the prisoners' impediment (107:14, 16) and leads them out of darkness and shadow (symbolic of death), but does *not* bring them to a final destination.

When one transfers the metaphor's power of evaluation to the target domain (the audience of the psalm), one clearly sees that the consequence of stubbornly rejecting Yhwh's will is complete stalemate (emotional as well as physical). However one understands one's life journey (e. g., raising a family, pursuing a trade, etc.), to resist Yhwh is to incur paralyzing stasis. And yet, this debilitating judgment is not irreversible. Just as we saw in strophe I, a person who is impeded along life's journey can appeal to Yhwh for help. A significant difference between the two strophes, however, is that in strophe I, neither the travelers nor Yhwh were the source of the impediment, while in strophe II the behavior of the "travelers" against Yhwh causes him to block their progress.

The exercise of the power of evaluation also reveals that moral culpability seems to influence the degree of assistance that Yhwh will provide in response to appeals for help. While the guilty prisoners' cries for help persuade Yhwh to reverse his punitive action, they are still very much mid-journey, not yet at their destination (and presumably could well return to confinement).

Strophe III (vv. 17 – 22) Illness

In this strophe, the psalmist represents the conceptual metaphor LIFE IS A JOURNEY by a linguistic metaphor that he develops without much specificity. The "vehicle" for the journey is "health." Poor health brings one to the gates of death (v. 18), while restored health carries one back from the edge of the pit (v. 20). The participants in the source domain are "fools" (אויל) and Yhwh. As noted above, such persons are not only intellectually lacking, but also willfully refuse to make moral choices. This characterization finds fitting expression in the fools' "rebellion" (פשע), presumably against Yhwh, who humbles them (Yhwh is apparently the agent – the text is not explicit) on account of their offenses.

The fools' impediment is not a hostile or confining environment, but rather their complete enervation due to their inability to eat. Their journey takes them to a lethal destination. Like those suffering tribulations in strophes I and II, they cry out (זעק) to Yhwh, who saves (ישע) them. In this case, salvation means restoring them to health and saving them from the pit of death. But as with the prisoners in strophe II, Yhwh only removes the impediment to the journey – there is no deliverance to a final, safe destination. The capacity for regression before the journey is completed remains quite real.

When transferred to the target domain, the lessons of the metaphor's power of evaluation are similar to those to be gleaned from strophe II. A corrupt moral attitude (like that of the fools) can fatally impair one's progress along life's journey and literally blind one to the sources of life's "sustenance" (e. g., healthy community relationships, self-discipline, etc.) so that those resources are freely rejected. In addition to suffering such self-inflicted impairment, the morally corrupt suffer at the hands of Yhwh because their behavior offends him. Even so, partial salvation is possible to those who reach out to Yhwh: not complete deliverance to a final destination, but at least a restored vigor. The consequences of moral failings are not irreversible.

Strophe IV (vv. 23 – 32) Stormy Seas

The final scenario presents the most fully developed of the four source domains that the psalmist employs in the LIFE IS A JOURNEY conceptual metaphor. The linguistic metaphor is a sea journey: the participants are sailors and Yhwh, the environment is the sea, and the vehicle (a ship) is mentioned explicitly. While the impediment to the journey is a storm, it is important to note that, within the context of the psalm, the environment is not inherently hostile. To be sure, water in the Bible often represents the destructive force of chaos, but here the psalmist contrasts the environment of the sea with that of the desert wilderness of strophe I. Unlike the desert, which is always foreboding and hostile to life, the sea can be calm and easily navigated at times. Only when the sea is stormy (or the ship is inadequate, or the crew unskilled) is the journey toward port endangered.[31]

As in the first strophe, there is no mention of moral culpability on the part of the sailors. And yet, as in strophes II and III, Yhwh is the agent who causes their impediment. Nevertheless, the source domain does not portray the storm as punishment for the sailors; rather, the storm simply represents one of the many natural manifestations of Yhwh's creative power. As in the first strophe, an external impediment to the journey (storm) gives rise to an internal impediment: the sailors' souls "melt" and they stagger, unable to walk straight.

With this exercise of the power of options (i. e., the psalmist's choice of sailors on a stormy sea to represent the conceptual metaphor LIFE IS A JOURNEY), the psalmist severely limits the metaphor's power of reason (i. e., the manner in which the scenario depicted by the metaphor governs the freedom of choice of the characters within the scenario)—even more so than in the previous strophes. In the midst of a stormy sea, there is no question of a "safe path" through the waves (as with a clearly marked road through desert wilderness) – the entire environment is threatening. Even if the sailors are healthy and skillful, they are limited by the seaworthiness of their ship, and the ship will always be weaker than the potential power of the storm. Indeed, in the scenario depicted, both sailors and ship are being overwhelmed. There is only one option open to them.

In their distress, the sailors cry out (צעק) to Yhwh and he brings them out (יצא) from their danger. He accomplishes this in two ways: first he transforms the hostile environment into a benign one (he calms the storm, v. 29), then he guides the sailors to their desired destination (safe port, v. 30). As a result, Yhwh also removes the sailors' internal impediment (their terror turns to calm, v. 30). From the perspective of the source domain, Yhwh provides more assistance to the sailors than to any other group in the psalm. He removes both external and internal impediments, and he provides directional guidance (in stro-

---

31 Mejía ("Some Observations," 63) fails to acknowledge this point when he notes that the fourth strophe "describes *the danger of chaos in the onslaught of the sea*, more active but no less dangerous, than the perils of the desert." (original emphasis)

phe I, Yhwh removed the internal impediment of hunger and also provided guidance, but did not change the hostile desert into fertile land).

The power of evaluation in evidence here is similar to that exhibited in strophe I. A lesson for the audience of the psalm (target domain) is that while life's struggles may well result from Yhwh's actions, they need not be understood as punishment for moral infractions. It is entirely possible that the least morally culpable may suffer the most hopeless plights. Yet even when one's situation appears so hopeless that no degree of human effort can provide relief, salvation is available solely from Yhwh, *if* he is sought out.[32]

Verses 33 – 41

The concluding verses of the psalm provide a summary reflection on Yhwh's actions in the world. Unlike the previous scenarios, the psalmist here describes Yhwh in general terms, not portraying him as responding to any particular situation. Nevertheless, many of the same types of divine acts that were represented in the earlier scenarios are depicted here. Only now the language is less metaphorical and more direct; hence, it refers more to the target domain of the psalm's conceptual metaphor than to its source domain.

In vv. 33 – 35, Yhwh treats the land much as he treated the sea in strophe IV. He directly changes benign environments into hostile ones (rivers into deserts, springs into parched ground) and hostile environments into benign ones (deserts into pools of water). Recall that in the first strophe Yhwh guided travelers through the hostile desert, but he did not change its character. Furthermore,

---

32 It is interesting to note that while the parties in distress in all four strophes "cry out" to Yhwh, in strophes II and III (in which the sufferers seem to carry culpability), the verb is זעק, while in strophes I and IV (in which no culpability is mentioned) the verb is צעק. *HALOT* labels these two verbs as by-forms. Upon surveying the MT for those instances in which human beings cry out to Yhwh for help (employing either צעק or זעק), it is interesting to note that זעק is used eight times to describe scenarios in which there is a cry for relief from affliction without any mention of culpability (Exod 2:23; 1 Sam 15:11; 2 Chr 20:9; 32:20; Ps 22:6; 142:2, 6; Lam 3:8), while it is used eighteen times to describe cries for relief from affliction after persons have sinned (Judg 3:9, 15; 6:6, 7; 10:10; 1 Sam 7:8, 9; Neh 9:4, 28; Isa 30:19; 57:13; Jer 11:11; 30:15; Hos 7:14; 8:2; Joel 1:14; Jonah 1:5; Mic 3:4). By comparison, צעק is used to describe the cry of the non-culpable eighteen times (Exod 14:10; 15:25; 17:4; 22:23 [bis], 27; Num 12:13; 20:16; Deut 26:7; Josh 24:7; 2 Chr 13:14; Job 19:7; 35:12; Ps 34:18; 77:2; 88:2; Isa 19:20; 33:7), while it describes the cry of the guilty four times (Judg 4:3; 10:12; Neh 9:27; Lam 2:18). While hardly conclusive, these distributions of usage may support the apparent difference with regard to culpability between the sufferers in strophes I and IV and those in strophes II and III.

the fact that fertile land is made sterile "because of the evil of those dwelling there" (v. 34) implies that, at least for a time, the wicked do live prosperously. While such an admission is not made in strophes I – IV, its appearance here indicates that the psalmist does not evade this difficult truth (cf., e.g., Ps 73:3–5).

Verses 36–37 recall Yhwh's role in leading people to cities to dwell in, but here (unlike in strophe I) the people are responsible for building the city and producing a fruitful harvest. Thus, Yhwh's assistance is not something that one simply receives, but also something with which one cooperates.

The juxtaposition of vv. 36–38 (blessings on the hungry) with v. 39 (diminishment due to oppression, trouble, and sorrow) reflects the unpredictable nature of life's sufferings that are represented in the four strophes. Those who have been blessed are not immune from future misfortunes. And yet, vv. 40–41 proclaim an irresistible justice: the prosperous wicked will be made to wander aimlessly while the lowly will be raised up.

What is missing from these closing verses of the psalm, however, is the very feature that unifies the previous four strophes and stands out so prominently by virtue of its ability to transcend the individual metaphorical constraints of each scenario: namely, the cry to Yhwh upon which the divine help appears to be contingent. While it might seem that this absence of the cry for help supports the hypothesis that vv. 33–41 were not originally associated with strophes I – IV, such a supposition is not necessary, as I shall argue in the conclusion of this chapter.

Worldview

In commenting upon Psalm 107, P. D. Miller sees it as representative of the worldview of the entire Psalter:

> This Psalm in its interaction of form and content is virtually a theological paradigm for the Psalter. It sets forth in its formal structure and repetition the movement from cry for help to divine deliverance to human response of praise. As it moves from strophe to strophe a significant area or metaphor of human need and human fulfillment is set forth: exile → place, hunger and thirst → sufficient food and drink, prison → liberation, sickness → healing. This structure is then climaxed by the familiar announcement of Yahweh's turning things around in behalf of the weak, the troubled, the needy.... In its final verse the extended hymn is given us for praise and instruction, to use to magnify the God of whom it speaks and as a guide for our lives.[33]

---

33 P. D. Miller, review of *Werden und Wesen des 107. Psalms.* BZAW 153, by W. Beyerlin, *VT* 32 (1982) 253–56, here 256.

To be sure, one of the most significant aspects of the worldview represented in the psalm is that one is always free to seek the salvific power of Yhwh and that (at least within the world of the psalm) Yhwh extends salvation liberally. The psalmist supports that point insofar as the sufferers' cries in each of the four scenarios transcend the metaphor which describes each scenario (see n. 30 above). The efficacy of an appeal to Yhwh is not specific to the particular plight portrayed, but rather extends to every potential life situation.

By a careful consideration of our metaphor analysis in the previous section, we can discern even more about the worldview of Psalm 107. For example, the pervasiveness of the LIFE IS A JOURNEY conceptual metaphor throughout the psalm highlights the metaphor's "power of being there" (i.e., the pervasiveness of the application of a metaphor throughout a given worldview; see chap. 1 for a further discussion of this power of metaphor) in helping to structure its associated worldview. This way of looking at life becomes the subconscious backdrop against which each person evaluates his or her life decisions and circumstances. If one understands life as a journey, then one should expect to have a goal or destination in life, a purpose for one's actions. When hardships are encountered, they are understood as impediments or "roadblocks" which get in the way of progress toward the destination, rather than as unavoidably insurmountable failures.

Perhaps most significantly, the psalm's metaphors reinforce the notion that, within this worldview, suffering is not necessarily tied to moral culpability and that even the wicked have access to divine salvation. Strophes I and IV reflect the conviction within the worldview that undeserved suffering can befall anyone. But these same strophes also acknowledge that if an innocent sufferer cries for help, Yhwh may provide fuller assistance: by removing a hostile environment (natural disasters, crowds of enemies, poor health, etc.), by calming internal fears, and by leading him safely through the midst of confusing alternatives.

The difference between this worldview and that of Psalm 1 is striking. From the perspective of Psalm 1, one would have to deem lost or faltering travelers as "wicked." Their state in life would constitute proof of their moral character and their crying out to Yhwh would be irrelevant to their situation. The suggestion that they might be *innocent* sufferers could simply not be accepted given the way in which the psalmist develops the PEOPLE ARE PLANTS conceptual metaphor in Psalm 1. It is important to note, however, that this conceptual metaphor is not *inherently* antithetical to the possibility of innocent sufferers (cf., for example, our discussion in chap. 6 of this study on the use of this same metaphor in Ps 90:5) – the psalmist's particular choices are determinative of how the conceptual metaphor will function.[34]

In spite of the liberality of Yhwh's salvific kindness, the worldview of Psalm 107 is hardly devoid of painful consequences for those who are obstinate against Yhwh and disregard his commands. Strophes II and III illustrate that one's moral choices can be so debilitating as to bring ruin upon oneself. Even in the midst of bounty and blessing, one may choose a wicked course (an unlikely option within the worldview of Psalm 1) and suffer terribly because of it. And yet, such actions do not render one irredeemable: crying out to Yhwh can mitigate the most debilitating of these consequences. Nevertheless, the redemption afforded to the repentant sinner (i.e., the "traveler" along life's way) only removes his impediments and frees him to resume his journey; it does not safely deliver him to his desired destination, and it is entirely possible that he could once again make choices that would return him to his suffering.

Epistemology

Social Epistemology

Applying the diagnostic tool developed at the end of chap. 1, we can summarize the primary proposition of Psalm 107 as: "Yhwh helps those who cry out to him." An important corollary to this proposition is that one's moral standing does not predict whether one will be in need of help or not. Neither need one be righteous in order to plead for help.

In broad terms, the psalmist supports his primary proposition by a coherentist justification scheme. Salvation at the hands of Yhwh follows from the basic premise of Yhwh's loving-kindness which endures forever (vv. 1 and 43). That premise is not "derived" from observations that provide new information. The specific scenarios described in the four strophes, as well as the more general descriptions of Yhwh's justice in vv. 33–41, all cohere with the basic proposition that divine salvation can be accessed through prayer. The scenarios do not provide unique "proof" of Yhwh's saving help, but they supply supporting evidence which bolsters one's justification for believing the primary proposition. That is, careful observation of the scenarios helps to establish the primary proposition as genuine knowledge.

---

34 Recall that every conceptual metaphor can be cast in numerous ways, depending on the choices made in the source domain.

If we compare the nature of this coherentist justification scheme with that evinced by the more starkly defined worldview of Psalm 1, we notice several important distinctions. For example, although the clearly delineated justice of Yhwh that is depicted in vv. 33–41 (in which the poor are elevated and the mighty are reduced; in which the righteous rejoice but the wicked are silenced) might seem to echo the portrayal of Yhwh's justice in Psalm 1, we saw above that these verses do at least allow for the fact that the wicked can temporarily thrive and the righteous can temporarily suffer. Yhwh alone determines the timing and the means for the restoration of justice.

The primary difference, however, between the portrayal of Yhwh's justice in Psalm 1 and Psalm 107 is evident in the complexity of the situations represented in the four strophes of Psalm 107. One cannot automatically conclude that the recipient of Yhwh's assistance is necessarily righteous, nor that one who pleads for divine help is necessarily suffering on account of Yhwh's punishment for his sins. Within the worldview of Psalm 107, the manner in which observations cohere with the primary proposition about Yhwh's redeeming salvation is nuanced and requires consideration of several variables (e. g., Was Yhwh asked for help? Were the sufferers innocent or guilty? What was the extent of the assistance provided in response to the plea?).

We find, therefore, that a careful observer of the four scenarios can clarify, expand, and enrich his understanding of the "truth-value" of the basic proposition put forth in Psalm 1: that is, Yhwh blesses the righteous and punishes the wicked. As we saw in chap. 4, when compared with the "real world" outside of the worldview of Psalm 1, an observer might question just exactly how a "righteous" or a "wicked" person could be identified. The basic proposition of Psalm 1 would suggest that a person who is suffering must be wicked. But to an outside observer, there might be no clear evidence of the person's wickedness. What constitutes a "wicked person?" If a righteous person steals one grape, is he still "righteous"? What about two grapes, or one hundred? Furthermore, what constitutes Yhwh's blessing or punishment? If a prosperous person loses one of his sheep, is that evidence of Yhwh's punishment? What if he loses two sheep? Is such a small loss proof that the prosperous person is, in fact, wicked, and not righteous?

It would seem, therefore, that the basic proposition of Psalm 1 contains an inherent ambiguity with regard to the precise definition of its terms. This inherent ambiguity underscores the proposition's "vagueness." Here, I employ the term "vague" in the technical sense with which it is applied in contemporary philosophy. The following brief consideration of this philosophical application will allow us to highlight the achievement of Psalm 107 in helping to substantially reduce the vagueness to which Psalm 1 gives rise. Furthermore, such a consideration will underscore the power of the psalmist in elucidating the nature of Yhwh's loving-kindness within the worldview of Psalm 107.

Epistemic Vagueness

As its everyday usage suggests, the technical philosophical term "vagueness" refers to how completely one can know a given proposition. C. S. Peirce's classic definition is still cited in contemporary research: "A proposition is vague when there are possible states of things concerning which it is *intrinsically uncertain* whether, had they been contemplated by the speaker, he would have regarded them as excluded or allowed by the proposition. By intrinsically uncertain we mean not uncertain in consequence of any ignorance of the interpreter, but because the speaker's habits of language were indeterminate."[35] A representative example of a vague proposition is "the woman is tall." At what measure of height, precisely, is a person classified as "tall"? If a woman is 1 cm shorter than a "tall" man, should she be considered "tall" as well?

Philosophically vague qualities are generally classified by three traits: (1) they admit "borderline" cases; (2) they lack sharp boundaries; (3) they suffer from "sorites" paradoxes.[36] A "borderline" case is one in which it is not obvious whether or not the vague quality applies (e. g., is a 5 ft. 11 in. man "tall"?). A sorites (from σωρός "heap") paradox can be illustrated by the following paradigmatic example. One may justifiably classify a huge pile of sand as a "heap." Now, if one grain of sand were removed from the pile, it could still reasonably be classified as a heap. This yields the proposition: "a heap of sand, less one grain, remains a heap of sand." Now imagine that one hundred million grains of sand are removed, one grain at a time. After each such removal, there is (according to our proposition) still a heap. By the end of the operation, however, we are left with a small pile, which is obviously no longer worthy of being called a "heap," although our proposition would seem to require this. Sorites paradoxes

---

35 C. S. Peirce, "Vague," in *Dictionary of Philosophy and Psychology* (ed. J.M. Baldwin; New York: MacMillan, 1902) 748 (original emphasis).
36 R. Keefe, *Theories of Vagueness* (Cambridge: Cambridge University Press, 2000) 6. There is a vast contemporary literature on this subject. In addition to Keefe, see, for example: T. Williamson, *Vagueness* (London: Routledge, 1994); R. A. Sorensen, *Vagueness and Contradiction* (Oxford: Oxford University Press, 2001); S. Shapiro, *Vagueness in Context* (Oxford: Oxford University Press, 2006); N. J. J. Smith, *Vagueness and Degrees of Truth* (Oxford: Oxford University Press, 2008).

force us to address the question of at what point a vague quality (such as "tall" or "happy") begins/ceases to apply to a given person or situation.

The issue of whether or not vague propositions (such as "the man is tall") can ever be "true" is the subject of a much-contested debate within contemporary philosophical scholarship. In this study, I shall follow the understanding of vagueness which is known as "epistemic vagueness," insofar as I believe it is the most relevant to the epistemology of the worldview of Psalm 107 (as I shall discuss below).[37] Adherents of epistemic vagueness contend that a vague proposition is unambiguously either true or false, even if it is not always possible for an observer to determine the proposition's truth-value. Thus, the borderline between "heap" and "not-heap" is sharply defined: one grain of sand more or less than the boundary value amount is enough to change the characterization of the pile. The fact that it may not always be possible to accurately identify that boundary value does not negate its existence (and thus it does not negate the truth-value of a statement such as "this pile is a heap").[38] Note that, with epistemic vagueness, sorites paradoxes are no longer possible: it is *not* the case that any heap, less one grain, is *always* still a heap. At some point, removal of one grain causes the pile to cross a critical boundary and to cease being a heap.

I employ the concept of epistemic vagueness as the most applicable to the psalms because while it is likely that an ancient psalmist would not have concerned himself with such formal logical considerations, it seems equally likely that he would have unequivocally accepted the truth of the proposition that Yhwh prospers the righteous and punishes the wicked (and that Yhwh unambiguously knows the "boundary" between a righteous person and a wicked one, even if human beings are not privy to that knowledge). What the Psalter clearly reveals, however, is that various psalmists do question the manner in which Yhwh metes out his justice. While Psalm 1 may not raise such questions, we have seen in this study that Psalms 73 and 90 certainly do (see, for example, Pss 73:1–5; 90:7–10). Epistemologically, this means that the true proposition

---

37 For a discussion of epistemeic vagueness, see, e. g., Keefe, *Theores of Vagueness*, 62–84. Extended, full-length arguments in support of epistemic vagueness are presented by Williamson (*Vagueness*) and Sorensen (*Vagueness and Contradiction*).

38 With this simple example, I do not pretend to have fully addressed the complexity of the arguments put forth by epistemicists in support of their principal understanding of vagueness. Suffice it to say that only epistemic vagueness preserves the principle of bi-valence (i.e., a proposition must be either true or false), one of the foundational tenets of traditional logic which epistemicists are loathe to surrender. Alternative theories of vagueness relax the requirement of bi-valence (i.e., it is *not* the case that a proposition must be either true or false) and thus generate entirely new logical systems.

constitutes actual knowledge (justified, true belief) to a greater or lesser degree in inverse proportion to the vagueness with which it is known.

We can now better appreciate how the scenarios presented in Psalm 107 address the vagueness inherent in a proposition such as "Yhwh prospers the righteous." For example, the suffering of the travelers in strophe I and the sailors in strophe IV makes clear that one cannot accurately discern the boundary between the righteous and the wicked simply by the presence (absence) of suffering. Similarly, the help offered by Yhwh to the prisoners in strophe II and the languishing rebels in strophe III demonstrates that the recipient of any degree of divine assistance is not necessarily to be identified as completely righteous.

Furthermore, the interaction between Yhwh and the sufferers in strophes II and III raises the question of whether the act of calling out to Yhwh is itself an act that renders the caller righteous (or at least more righteous than he previously was). One can imagine a kind of sorites paradox in which an observer of the scenarios in strophes II and III wonders whether a wicked man who calls out only once to Yhwh is still wicked. If the answer is yes, then (by induction) a wicked man who calls out to Yhwh every second of the day must still be classified as wicked, which seems absurd. The fact that Yhwh *does* help everyone who calls to him in Psalm 107 clearly establishes that there is some connection between appealing for divine assistance and being deemed worthy by Yhwh to receive it. While only Yhwh knows exactly where the boundary exists between the righteous person and the wicked person, an observer of the scenarios in Psalm 107 can at least entertain the possibility that the righteous and the wicked are able to cross over that boundary. One could not even imagine such a transition within the worldview of Psalm 1.

Finally, we must note that while the scenarios depicted in Psalm 107 might offer new insights that help address the vagueness that persons encounter when they observe Yhwh's justice, those insights will only contribute to actual knowledge if they seem reasonable ("justified") to the observer. Upon considering whether or not the primary proposition of the worldview of Psalm 107 can count as knowledge, we should recall Kearney's requirement that any successful worldview must be both internally and externally consistent (see chap. 4). The worldview depicted in Psalm 107 meets this criterion insofar as the circumstances described in the four scenarios, and the interactions they portray between human beings and Yhwh, appear neither arbitrary nor unreasonable.

The audience of the psalm knows well from everyday life experience that suffering can befall any person, irrespective of their perceived righteousness or wickedness. The psalm's realistic portrayal of the universality of human suffering, among both the morally culpable and inculpable, lends significant "credibility" to the worldview of Psalm 107 insofar as that portrayal is consistent with the human condition. Furthermore, the worldview of the psalm maintains an internal consistency in that Yhwh does not extend the same degree of assistance to every person. As we saw in our analysis of the four scenarios, there does seem to be a correlation between the extent of Yhwh's help and the moral (non) culpability of the person in need. It is not simply the case that Yhwh saves everyone, regardless of their moral standing. In fact, there are consequences to one's moral actions, and the degree and nature of the salvific help that Yhwh extends reflect those consequences.

Conclusion: New Knowledge for the Wise Person to Learn

As argued above, upon a casual reading of Ps 107:33–41, isolated from the rest of the psalm, one might surmise those verses as a simple reprise of the deuteronomistic theology represented in Psalm 1, in which the wicked suffer and the righteous thrive, and one cannot truly "know" (in the epistemological sense of having a justified, true belief) that a suffering person may be just, or that a thriving person may be wicked. Nor would there be much reason for believing that Yhwh would ever extend his assistance to anyone other than a just person. Human beings should simply endure their status and await Yhwh's actions.

When one considers the entire psalm as a whole, however, the possibility for the acquisition of new knowledge is significantly expanded. The scenarios of the four strophes represent a worldview that offers a nuanced complexity which is completely lacking in Psalm 1. Here, Yhwh renders his justice in response to the cry of those who suffer. And he responds with some sort of assistance, *whether the sufferers are morally culpable or not*. This is the new lesson that the wise person is challenged to learn in v. 43.

We have shown that the degree and quality of help that Yhwh metes out to the various classes of sufferers does vary, depending on their moral status. Such differentiation among Yhwh's responses helps to address the vagueness inherent in the question of who is righteous and who is wicked. The apparent contradiction of a suffering righteous person or a prosperous wicked person is placed within a broader context once one recognizes the possibility for calling out to Yhwh. Thus, while the proposition that Yhwh prospers the righteous is true (as vv. 33–41 unambiguously reaffirm), Psalm 107 underscores and strengthens one's justification for believing that truth; that is, one can more deservedly classify the proposition as actual knowledge.

By a careful analysis of the conceptual metaphor of Psalm 107 – as it is represented in each of the four scenarios described in the poem – we see then that the psalmist develops a new worldview in which it is possible to "know" Yhwh's חסד with greater perception and depth.

Conclusion:
Implications for the Canonical Study of the Psalter

In this concluding chapter, I briefly explore some of the implications of the findings of this study for an understanding of the canonical structure of the Psalter,
focusing on how the epistemology of particular psalms can contribute to the ongoing dialogue concerning the shape and shaping of the entire collection.

Psalm Exegesis and Psalter Exegesis

In their commentary on Psalms 51–100, Hossfeld and Zenger note that traditional psalms exegesis often failed to adequately account for the contextual (canonical) setting within which each psalm is situated, and they stress that one can
only fully comprehend the meaning and significance of a psalm text by considering its place in the overall Psalter.[1] Any such lack in traditional psalms scholarship has been extensively addressed by the growing body of research into the
canonical structure of the Psalter.[2]

---

1 Hossfeld and Zenger, *Psalmen: 51–100*, 35.
2 I list here only a representative sampling of such research: B.S. Childs, *Introduction to the Old
Testament as Scripture* (Philadelphia: Fortress, 1979); G. H. Wilson, *The Editing of the Hebrew
Psalter* (SBLDS 76; Chico, CA: Scholars Press, 1985); F.-L. Hossfeld and E. Zenger, *Psalmen* and
Die Psalmen commentaries (1993–2012; see chap. 3, n. 46); *The Shape and Shaping of the Psalter*
(J. C. McCann, ed.; JSOTSup 159. Sheffield: JSOT Press, 1993); M. Millard, *Die Komposition des
Psalters: Ein Formgeschichtlicher Ansatz* (FAT 9; Tübingen: Mohr, 1994); K. Koenen, *Jahwe wird
kommen, zu herrschen über die Erde: Ps 90–110 als Komposition* (BBB 101; Weinheim: Beltz
Athenäum Verlag, 1995); R. G. Kratz, "Die Tora Davids : Psalm 1 und die Doxologische Fünfteilung des Psalters," *ZTK* 93 (1996) 1–34; R. N. Whybray, *Reading the Psalms as a Book* (JSOTSup
222; Sheffield: Sheffield Academic Press, 1996); E. Zenger, "Der Psalter als Buch: Beobachtungen
zu seiner Entstehung, Komposition und Funktion," in *Der Psalter in Judentum und Christentum*
(eds. H.-J. Klauck and E. Zenger; Herders Biblische Studien 18; Freiburg: Herder, 1998) 1–57; B.
Janowski, *Konfliktgespräche mit Gott: Eine Anthropologie der Psalmen* (Neukirchen-Vluyn: Neukirchener Verlag, 2003); M. Leuenberger, *Konzeptionen des Königtums Gottes im Psalter. Untersuchungen zu Komposition und Redaktion der theokratischen Bücher IV-V innerhalb des Psalters*
(ATANT 83; Zürich: Theologischer Verlag, 2004); C. Süssenbach, *Der elohistische Psalter: Un-
tersuchungen zur Komposition und Theologie von Ps 42–83* (FAT 2.7; Tübingen: Mohr, 2005); *The
Book of Psalms: Composition and Reception* (eds. P. W. Flint and P. D. Miller; VTSup 99. Leiden:
Brill, 2005); M. Marttila, *Collective Reinterpretation in the Psalms: A Study of the Redaction
History of the Psalter* (FAT 2.13; Tübingen: Mohr, 2006); *The Composition of the Book of Psalms*

As many scholars have indicated, a complete canonical analysis can be neither purely synchronic nor diachronic, but must be attentive to the possible historical progressions that produced not only the development of individual psalm texts but also the collections of such texts into subgroupings (based on lexical and/or thematic ties), and then the further grouping of those small collections into larger ones. For example, we saw in chap. 4 of this study how it is likely that Psalms 1 and 2 were combined to achieve a particular perspective for the entire Psalter (numerous similar subgroupings have been suggested, e.g., Psalms 50—51; Psalms 90—92). In the Psalter's final redaction, each such cluster holds a place within the five "Books" (a cluster might extend across the boundaries of a single Book) and thus relates to the other psalms within its respective Book(s), while each of the five Books further stand in relationship to each other.[3] It is unlikely that such collections were assembled in a purely random fashion. In their recent overview of the current status of canonical Psalter research, Hossfeld and Steiner note that "a synchronic exploration of the structure of the Psalter leads necessarily into a diachronic exploration. The diachronic and synchronic approaches are two parameters, which in a correlative way lead to the understanding of the growth of the final message(s) of the Psalter and of the final message itself."[4]

Thus, even a purely synchronic analysis is useful both for understanding the Psalter as we have received it today, as well as for providing a helpful beginning to guide diachronic explorations of the texts. One of the least speculative synchronic claims concerning the layout of the Psalter is the observation that there seems to be a significant distinction between Books I—III and Books

---

(ed. E. Zenger; BETL 238; Leuven: Uitgeverij Peeters, 2010) – see esp. E. Zenger, "Psalmenexegese *und* Psalterexegese: Eine Forschungsskizze," 17–65 and B. Janowski, "Ein Tempel aus Worten: Zur Theologischen Architektur des Psalters," 279–306; J. Gärtner, *Die Geschichtspsalmen: Eine Studie zu den Psalmen 78, 105, 106, 135 und 136 als Hermeneutische Schlüsseltexte im Psalter* (FAT 84; Tübingen: Mohr, 2012); F.-L. Hossfeld and T. M. Steiner, "Problems and Prospects in Psalter Studies," in *Jewish and Christian Approaches to the Psalms: Conflict and Convergence* (ed. Susan Gillingham; Oxford: Oxford University Press, 2013) 240–58; K. Seybold, "The Psalter as a Book," in *Jewish and Christian Approaches to the Psalms: Conflict and Convergence* (ed. Susan Gillingham; Oxford: Oxford University Press, 2013) 168–81.

3 For detailed examples of the fruitfulness of a combined synchronic and diachronic analysis of a large grouping of psalms, see Leuenberger's study of Books IV and V of the Psalter (*Konzeptionen des Königtums Gottes im Psalter*) and Süssenbach's study of the Elohist psalms (*Der elohistische Psalter: Untersuchungen zur Komposition und Theologie von Ps 42–83*).

4 Hossfeld and Steiner, "Problems and Prospects," 248. See also J. S. Burnett, W. H. Bellinger, Jr., and W. Dennis Tucker Jr., eds., *Diachronic and Synchronic: Reading the Psalms in Real Time. Proceedings of the Baylor Symposium on the Book of Psalms* (LHBOTS 488; London: T&T Clark, 2009).

IV—V.[5] Given the scope and parameters of the present study, we are invited to explore whether the epistemological traits of Psalms 1, 73, 90, and 107 reflect any such distinctions.

Epistemological Comparison of Psalms 1, 73, 90, and 107

Psalm 1

Psalm 1 is the least epistemologically complex of the psalms considered in this study. Its primary proposition ("the good flourish, the wicked perish") is presented axiomatically, and the worldview represented within the text is incapable of adequately addressing the inevitable challenges to that proposition which are posed by everyday life experience. Such challenges (e. g., why do the good suffer and the wicked prosper?) are never raised within the context of the psalm. For the psalmist, human beings presumably have no inclination to change their moral state (from wicked to good, or vice versa) and they do not interact with God other than to either continually contemplate God's law or else to categorically reject it.

From the perspective of social epistemology, Psalm 1 reflects a rigid society that requires the indoctrination of each new generation with the above-cited primary proposition about good and evil. Nihilation is practiced in the strictest possible fashion: dissenting voices (claiming, for example, that good people might suffer, or that the wicked might prosper) are simply not acknowledged to exist.

Psalm 73

Psalm 73 provides a significant epistemological advance over Psalm 1 insofar as the psalmist at least acknowledges the reality that wicked people do sometimes

---

5 For example, Psalms 1—89 (the so-called "Messianic Psalter") contain the majority of psalms that are attributed to David in their superscriptions, while the thematic focus of these Books appears to be centered around properties of the Davidic kingship. By contrast, Books IV and V contain relatively few psalms with "author designation" superscriptions and the thematic focus appears to be much more centered on the kingship of Yhwh. Rather than repeat arguments here regarding past research on the Psalter's canonical structure that are amply treated in other sources, I refer the reader to the excellent reviews by Leuenberger (*Konzeptionen des Königtums Gottes im Psalter*, 93–123), Kratz (*Die Tora Davids*), Zenger (*Der Psalter als Buch*), and McCann, ed. (*The Shape and Shaping of the Psalter*).

prosper, and that this situation can lead to deep anguish among the righteous. Within the worldview represented within the psalm, however, the one who is pure of heart has no direct recourse for resolving his crisis. While he holds the same axiomatic truth that sustained the psalmist in Psalm 1, that truth provides no succor to him in the face of the apparent grave injustices he witnesses. Relief finally comes to him, not because he has judiciously followed a prescribed plan for the acquisition of deeper insight and clarity, but rather as the result of a purely gratuitous revelation from God. The psalmist put himself in the position to receive such a gift (by entering God's sanctuary), but he gives no indication that he deliberately entered the sanctuary in expectation of receiving the revelation. Furthermore, the resolution to his crisis – a crisis that was precipitated by the material wellbeing of the wicked – comes not via the granting of material wealth (at least not initially), but rather via an intellectual insight.

Unlike the situation in Psalm 1, here the psalmist has both the capacity to recognize his lack of knowledge as well as the desire to acquire what he does not know. He does not, however, have a method for learning. And while God is the ultimate source of the knowledge he lacks, the psalmist does not seem to know how to access that knowledge; when the psalmist actually receives the knowledge, it arrives unexpectedly.

Viewed from a social perspective, we note that the "education" of this psalmist is a highly individualistic affair. He wanders into the sanctuary alone and is enlightened. He gives no indication that he carries an intellectual burden which is shared by all the "pure of heart." He is not sent as a representative to acquire an answer for his people, nor does he indicate a desire to share his new-found wisdom either with his peers or with future generations. The epistemological gains of the psalmist are largely a private matter. If one were to doubt that the pure of heart will always prosper (or that the wicked will be punished), there is no suggestion in Psalm 73 that such a one would be silenced by his society. But neither is there any indication that he would necessarily be enlightened with the truth.

Psalm 90

Psalm 90 begins with an intellectual crisis that is even broader than that voiced in Psalm 73. Here the problem is not only that the righteous sometimes suffer, but that all humanity is under the burden of a toilsome and relatively brief life. The crisis gives rise to "existential questions" about the purpose of lives that vanish like a sigh.[6]

As in Psalms 1 and 73, the psalmist holds an axiomatic truth about Yhwh: in this case, that Yhwh has been a safe refuge for Israel for all eternity. As in Psalm 73, the usefulness of that truth is questioned (at least implicitly). Unlike Psalm 73, however, here the psalmist has a deliberate plan for attempting to resolve his intellectual crisis. He directly appeals to Yhwh and asks to be *taught*, so that he might gain a heart of wisdom. Furthermore, he names the explicit lesson that he would like to learn: how to number his days rightly. While the psalmist in Psalm 73 receives the help he desires, Psalm 90 offers no such resolution: the audience is left, along with the psalmist, still awaiting a reply. Nevertheless, the psalmist in Psalm 90 conveys a greater sense of confidence than does the psalmist in Psalm 73, for the former clearly knows whom to ask, and what to ask for, in order to gain understanding about the nature of life.

We should also note that the psalmist in Psalm 90 is speaking on behalf of the entire community. The crisis posed by the brevity and harshness of life is common to all, and the psalmist voices the desire of his people when he tells Yhwh: "to number *our* days rightly teach *us*" (Ps 90:12a). Thus, there is no need for anyone voicing the psalmist's lament to be singled out and silenced, as a threat to social stability. Furthermore, because the acknowledgement of the crisis, as well as the assistance sought, are expressed communally, the effect of any lesson that Yhwh might teach in response to the psalmist's pleas would have the potential to shape the worldview of the entire society represented within the psalm (rather than just the psalmist's personal outlook, as in Psalm 73). This communal application renders Psalm 90 particularly useful for the social epistemological task of legitimation (see chap. 1). Recall that legitimation addresses the need of the members of a society to understand why their worldview (which, in the case of Psalm 90, includes universal suffering and the brevity of life) is structured the way that it is. Equipped with such an understanding, they would be better able to transmit their worldview to the next generation. Thus, the knowledge that is sought in Ps 90:12 has profound social significance.

---

6 To be sure, such questions are not explicitly posed by the psalmist, but they are implicitly raised in the minds of the audience.

Psalm 107

Psalm 107 is the most epistemologically complex of the four psalms considered in this study. As in the previous psalms, there is an opening axiomatic declaration of confidence in Yhwh's goodness and loving-kindness, which is quickly followed by real-life scenarios which bring the axiom into question. As in Psalm 90, there is a global quality to the poem, suggesting that the situations portrayed in its verses apply to all humanity. But there is also a specificity and a level of detail in Psalm 107 that is lacking in Psalm 90. The psalmist goes to some length to describe people who are both morally culpable and those who are innocent; and provides examples drawn from several different strata of society. As in Psalm 90, hardships and struggles are experienced by everyone, but here the nature of the hardship is unique to each group described within the psalm (compared to a general hardship that everyone must undergo in Psalm 90). Thus, there is a level of sophistication and realism in Psalm 107 that increases its epistemological relevance to the audience, insofar as they can more readily identify their own life situations with those of the characters depicted within the worldview of the psalm.

Along with this higher degree of realism in Psalm 107, we also find a more direct level of human engagement in the epistemological process. In Psalm 90, the psalmist calls out to Yhwh and pleads to be taught, so that he might gain wisdom. Any new knowledge that might be conveyed must come directly from Yhwh. By the end of the psalm, we still do not know whether or not the psalmist has in fact learned anything new; his education is totally dependent upon Yhwh's will. In Psalm 107, by contrast, the teacher is the psalmist himself, not Yhwh. The lesson comes directly from the scenarios depicted in the psalm. The characters within the psalm (not the psalmist) cry out to Yhwh, and in every instance they are given aid; there is no question here of uncertainty about whether Yhwh will offer help or not. The aid given is not knowledge, but rather physical assistance (guidance through deserts, liberation from prison, etc.). Knowledge in Psalm 107 will only be received via the careful attention of the audience. The psalmist is the instructor, telling "whoever is wise" to learn from his poem. Note that the psalmist is not just directing his message to his own people alone, but rather to all humanity (or at least to all those people who are wise enough to heed his words).

Thus we find that Psalm 107 itself is an extended instruction, intended for any person who cares to glean new knowledge from its verses. The source of that knowledge cannot be attributed solely to Yhwh. Indeed, the "lesson" of Psalm 107 depends upon the sufferers whom the psalmist describes (and their free-will choice to cry out for help) as much as it does upon Yhwh and his salvific actions. While Yhwh does not directly instruct anyone in the psalm, a wise person might acquire new knowledge by simply observing the divine response to the prayers of both the wicked and the righteous. Thus, the level of personal responsibility for one's own acquisition of knowledge is higher in Psalm 107 than in any of the other three psalms we have analyzed. Insofar as the psalmist in this poem functions as a wise teacher, Psalm 107 could readily be employed in the social epistemological process of internalization (see chap. 1), by which the members of a society come to receive and absorb that society's prevailing worldview.

Epistemological Progression

We therefore find an epistemological progression as we take up Psalms 1, 73, 90, and 107 in their canonical order. The psalmists are increasingly more forthright in acknowledging the moral paradox that the righteous can suffer, while the wicked can prosper.[7] At the same time, the psalmists confront and engage that paradox with increasingly more complex and sophisticated responses while assuming more personal responsibility for growing in wisdom.

In Psalm 1, there is no opportunity to even acknowledge the paradox, and thus there is no need to resolve it. In Psalm 73, however, the psalmist proclaims his anxiety over the paradox with blunt honesty. Eventually he gains the necessary insight to resolve the paradox, but the level of human involvement in that resolution is minimal; the psalmist is simply given fresh knowledge by Yhwh without directly seeking it. Furthermore, the knowledge is given individually, not to the psalmist's entire community. Thus, there is no obvious reason to expect that this process for conveying knowledge will have social epistemological consequences.

In Psalm 90, the moral paradox is recognized with as much stark realism as in Psalm 73. Now, however, the psalmist undertakes an explicitly epistemological solution: he directly appeals to Yhwh to teach him wisdom. And because he makes this appeal on behalf of his community, his actions have the potential for affecting social epistemological change.

In Psalm 107, not only is the paradox of universal suffering recognized but also Yhwh's response of universal mercy to all who pray to him. The new knowledge to be gained is directly presented in the psalm, for all who are able to grasp

---

7 This is the fundamental core of the problem, although it is formulated in somewhat different ways in the four psalms. Thus, in Psalm 90 the question focuses on why all human beings are subjected to harsh lives (there is no attempt to distinguish the righteous from the wicked). In Psalm 107, the issue concerns the fact that both the righteous and the wicked undergo suffering.

it. The only hindrance to the growth of knowledge lies in the heart and mind of the audience; the psalmist holds nothing back. In this epistemological process, Yhwh must be approached not as a teacher but rather as a source of salvific mercy and love. Insofar as any (wise) member of the psalmist's society is free to access the knowledge contained within the poem, Psalm 107 has the capacity to function as a powerful agent for epistemological social change (or for firmly establishing and propagating the values of a society that already embraces the psalm's worldview).[8]

Epistemology and the Canonical Structure of the Psalter

The epistemological progression we have noted calls for human beings to take on a greater responsibility for their own wisdom, which in turn equips them to better address the puzzle posed by the apparent success of the wicked and the suffering of the righteous. This does not mean, however, a prideful rejection of dependence on Yhwh. On the contrary, Yhwh's actions constitute the epistemological core of the psalms considered in this study. What these psalms reveal, however, is that the acquisition of knowledge is advanced when Yhwh is sought out intentionally, is questioned directly, and is observed with a heart focused on learning.

It is important to observe that this epistemological progression does not lend support to the notion that (as has sometimes been suggested) Psalm 89 marks the demise of the Davidic kingship and that Books IV and V point to a new reliance upon Yhwh's kingship alone.[9] As we noted, the role for human reason increases substantially as the social epistemology becomes more complex. Further-

---

8 These epistemological findings would seem to concur with H. Angel's comparison of the responses of the "wise" and the "foolish" in the Psalter to the problem of suffering (his study includes the analysis of Psalms 1, 73, and 107). "Because of unfairness in this world, the wicked abandon God: *The benighted man thinks, 'God does not care'* (14:1). In contrast, the righteous develop their relationship with God, sometimes by remaining steadfast in their belief that everything must ultimately be fair, and sometimes by protesting or pleading. Whatever their response, they create a dynamic connection to God. *Yet I was always with You* (73:23), proclaims the troubled psalmist." (H. Angel, "The Differences Between the Wise and the Foolish in Psalms: Theodicy, Understanding Providence, and Religious Responses," *JBQ* 38 [2010] 164). This "dynamic connection to God," I suggest, is not only the foundation for religious succor but also a necessary condition if the wise man is to grow in his knowledge about the nature of suffering.
9 See, e.g., the discussion of this issue in D. M. Howard, "The Proto-MT Psalter, the King, and Psalms 1 and 2: A Response to Klaus Seybold," in *Jewish and Christian Approaches to the Psalms: Conflict and Convergence* (ed. S. Gillingham; Oxford: Oxford University Press, 2013) 185–86.

more, at each "stage" of the epistemological progression (moving sequentially from Psalm 1 through 107), one who is fully integrated into the worldview of that stage (i.e., participates in the society's "internalization" of its worldview, to use the social epistemological language of chap. 1) builds upon the epistemological capacities of prior stages. For example, when a person who is fully integrated into the worldview of Psalm 107 meditates upon Yhwh's torah (Ps 1:2), he is not limited by the static epistemology of Psalm 1 but rather is open to receiving special revelation of the type given in Psalm 73 (v. 17)—he cannot *cause* such revelation, but he can watch for it, as part of his diligent observing (cf. Ps 107:43). Similarly, the person who has learned the importance of crying out to the Lord in his distress (cf. Ps 107:6, 13, 19, 28) would presumably be comfortable asking the Lord to teach him wisdom (Ps 90:12).

It therefore follows that if a human king were fully integrated into the worldview of Psalm 107, he would possess such wisdom and could convey it to his people (just as the psalmist is able to teach his audience [cf. Ps 107:43]). For the king (or his subjects) to actually receive newfound wisdom, however, he must carefully observe (107:43) and actively engage (107:6, 13, 19, 28) Yhwh. Even as he does so, he will continue to inhabit a world in which seemingly unjust suffering and undeserved prosperity remain, but he will nevertheless know that he can call out to the Lord and place his trust in him.[10]

Such an epistemological turning toward Yhwh is consonant with the growing desire to praise him that is evident in the latter half of the Psalter. Yhwh cannot, however, be fully praised if he is not first carefully observed. And if he is carefully observed, then, our epistemological study suggests, he can be learned from. While observing Yhwh may not be the beginning of wisdom (cf. Prov 1:7), the Psalter seems to imply that such observation is a critical step toward enabling wisdom to grow.

---

10 This view of kingship is not unlike the qualities of David that R. Rendtorff lists from his survey of the images of David throughout the Psalter. Namely, David is portrayed as: (1) the "messianic king whom God has enthroned on Zion," as in Psalm 2; (2) the "exemplary righteous king who follows the divine Torah," as in Psalm 1; (3) a "suffering and lamenting" figure, but at the same time "hoping and trusting in God's help," as in Psalm 3. Rendtorff notes that it is by the third of these categories that David is most frequently portrayed in Books I—III. As such, David stands as an example for every suffering person, "because almost every lamentation psalm related to David's name ends with an expression of hope and confidence in God's help. David is not only the exemplary sufferer, but also the exemplary believer." See R. Rendtorff, "The Psalms of David: David in the Psalms," in *The Book of Psalms: Composition and Reception* (ed. P. W. Flint and P. D. Miller; VTSup 99; Leiden: Brill, 2005) 63.

Bibliography

Primary Sources

Biblia Hebraica Stuttgartensia, 5th ed. Edited by K. Elliger and W. Rudolph. Stuttgart: Deutsche Bibelgesellschaft, 1967/77.

Biblia Sacra iuxta Vulgatam Versionem, editionem quartam emendatam. Edited by R. Weber. Stuttgart: Deutsche Bibelgesellschaft, 1994.

Psalmi cum Odis. Edited by A. Rahlfs. Septuaginta: Vetus Testamentum Graecum: auctoritate Societatis Litterarum Gottingensis editum; Vol. X. Göttingen: Vandenhoeck & Ruprecht, 1979.

Psalms. Edited by L. G. Rignell. The Old Testament in Syriac according to the Peshitta Version; Vol. II/3. Leiden: Brill, 1980.

Lexicons and Grammars

Baldwin, J. M., ed. *Dictionary of Philosophy and Psychology.* New York: MacMillan, 1902.

Botterweck, G. Johannes, and Helmer Ringgren, eds. *Theological Dictionary of the Old Testament.* 15 vols. Grand Rapids: Eerdmans, 1977–2006.

Hatch, Edwin, and Henry A. Redpath. *A Concordance to the Septuagint and the Other Greek Versions of the Old Testament (Including the Apocryphal Books).* 2nd ed. Grand Rapids: Baker Academic, 1998.

Joüon, Paul. *A Grammar of Biblical Hebrew.* 2 vols. Subsidia Biblica 14/I,II. Translated and revised by T. Muraoka. Rome: Editrice Pontifico Istituto Biblico, 2003.

Kautzsch, E., ed. *Gesenius' Hebrew Grammar.* Translated and edited by A. E. Cowley. New York: Oxford University Press, 1910.

Koehler, Ludwig, and Walter Baumgartner. *The Hebrew and Aramaic Lexicon of the Old Testament.* Revised by Walter Baumgartner and Johann J. Stamm; trans. M. E. J. Richardson. Leiden: Brill, 1994–2000.

Waltke, Bruce K., and M. O'Connor. *An Introduction to Biblical Hebrew Syntax.* Winona Lake, IN: Eisenbrauns, 1990.

Commentaries

Allen, Leslie C. *Psalms 101–150.* WBC 21. Waco: Word Books, 1983.

Anderson, A. A. *The Book of Psalms.* 2 vols. New Century Bible Commentary. Grand Rapids: Eerdmans, 1981.

Anderson, Bernhard W., and Steven Bishop. *Out of the Depths: The Psalms Speak for Us Today.* 3rd rev. ed. Louisville: Westminster John Knox, 2000.

Briggs, Charles Augustus, and Emilie Grace Briggs. *A Critical and Exegetical Commentary on the Book of Psalms.* 2 vols. ICC. Edinburgh: T&T Clark, 1906.

Brueggemann, Walter. *The Message of the Psalms: A Theological Commentary.* Minneapolis: Augsburg Publishing House, 1984.

—. *The Psalms: The Life of Faith*. Minneapolis: Fortress, 1995.

—. *An Introduction to the Old Testament: The Canon and Christian Imagination*. Louisville: Westminster John Knox, 2003.

Bullock, C. Hassell. *Encountering the Book of Psalms*. Grand Rapids: Baker, 2001.

Clifford, Richard J. *Proverbs: A Commentary*. OTL. Louisville: Westminster John Knox, 1999.

Craigie, Peter, C. *Psalms 1–50*. WBC 19. Waco, TX: Word Books, 1983.

Crenshaw, James L. *Ecclesiastes: A Commentary*. OTL. Philadelphia: Westminster, 1987.

Dahood, Mitchell. *Psalms*. 3 vols. AB 16, 17, 17 A. Garden City, NY: Doubleday, 1966–1970.

Day, J. *Psalms*. OTG. Sheffield: JSOT Press, 1990.

Delitzsch, Franz. *Biblischer Kommentar über die Psalmen*. 5th ed. BKAT. Leipzig: Dörffling & Franke, 1894.

Duhm, Bernhard. *Die Psalmen*. Kurzer Hand-Commentar zum Alten Testament 14. Freiburg i. B.: Mohr, 1899.

—. *Die Psalmen*. 2nd ed., rev. and exp. Kurzer Hand-Commentar zum Alten Testament 14. Freiburg i. B.: Mohr, 1922.

Fitzmyer, Joseph A. *The Acts of the Apostles*. AB 31. New York: Doubleday, 1998.

Fox, Michael V. *A Time to Tear Down and a Time to Build Up: A Rereading of Ecclesiastes*. Grand Rapids: Eerdmans, 1999.

—. *Proverbs 1–9: A New Translation with Introduction and Commentary*. AB 18 A. New York: Doubleday, 2000.

—. *Ecclesiastes*. JPS Bible Commentary. Philadelphia: Jewish Publication Society, 2004.

Gerstenberger, Erhard S. *Psalms: Part 1, with an Introduction to Cultic Poetry*. FOTL 14. Grand Rapids: Eerdmans, 1988.

—. *Psalms: Part 2, and Lamentations*. FOTL 15. Grand Rapids: Eerdmans, 2001.

Goldingay, John. *Psalms*. 3 vols. Baker Commentary on the Old Testament. Grand Rapids: Baker Academic, 2006–2008.

Grogan, Geoffrey W. *Psalms*. Two Horizons Old Testament Commentary. Grand Rapids: Eerdmans, 2008.

Gunkel, Hermann. *Einleitung in die Psalmen: Die Gattungen der religiösen Lyrik Israels*. HKAT. Abt. 2 Suppl. Göttingen: Vandenhoeck & Ruprecht, 1933.

—. *Die Psalmen: Übersetzt und Erklärt*. 5th ed. HKAT II/2. Göttingen: Vandenhoeck & Ruprecht, 1968.

Hossfeld, Frank-Lothar, and Erich Zenger. *Die Psalmen: Psalm 1—50*. NEchtB. Würzburg: Echter Verlag, 1993.

—. *Psalmen 51–100*. HThKAT. Freiburg: Herder, 2000.

—. *Die Psalmen: Psalm 51—100*. NEchtB. Würzburg: Echter Verlag, 2002.

—. *Psalmen 101–150*. HThKAT. Freiburg: Herder, 2008.

—. *Die Psalmen: Psalm 101—150*. NEchtB. Würzburg: Echter Verlag, 2012.

Kraus, Hans-Joachim. *Psalmen*. 2 vols. BKAT XV/2. Neukirchen-Vluyn: Neukirchener Verlag, 1960.

Krüger, Thomas L. *Qoholeth: A Commentary*. Hermeneia. Translated by O. C. Dean, Jr. Minneapolis: Fortress, 2004.

Lohfink, Norbert. *Qoheleth: A Continental Commentary*. Translated by Sean McEvenue. Minneapolis: Fortress, 2003.

McCann, J. Clinton. *A Theological Introduction to the Book of Psalms*. Nashville: Abingdon, 1993.

McCarter, P. Kyle, Jr. *II Samuel: A New Translation with Introduction, Notes and Commentary.* AB 9. Garden City, NY: Doubleday, 1984.

Miller, Patrick D. *Deuteronomy.* Interpretation. Louisville: John Knox, 1990.

Murphy, Roland E. *Proverbs.* WBC 22. Nashville: Thomas Nelson, 1998.

Perdue, Leo G. *Proverbs.* Interpretation. Louisville: John Knox, 2000.

Sabourin, Leopold. *The Psalms: Their Origin and Meaning.* New York: Alba House, 1974.

Seybold, Klaus. *Die Psalmen.* HAT I/15. Tübingen: Mohr, 1996.

Skehan, Patrick W., and Alexander A. Di Lella. *The Wisdom of Ben Sira: A New Translation with Notes, Introduction, and Commentary.* AB 39. New York: Doubleday, 1987.

Tate, Marvin E. *Psalms 51–100.* WBC 20. Dallas: Word Books, 1990.

Terrien, Samuel. *The Psalms: Strophic Structure and Theological Commentary.* Grand Rapids: Eerdmans, 2003.

Van Leeuwen, Raymond C. *Proverbs.* NIB 5. Nashville: Abingdon, 1997.

Westermann, Claus. *Der Psalter.* Stuttgart: Calwer Verlag, 1967.

——. *Ausgewählte Psalmen.* Göttingen: Vandenhoeck & Ruprecht, 1984.

Articles and Monographs

Aaron, David H. *Biblical Ambiguities: Metaphor, Semantics and Divine Imagery.* Brill Reference Library of Ancient Judaism 4. Leiden: Brill, 2001.

Achenbach, Reinhard, and Martin Arneth, eds. *"Gerechtigkeit und Recht zu üben" (Gen 18,19): Studien zur altorientalischen und biblischen Rechtsgeschichte, zur Religionsgeschichte Israels und zur Religionssoziologie: Festschrift für Eckart Otto zum 65. Geburtstag.* Beihefte zur Zeitschrift für Biblische Rechtsgeschichte 13. Wiesbaden: Harrassowitz, 2009.

Allen, Leslie C. "Psalm 73: An Analysis." *TynBul* 33 (1982): 93–118.

——. "Psalm 73: Pilgrimage from Doubt to Faith." *Bulletin for Biblical Research* 7 (1997): 1–10.

Alonso Schökel, Luis. *A Manual of Hebrew Poetics.* Subsidia Biblica 11. Rome: Pontifical Biblical Institute, 1998.

Alter, Robert. *The Art of Biblical Poetry.* New York, NY: Basic Books, 1985.

Anderson, G. W. "A Note on Psalm I 1." *VT* 24 (1974): 231–33.

Anderson, R. Dean. "The Division and Order of the Psalms." *WTJ* 56 (1994): 219–41.

André, Gunnel. "'Walk,' 'Stand,' and 'Sit' in Psalm I 1–2." *VT* 32 (1982): 327.

Angel, Hayyim. "The Differences Between the Wise and the Foolish in Psalms: Theodicy, Understanding Providence, and Religious Responses." *JBQ* 38 (2010): 157–65.

Apple, Raymond. "The Happy Man of Psalm 1." *Jewish Bible Quarterly* 40 (2012): 179–82.

Arnold, Tina. "Die Einladung zu einem 'Glücklichen' Leben: Tora als Lebensraum nach Ps 119,1–3." In *The Composition of the Book of Psalms,* ed. Erich Zenger, 401–12. BETL 238. Leuven: Uitgeverij Peeters, 2010.

Attard, Stefan. "Establishing Connections between Pss 49 and 50 within the Context of Pss 49—52: A Synchronic Analysis." In *The Composition of the Book of Psalms,* ed. Erich Zenger, 413–24. BETL 238. Leuven: Uitgeverij Peeters, 2010.

Auffret, Pierre. "Essai sur la structure littéraire du Psaume 1." *BZ* 22 (1978): 27–45.

——. "Essai sur la structure littéraire du Psaume 90." *Bib* 61 (1980): 262–76.

——. "Compléments sur la structure littéraire du Ps 2 et son rapport au Ps 1." *BN* 35 (1986): 7–13.

——. "Et moi sans cesse avec toi: Etude structurelle du psaume 73." *SJOT* 9 (1995): 241–76.

——. "Ses merveilles pour les fils d'Adam: Étude structurelle du Psaume 107." In *Merveilles à nos yeux: Etude structurelle de vingt psaumes dont celui de 1Ch 16,8–36*, 105–29. BZAW 235. Berlin: de Gruyter, 1995.

Auvray, Paul. "Le Psaume 1." *RB* 53 (1946): 365–71.

Auwers, Jean-Marie. "Le Psautier comme livre biblique: Édition, redaction, function." In *The Composition of the Book of Psalms*, ed. Erich Zenger, 67–89. BETL 238. Leuven: Uitgeverij Peeters, 2010.

Bailey, Noel. "David's Innocence: A Response to J. Wright." *JSOT* 64 (1994): 83–90.

——. "David and God in 1 Chronicles 21: Edged with Mist." In *The Chronicler as Author: Studies in Text and Texture*, eds. M. P. Graham and S. L. McKenzie, 337–59. JSOTSup 263. Sheffield: Sheffield Academic Press, 1999.

Ballhorn, Egbert. "Der Torapsalter: Vom Gebetbuch zum Buch der Weisung." *BK* 65 (2010): 24–27.

——. *Zum Telos des Psalters: Der Textzusammenhang des Vierten und Fünften Psalmenbuches (Ps 90–150)*. BBB 138. Berlin: Philo, 2004.

Bardtke, Hans. "Erwägungen zu Psalm 1 und Psalm 2." In *Symbolae Biblicae et Mesopotamicae. Festschrift Francisco Mario Theodore de Liagre Böhl*, eds. M. A. Beek, A. A. Kampman, and C. Nijland, J. Ryckmans, 1–18. Leiden: Brill, 1973.

Barré, Michael L., ed. *Wisdom, You Are My Sister: Studies in Honor of Roland E. Murphy, O. Carm., on the Occasion of His Eightieth Birthday*. CBQMS 29. Washington: Catholic Biblical Association of America, 1997.

Basson, Alec. *Divine Metaphors in Selected Hebrew Psalms of Lamentation*. FAT 2.15. Tübingen: Mohr, 2006.

Beaucamp, Évode. "Le Sens de ki-im en Psaume 1, vv. 2 et 4." *RSR* 57 (1969): 435–37.

Begg, Christopher. "Josephus' Version of David's Census." *Hen* 16 (1994): 199–226.

Bellinger, W. H., Jr. "The Psalter as Theodicy Writ Large." In *Jewish and Christian Approaches to the Psalms: Conflict and Convergence*, ed. Susan Gillingham, 147–60. Oxford: Oxford University Press, 2013.

Bender, John W. "Coherentism." In *Encyclopedia of Philosophy*, 2nd ed., ed. Donald M. Borchert, 2. 313–15. New York: Thomson Gale, 2006.

Benson, Hugh H. *Socratic Wisdom: The Model of Knowledge in Plato's Early Dialogues*. New York: Oxford University Press, 2000.

Berger, Peter L. *The Precarious Vision: A Sociologist Looks at Social Fictions and Christian Faith*. Garden City, NY: Doubleday, 1961.

——. *The Sacred Canopy: Elements of a Sociological Theory of Religion*. Garden City, NY: Doubleday, 1967.

——. *A Rumor of Angels: Modern Society and the Rediscovery of the Supernatural*. Expanded ed. New York: Doubleday, 1969/90.

Berger, Peter L., and Thomas Luckmann. *The Social Construction of Reality: A Treatise in the Sociology of Knowledge*. New York: Anchor Books, 1966.

Bergmeier, Roland. "Zum Ausdruck עצת רשעים in Ps 1:1; Hi 10:3; 21:16 und 22:18." *ZAW* 79 (1967): 229–32.

Berlin, Adele. "On Reading Biblical Poetry: The Role of Metaphor." In *Congress Volume: Cambridge 1995*, ed. J. A. Emerton, 25–36. VTSup 66. Leiden: Brill, 1997.

——. "The Wisdom of Creation in Psalm 104." In *Seeking Out the Wisdom of the Ancients: Essays Offered to Honor Michael V. Fox on the Occasion of His Sixty-Fifth Birthday*, eds. Ronald L. Troxel, Kelvin G. Friebel, and Dennis R. Magary, 71–83. Winona Lake, IN: Eisenbrauns, 2005.

——. *The Dynamics of Biblical Parallelism*. Rev. and exp. ed. Grand Rapids: Eerdmans, 2008.

Bertrand, J. Mark. *(Re)Thinking Worldview: Learning to Think, Live, and Speak in This World*. Wheaton, IL: Crossway Books, 2007.

Beyerlin, Walter. *Werden und Wesen des 107. Psalms*. BZAW 153. Berlin: de Gruyter, 1979.

Biderman, Shlomo. *Scripture and Knowledge: An Essay on Religious Epistemology*. Studies in the History of Religions 69. Leiden: Brill, 1995.

Birkeland, Harris. "The Chief Problems of Ps 73:17 ff." *ZAW* 67 (1955): 99–103.

Black, Max. *Models and Metaphors: Studies in Language and Philosophy*. Ithaca, NY: Cornell University Press, 1962.

Boadt, Lawrence. "The Use of 'Panels' in the Structure of Psalms 73–78." *CBQ* 66 (2004): 533–50.

Boer, Pieter A. H. de. "The Meaning of Psalm LXXIII 9." *VT* 18 (1968): 260–64.

Boeve, Lieven, and Kurt Feyaerts, eds. *Metaphor and God-Talk*. Religions and Discourse 2. Bern: Peter Lang, 1999.

Boeve, Lieven, and Kurt Feyaerts. "Religious Metaphors in a Postmodern Culture: Transverse Links Between Apophatical Theology and Cognitive Semantics." In *Metaphor and God-Talk*, eds. Lieven Boeve and Kurt Feyaerts, 153–85. Religions and Discourse 2. Bern: Peter Lang, 1999.

BonJour, Laurence. "Can Empirical Knowledge Have a Foundation?" *American Philosophical Quarterly* 15 (1978): 1–13.

——. *The Structure of Empirical Knowledge*. Cambridge: Harvard University Press, 1985.

——. *Epistemology: Classic Problems and Contemporary Responses*. Lanham, MD: Rowman & Littlefield, 2002.

Booij, Th. "Psalm 90,5–6: Junction of Two Traditional Motifs." *Bib* 68 (1987): 393–96.

Boston, James R. "The Wisdom Influence upon the Song of Moses." *JBL* 87 (1968): 198–202.

Boström, Lennart. *The God of the Sages: The Portrayal of God in the Book of Proverbs*. ConBOT 29. Stockholm: Almqvist & Wiksell International, 1990.

Botha, Phil J. "Intertextuality and the Interpretation of Psalm 1." *OTE* 18 (2005): 503–20.

——. "Interpreting 'Torah' in Psalm 1 in the Light of Psalm 119." *HTS Teologiese Studies/Theological Studies* 68 (2012), Art. #1274, 7 pages. http://dx.DOI.org/10.4102/hts.v68i1.1274.

——. "Pride and the Suffering of the Poor in the Persian Period: Psalm 12 in its Post-Exilic Context." *OTE* 25 (2012): 40–56.

——. "Psalm 91 and Its Wisdom Connections." *OTE* 25 (2012): 260–76.

Brandscheidt, Renate. "'Unsere Tage zu zählen, so lehre du' (Psalm 90,12): Literarische Gestalt, theologische Aussage und Stellung des 90. Psalms im vierten Psalmenbuch." *TTZ* 113 (2004): 1–33.

Brekelmans, C. "Wisdom Influence in Deuteronomy." In *A Song of Power and the Power of Song: Essays on the Book of Deuteronomy*, ed. Duane L. Christensen, 123–34. Sources for Biblical and Theological Study. Winona Lake, IN: Eisenbrauns, 1993.

Brennan, Joseph P. "Psalms 1–8: Some Hidden Harmonies." *BTB* 10 (1980): 25–29.

Brent, Allen. "The Sociology of Knowledge and Epistemology." *British Journal of Educational Studies* 23 (1975): 209–24.

Brettler, Marc Zvi. *God is King: Understanding an Israelite Metaphor.* JSOTSup 76. Sheffield: Sheffield Academic Press, 1989.

Brown, William P. *Seeing the Psalms: A Theology of Metaphor.* Louisville: Westminster John Knox, 2002.

——. "'Come, O Children … I Will Teach You the Fear of the Lord' (Psalm 34:12): Comparing Psalms and Proverbs." In *Seeking Out the Wisdom of the Ancients: Essays Offered to Honor Michael V. Fox on the Occasion of His Sixty-Fifth Birthday*, eds. Ronald L. Troxel, Kelvin G. Friebel, and Dennis R. Magary, 85–102. Winona Lake, IN: Eisenbrauns, 2005.

——. "The Law and the Sages: A Reexamination of *Tôrâ* in Proverbs." In *Constituting the Community: Studies on the Polity of Ancient Israel in Honor of S. Dean McBride Jr.*, eds. John T. Strong and Steven S. Tuell, 251–80. Winona Lake, IN: Eisenbrauns, 2005.

——. "'Here Comes the Sun!': The Metaphorical Theology of Psalms 15—24." In *The Composition of the Book of Psalms*, ed. Erich Zenger, 259–77. BETL 238. Leuven: Uitgeverij Peeters, 2010.

Brownlee, William H. "Psalms 1–2 as a Coronation Liturgy." *Bib* 52 (1971): 321–36.

Brueggemann, Walter. "Psalms and the Life of Faith: A Suggested Typology of Function." *JSOT* 17 (1980): 3–32.

——. "'Impossibility' and Epistemology in the Faith Tradition of Abraham and Sarah (Gen 18:1–15)." *ZAW* 94 (1982): 615–34.

——. *Israel's Praise: Doxology Against Idolatry and Ideology.* Philadelphia: Fortress, 1988.

——. "Bounded by Obedience and Praise: The Psalms as Canon." *JSOT* 50 (1991): 63–92.

——. "The Epistemological Crisis of Israel's Two Histories (Jeremiah 9:22–23)." In *Old Testament Theology: Essays on Structure, Theme, and Text*, ed. Patrick D. Miller, 270–95. Minneapolis: Fortress, 1992.

——. "Psalm 37: Conflict of Interpretation." In *Of Prophets' Visions and the Wisdom of Sages: Essays in Honor of R. Norman Whybray on His Seventieth Birthday*, eds. Heather A. McKay and David J. A. Clines, 229–56. JSOTSup 162. Sheffield: JSOT Press, 1993.

——. "The Psalms in Theological Use: On Incommensurability and Mutuality." In *The Book of Psalms: Composition and Reception*, ed. Peter W. Flint and Patrick D. Miller, 581–602. VTSup 99. Leiden: Brill, 2005.

——. "The Psalms and the Life of Faith: A Suggested Typology of Function." In *Soundings in the Theology of Psalms: Perspectives and Methods in Contemporary Scholarship*, ed. Rolf A. Jacobson, 1–25. Minneapolis: Fortress, 2011.

Brueggemann, Walter, and Patrick D. Miller. "Psalm 73 as a Canonical Marker." *JSOT* 72 (1996): 45–56.

Bryce, Glendon E. *A Legacy of Wisdom: The Egyptian Contribution to the Wisdom of Israel.* Cranbury, NJ: Associated University Presses, 1979.

Buber, Martin. "Das Herz Entscheidet: Psalm 73." In *Werke*. 2 vols. 2. 971–83. Munich and Heidelberg: Kösel, 1964.

Buccellati, Giorgio. "Wisdom and Not: The Case of Mesopotamia." *JAOS* 101 (1981): 35–47.

Burnett, Joel S., W. H. Bellinger, Jr., and W. Dennis Tucker Jr., eds. *Diachronic and Synchronic: Reading the Psalms in Real Time. Proceedings of the Baylor Symposium on the Book of Psalms.* LHBOTS 488. London: T&T Clark, 2009.

Butler, Christopher, S., María de los Ángeles Gómez-Gonzáles, and Susana M. Doval-Suárez. *The Dynamics of Language Use: Functional and Contrastive Perspectives.* Pragmatics and Beyond, New Series 140. Amsterdam: John Benjamins, 2005.

Callaway, Phillip R. "Deut 21:18–21: Proverbial Wisdom and Law." *JBL* 103 (1984): 341–52.

Carbajosa, I. "Salmo 107: Unidad, Organización y Teología." *EstBib* 59 (2001): 451–85.

Ceresko, Anthony R. "The Sage in the Psalms." In *The Sage in Israel and the Ancient Near East*, eds. John G. Gammie and Leo G. Perdue, 217–30. Winona Lake, IN: Eisenbrauns, 1990.

Chester, Ray. "Faith on Trial: Psalm 73." *ResQ* 20 (1977): 88–92.

Childs, Brevard. "Psalm Titles and Midrashic Exegesis." *JSS* 16 (1971): 137–50.

——. S. *Introduction to the Old Testament as Scripture*. Philadelphia: Fortress, 1979.

Chisholm, Robert B., Jr. "'Drink Water From Your Own Cistern:' A Literary Study of Proverbs 5:15–23." *BSac* 157 (2000): 397–409.

Clayton, J. Nathan. "An Examination of Holy Space in Psalm 73: Is Wisdom's Path Infused with an Eschatologically Oriented Hope?" *Trinity Journal* 27 (2006): 117–42.

Clifford, Richard J. *The Cosmic Mountain in Canaan and the Old Testament*. HSM 4. Cambridge: Harvard University Press, 1972.

——. "What Does the Psalmist Ask for in Psalms 39:5 and 90:12?" *JBL* 119 (2000): 59–66.

——. "Psalm 90: Wisdom Meditation or Communal Lament?" In *The Book of Psalms: Composition and Reception*, ed. Peter W. Flint and Patrick D. Miller, 190–205. VTSup 99. Leiden: Brill, 2005.

Cole, Robert L. *The Shape and Message of Book III (Psalms 73–89)*. JSOTSup 307. Sheffield: Sheffield Academic Press, 2000.

——. "An Integrated Reading of Psalms 1 and 2." *JSOT* 98 (2002): 75–88.

——. *Psalms 1–2: Gateway to the Psalter*. Hebrew Bible Monographs 37. Sheffield: Sheffield Phoenix Press, 2013.

Collins, C. John. "Psalm 1: Structure and Rhetoric." *Presbyterion* 31 (2005): 37–48.

Conee, Earl, and Richard Feldman. "Epistemology." In *Encyclopedia of Philosophy*, 2nd ed., ed. Donald M. Borchert, 3. 270–77. New York: Thomson Gale, 2006.

Coulson, Seana. *Semantic Leaps: Frame-Shifting and Conceptual Blending in Meaning Construction*. Cambridge: Cambridge University Press, 2001.

Cox, D. "Fear or Conscience? *yir'at yhwh* in Proverbs 1–9." In *Studia Hierosolymitana* 3, ed. G. C. Bottini, 83–90. Studium Biblicum Franciscanum, Collectio 30. Jerusalem: Franciscan Printing Press, 1982.

Craig, William Lane, ed. *Philosophy of Religion: A Reader and Guide*. New Brunswick, NJ: Rutgers University Press, 2002.

Creach, Jerome F. D. *Yahweh as Refuge and the Editing of the Hebrew Psalter*. JSOTSup 217. Sheffield: Sheffield Academic Press, 1996.

——. "The Shape of Book Four of the Psalter and the Shape of Second Isaiah." *JSOT* 80 (1998): 63–76.

——. "Like a Tree Planted by the Temple Stream: The Portrait of the Righteous in Psalm 1:3." *CBQ* 61 (1999): 34–46.

——. *The Destiny of the Righteous in the Psalms*. St. Louis: Chalice, 2008.

——. "The Destiny of the Righteous and the Theology of the Psalms." In *Soundings in the Theology of Psalms: Perspectives and Methods in Contemporary Scholarship*, ed. Rolf A. Jacobson, 49–61. Minneapolis: Fortress, 2011.

Crenshaw, James L. *Prophetic Conflict: Its Effect Upon Israelite Religion*. BZAW 124. Berlin: de Gruyter, 1971.

——. "Standing Near the Flame: Psalm 73." In *A Whirlpool of Torment: Israelite Traditions of God as an Oppressive Presence*, 93–109. OBT 12. Philadelphia: Fortress, 1984.

——. "Education in Ancient Israel." *JBL* 104 (1985): 601–15.

——. "Wisdom Literature: Retrospect and Prospect." In *Of Prophets' Visions and the Wisdom of Sages: Essays in Honor of R. Norman Whybray on His Seventieth Birthday*, eds. Heather A. McKay and David J. A. Clines, 161–78. JSOTSup 162. Sheffield: JSOT Press, 1993.

——. "Murphy's Axiom: Every Gnomic Saying Needs a Balancing Corrective." In *Urgent Advice and Probing Questions: Collected Writings on Old Testament Wisdom*, 344–54. Macon, GA: Mercer, 1995.

——. "The Acquisition of Knowledge in Israelite Wisdom Literature." In *Urgent Advice and Probing Questions: Collected Writings on Old Testament Wisdom*, 292–99. Macon, GA: Mercer, 1995.

——. "The Expression מי יודע in the Hebrew Bible." In *Urgent Advice and Probing Questions: Collected Writings on Old Testament Wisdom*, 279–91. Macon, GA: Mercer, 1995.

——. "Wisdom and Authority: Sapiential Rhetoric and Its Warrants." In *Urgent Advice and Probing Questions: Collected Writings on Old Testament Wisdom*, 326–43. Macon, GA: Mercer, 1995.

——. *Urgent Advice and Probing Questions: Collected Writings on Old Testament Wisdom.* Macon, GA: Mercer, 1995.

——. "The Primacy of Listening in Ben Sira's Pedagogy." In *Wisdom, You Are My Sister: Studies in Honor of Roland E. Murphy, O. Carm., on the Occasion of His Eightieth Birthday*, ed. Michael L. Barré, 172–87. CBQMS 29. Washington: Catholic Biblical Association of America, 1997.

——. *Education in Ancient Israel: Across the Deadening Silence.* ABRL. New York: Doubleday, 1998.

——. "Qoheleth's Understanding of Intellectual Inquiry." In *Qohelet in the Context of Wisdom*, ed. A. Schoors, 205–24. BETL 136. Leuven: Leuven University Press, 1998.

——. "Wisdom Psalms?" *Currents in Research: Biblical Studies* 8 (2000): 9–17.

——. "A Proverb in the Mouth of a Fool." In *Seeking Out the Wisdom of the Ancients: Essays Offered to Honor Michael V. Fox on the Occasion of His Sixty-Fifth Birthday*, eds. Ronald L. Troxel, Kelvin G. Friebel, and Dennis R. Magary, 103–15. Winona Lake, IN: Eisenbrauns, 2005.

——. *Prophets, Sages, and Poets.* St. Louis: Chalice, 2006.

Dahmen, Ulrich. "'Gepriesen sei der Herr, der Gott Israels, vom Anfang bis ans Ende der Zeiten' (Ps 106,48): Beobachtungen zur Entstehungsgeschichte des Psalters im vierten und fünften Psalmenbuch." *BZ* 49 (2005): 1–25.

Dahood, Mitchell. "Interrogative *kî* in Psalm 90,11; Isaiah 36,19 and Hosea 13,9." *Bib* 60 (1979): 573–74.

Davidson, Donald. "A Coherence Theory of Truth and Knowledge." In *Truth and Interpretation: Perspectives on the Philosophy of Donald Davidson*, ed. Ernest LePore, 307–19. New York: Blackwell, 1989.

Day, John. "Foreign Semitic Influence on the Wisdom of Israel and its Appropriation in the Book of Proverbs." In *Wisdom in Ancient Israel*, eds. John Day, Robert P. Gordon, and H. G. M. Williamson, 55–70. Cambridge: Cambridge University Press, 1995.

Day, John, ed. *Temple and Worship in Biblical Israel.* Library of Hebrew Bible/Old Testament Studies (formerly JSOTSup) 422. London: T&T Clark, 2005.

Day, John, Robert P. Gordon, and H. G. M. Williamson, eds. *Wisdom in Ancient Israel: Essays in Honour of J. A. Emerton.* Cambridge: Cambridge University Press, 1995.

Day, Peggy L. *An Adversary in Heaven: Satan in the Hebrew Bible.* HSM 43. Atlanta: Scholars, 1988.

——. "Metaphor and Social Reality: Isaiah 23.17–18, Ezekial 16.35–37 and Hosea 2.4–5." In *Inspired Speech: Prophecy in the Ancient Near East. Essays in Honour of Herbert B. Huffman*, eds. John Kaltner and Louis Stulman, 63–71. JSOTSup 378. London: T&T Clark, 2004.

deClaissé-Walford, Nancy L. "The Canonical Shape of the Psalms." In *Introduction to Wisdom Literature and the Psalms: Festschrift Martin E. Tate*, eds. H. Wayne Ballard, Jr. and W. Dennis Tucker, Jr., 93–110. Macon, GA: Mercer, 2000.

Dell, Katharine J., and Margaret Barker, eds. *Wisdom: The Collected Articles of Norman Whybray.* SOTSMS. Aldershot: Ashgate, 2005.

Di Lella, Alexander A., O.F.M. "The Deuteronomic Background of the Farewell Discourse in Tob 14:3–11." *CBQ* 41 (1979): 380–89.

——. "Fear of the Lord and Belief and Hope in the Lord amid Trials: Sirach 2:1–18." In *Wisdom, You Are My Sister: Studies in Honor of Roland E. Murphy, O. Carm., on the Occasion of His Eightieth Birthday*, ed. Michael L. Barré, 188–204. CBQMS 29. Washington: Catholic Biblical Association of America, 1997.

Dille, Sarah J. *Mixing Metaphors: God as Mother and Father in Deutero-Isaiah.* JSOTSup 398. London: T&T Clark, 2004.

Dirksen, Piet B. "Why Was David Disqualified as Temple Builder? The Meaning of 1 Chronicles 22.8." *JSOT* 70 (1996): 51–56.

Doyle, Brian. "Where is God When You Need Him Most? The Divine Metaphor of Absence and Presence as a Binding Element in the Composition of the Book of Psalms." In *The Composition of the Book of Psalms*, ed. Erich Zenger, 377–90. BETL 238. Leuven: Uitgeverij Peeters, 2010.

Driver, G. R. "Old Problems Re-examined." *ZAW* 80 (1968): 174–83.

Driver, S. R. *An Introduction to the Literature of the Old Testament.* Edinburgh: T&T Clark, 1913.

Driver, Tom F. *Liberating Rites: Understanding the Transformative Power of Ritual.* BookSurge, 2006.

Dundes, Allan. "Folk Ideas as Units of Worldview." *The Journal of American Folklore* 84 (1971): 93–103.

Durlesser, James A. "Poetic Style in Psalm 1 and Jeremiah 17:5–8: A Rhetorical Critical Study." *Semitics* 9 (1984): 30–48.

Eberle, Thomas Samuel. "A New Paradigm for the Sociology of Knowledge: 'The Social Construction of Reality' After 25 Years." *Revue Suisse de Sociologie* 2 (1992): 493–502.

Eidevall, Göran. *Grapes in the Desert: Metaphors, Models, and Themes in Hosea 4–14.* ConBOT 43. Stockholm: Almqvist & Wiksell International, 1996.

——. "Images of God, Self, and the Enemy in the Psalms: On the Role of Metaphor in Identity Construction." In *Metaphor in the Hebrew Bible*, ed. P. Van Hecke, 55–65. BETL 187. Leuven: Leuven University Press, 2005.

——. "Metaphorical Landscapes in the Psalms." In *Metaphors in the Psalms*, eds. Pierre van Hecke, and Antje Labahn, 13–21. BETL 231. Leuven: Uitgeverij Peeters, 2010.

Emanatian, Michele. "Congruence by Degree: On the Relation Between Metaphor and Cultural Models." In *Metaphor in Cognitive Linguistics*, eds. Raymond W. Gibbs, Jr. and Gerard J. Steen, 205–18. Amsterdam Studies in the Theory and History of Linguistic Science 175. Amsterdam: John Benjamins, 1999.

Esteban, Eduardo I. "Salmo 1: Reflexiones Teológicas y Escatológicas Acerca del Juicio." *Theologika* 26 (2011): 28–45.

Estes, Daniel J. *Hear, My Son: Teaching and Learning in Proverbs 1–9.* New Studies in Biblical Theology. Grand Rapids: Eerdmans, 1997.

Fauconnier, Gilles. *Mappings in Thought and Language.* Cambridge: Cambridge University Press, 1997.

Fauconnier, Gilles, and Mark Turner. "Blending as a Central Process of Grammar." In *Conceptual Structure, Discourse, and Language,* ed. Adele Goldberg, 113–29. CSLI Lecture Notes. Stanford: Center for the Study of Language and Information, 1996.

——. "Conceptual Integration Networks." *Cognitive Science* 22 (1998): 133–87.

——. *The Way We Think: Conceptual Blending and the Mind's Hidden Complexities.* New York, NY: Basic Books, 2002.

——. "Rethinking Metaphor." In *The Cambridge Handbook of Metaphor and Thought,* ed. Raymond W. Gibbs, Jr., 53–66. Cambridge: Cambridge University Press, 2008.

Feldman, Richard. *Epistemology.* Upper Saddle River, NJ: Prentice Hall, 2003.

Flint, Peter W. *The Dead Sea Psalms Scrolls and the Book of Psalms.* STDJ 17. Leiden: Brill, 1997.

Flint, Peter W., and Patrick D. Miller, eds. *The Book of Psalms: Composition and Reception.* VTSup 99. Leiden: Brill, 2005.

Fouts, David M. "A Defense of the Hyperbolic Interpretation of Large Numbers in the Old Testament." *JETS* 40 (1997): 377–87.

Fox, Michael V. "Two Decades of Research in Egyptian Wisdom Literature." *ZÄS* 107 (1980): 120–35.

——. "Ancient Egyptian Rhetoric." *Rhetorica* 1 (1983): 9–22.

——. "Egyptian Onomastica and Biblical Wisdom." *VT* 36 (1986): 302–10.

——. "The Meaning of *hebel* for Qohelet." *JBL* 105 (1986): 409–27.

——. "Qohelet's Epistemology." *HUCA* 58 (1987): 137–55.

——. *Qohelet and His Contradictions.* JSOTSup 71. Sheffield: Almond, 1989.

——. "Words for Wisdom." *ZAH* 6 (1993): 149–69.

——. "The Pedagogy of Proverbs 2." *JBL* 113 (1994): 233–43.

——. "The Social Location of the Book of Proverbs." In *Texts, Temples, and Traditions: A Tribute to Menaham Haran,* eds. M. V. Fox, V. A. Hurowitz, A. Hurvitz, M. L. Klein, B. J. Schwartz, and N. Shupak, 227–39. Winona Lake, IN: Eisenbrauns, 1996.

——. "Ideas of Wisdom in Proverbs 1–9." *JBL* 116 (1997): 613–33.

——. "Who Can Learn? A Dispute in Ancient Pedagogy." In *Wisdom, You Are My Sister: Studies in Honor of Roland E. Murphy, O. Carm., on the Occasion of His Eightieth Birthday,* ed. Michael L. Barré, 62–77. CBQMS 29. Washington: Catholic Biblical Association of America, 1997.

——. "Words for Folly." *ZAH* 10 (1997): 1–12.

——. "The Inner-Structure of Qohelet's Thought." In *Qohelet in the Context of Wisdom,* ed. A. Schoors, 225–38. BETL 136. Leuven: Leuven University Press, 1998.

——. "The Epistemology of the Book of Proverbs." *JBL* 126 (2007): 669–84.

Fox, Michael V., V. A. Hurowitz, A. Hurvitz, M. L. Klein, B. J. Schwartz, and N. Shupak, eds. *Texts, Temples, and Traditions: A Tribute to Menahem Haran.* Winona Lake, IN: Eisenbrauns, 1996.

Freedman, David N. "Other than Moses…Who Asks (or Tells) God to Repent?" *Bible Review* 1.4 (1985): 56–9.

Fricker, Miranda. "Rational Authority and Social Power: Towards a Truly Social Epistemology." *Proceedings of the Aristotelian Society*, Ser. 2. 98 (1998): 159–77.

Frydrych, Tomáš. *Living Under the Sun: Examinations of Proverbs and Qoheleth*. VTSup 90. Leiden: Brill, 2002.

Fuller, Steve. *Social Epistemology*. 2nd ed. Bloomington, IN: Indiana University Press, 2002.

Fumerton, Richard. "Classical Foundationalism." In *Encyclopedia of Philosophy*, 2nd ed., ed. Donald M. Borchert, 2. 275–79. New York: Thomson Gale, 2006.

Gammie, John G., and Leo G. Perdue, eds. *The Sage in Israel and the Ancient Near East*. Winona Lake, IN: Eisenbrauns, 1990.

Gärtner, Judith. "The Torah in Psalm 106: Interpretations of JHWH's Saving Act at the Red Sea." In *The Composition of the Book of Psalms*, ed. Erich Zenger, 479–88. BETL 238. Leuven: Uitgeverij Peeters, 2010.

Gärtner, Judith. *Die Geschichtspsalmen: Eine Studie zu den Psalmen 78, 105, 106, 135 und 136 als Hermeneutische Schlüsseltexte im Psalter*. FAT 84. Tübingen: Mohr, 2012.

Geivett, R. Douglas, and Brendan Sweetman, eds. *Contemporary Perspectives on Religious Epistemology*. Oxford: Oxford University Press, 1992.

Geller, Stephen A. "Wisdom, Nature and Piety in Some Biblical Psalms." In *Riches Hidden in Secret Places: Ancient Near Eastern Studies in Memory of Thorkild Jacobsen*, ed. Tzvi Abusch, 101–21. Winona Lake, IN: Eisenbrauns, 2002.

Gelston, Anthony. "Editorial Arrangement in Book IV of the Psalter." In *Genesis, Isaiah and Psalms: A Festschrift to Honour Professor John Emerton for his Eightieth Birthday*, eds. Katharine J. Dell, Graham Davies, and Yee Von Koh, 165–76. VTSup 135. Leiden/Boston: Brill, 2010.

Gennep, Arnold van. *The Rites of Passage*. Translated by Monika B. Vizedom and Gabrielle L. Caffee. Chicago: University of Chicago Press, 1960.

Gericke, Jaco. "The Epistemology of Israelite Religion: Introductory Proposals for a Descriptive Approach." *OTE* 24 (2011): 49–73.

Gerstenberger, Erhard S. "Der Psalter als Buch und als Sammlung." In *Neue Wege der Psalmenforschung: Für Walter Beyerlin*, eds. Klaus Seybold und Erich Zenger, 3–13. Herders Biblische Studien 1. Freiburg: Herder, 1994.

——. "Theologies in the Book of Psalms." In *The Book of Psalms: Composition and Reception*, ed. Peter W. Flint and Patrick D. Miller, 603–25. VTSup 99. Leiden: Brill, 2005.

——. "Die 'Kleine Biblia': Theologien im Psalter." In *The Composition of the Book of Psalms*, ed. Erich Zenger, 391–97. BETL 238. Leuven: Uitgeverij Peeters, 2010.

——. "Modes of Communication with the Divine in the Hebrew Psalter." In *Mediating Between Heaven and Earth: Communication with the Divine in the Ancient Near East*, eds. C. L. Crouch, Jonathan Stökl, Anna Elise Zernecke, 93–113. LHB/OTS 566. London: T&T Clark, 2012.

Gettier, Edmund. "Is Justified True Belief Knowledge?" *Analysis* 23 (1963): 121–23.

Gibbs, Raymond W., Jr. *The Poetics of Mind: Figurative Thought, language, and Understanding*. Cambridge: Cambridge University Press, 1994.

——. "Taking Metaphor Out of Our Heads and Putting It Into the Cultural World." In *Metaphor in Cognitive Linguistics*, eds. Raymond W. Gibbs, Jr. and Gerard J. Steen, 145–66. Amsterdam Studies in the Theory and History of Linguistic Science 175. Amsterdam: John Benjamins, 1999.

——, ed. *The Cambridge Handbook of Metaphor and Thought*. Cambridge: Cambridge University Press, 2008.

Gibbs, Raymond W., Jr., and Gerard J. Steen, eds. *Metaphor in Cognitive Linguistics: Selected Papers from the Fifth International Cognitive Linguistics Conference*. Amsterdam Studies in the Theory and History of Linguistic Science 175. Amsterdam: John Benjamins, 1999.

Gibbs, Raymond W., Jr., and Julia E. Lonergan. "Studying Metaphor in Discourse: Some Lessons, Challenges, and New Data." In *Metaphor and Discourse*, eds. Andreas Musolff and Jörg Zinken, 251–61. Basingstoke: Palgrave MacMillan, 2009.

Gilbert, Margaret. "Modelling Collective Belief." *Synthese* 73 (1987): 185–204.

Gilbert, Maurice. *Les cinq livres des Sages: Proverbes, Job, Qohélet, Ben Sira, Sagesse*. Lire la Bible 129. Paris: Cerf, 2003.

Gillingham, Susan E. *The Poems and Psalms of the Hebrew Bible*. Oxford: Oxford University Press, 1994.

——. "The Zion Tradition and the Editing of the Hebrew Psalter." In *Temple and Worship in Biblical Israel*, ed. John Day, 308–41. Library of Hebrew Bible/Old Testament Studies (formerly JSOTSup) 422. London: T&T Clark, 2005.

——. "Studies of the Psalms: Retrospect and Prospect." *ExpTim* 119 (2008): 209–16.

——. "The Levitical Singers and the Editing of the Hebrew Psalter." In *The Composition of the Book of Psalms*, ed. Erich Zenger, 91–123. BETL 238. Leuven: Uitgeverij Peeters, 2010.

——. "Entering and Leaving the Psalter: Psalms 1 and 150 and the Two Polarities of Faith." In *Let Us Go Up to Zion: Essays in Honour of H. G. M. Williamson on the Occasion of his Sixty-Fifth Birthday*, eds. Iain Provan and Mark J. Boda, 383–93. Leiden: Brill, 2012.

Gillingham, S. E., ed. *Jewish and Christian Approaches to the Psalms: Conflict and Convergence*. Oxford: Oxford University Press, 2013.

Glucksberg, Sam, with a contribution by Matthew S. McGlone. *Understanding Figurative Language: From Metaphors to Idioms*. Oxford Psychology Series 36. Oxford: Oxford University Press, 2001.

Glucksberg, Sam. "How Metaphors Create Categories – Quickly." In *The Cambridge Handbook of Metaphor and Thought*, ed. Raymond W. Gibbs, Jr., 67–83. Cambridge: Cambridge University Press, 2008.

Goldman, Alvin I. "Foundations of Social Epistemics." *Synthese* 73 (1987): 109–44.

——. "Experts: Which Ones Should You Trust?" *Philosophy and Phenomenological Research* 63 (2001): 85–110.

——. "Group Knowledge Versus Group Rationality: Two Approaches to Social Epistemology." *Episteme: A Journal of Social Epistemology* 1 (2004): 11–22.

——. "Social Epistemology." In *The Stanford Encyclopedia of Philosophy (Spring 2007 Edition)* [database online; article at <http://plato.stanford.edu/archives/spr2007/entries/epistemology-social/> SEP; ed. Edward N. Zalta; Stanford: Stanford University; accessed June 23, 2008].

Goulder. Michael D. *The Psalms of the Sons of Korah*. JSOTSup 20. Sheffield: Sheffield Academic Press, 1982.

——. *The Prayers of David (Psalms 51–72). Studies in the Psalter, II*. JSOTSup 102. Sheffield: Sheffield Academic Press, 1990.

——. *The Psalms of Asaph and the Pentateuch. Studies in the Psalter, III*. JSOTSup 233. Sheffield: Sheffield Academic Press, 1996.

——. *The Psalms of the Return (Book V, Psalms 107–150). Studies in the Psalter, IV*. JSOTSup 258. Sheffield: Sheffield Academic Press, 1998.

——. "The Social Setting of Book II of the Psalter." In *The Book of Psalms: Composition and Reception*, ed. Peter W. Flint and Patrick D. Miller, 349–67. VTSup 99. Leiden: Brill, 2005.

Grady, Joseph E. "A Typology of Motivation for Conceptual Metaphor: Correlation vs. Resemblance." In *Metaphor in Cognitive Linguistics*, eds. Raymond W. Gibbs, Jr. and Gerard J. Steen, 79–100. Amsterdam Studies in the Theory and History of Linguistic Science 175. Amsterdam: John Benjamins, 1999.

Grady, Joseph E., Todd Oakley, and Seana Coulson. "Blending and Metaphor." In *Metaphor in Cognitive Linguistics: Selected Papers from the Fifth International Cognitive Linguistics Conference*, eds. R. W. Gibbs, Jr. and G. J. Steen, 101–24. Amsterdam Studies in the Theory and History of Linguistic Science 175. Amsterdam: John Benjamins, 1999.

Grant, Jamie A. *The King as Exemplar: The Function of Deuteronomy's Kingship Law in the Shaping of the Book of Psalms*. SBL Academia Biblica 17. Atlanta: Society of Biblical Literature, 2004.

Gray, Alison Ruth. *Psalm 18 in Words and Pictures: A Reading Through Metaphor*. BIS 127. Leiden: Brill, 2014.

Griffiths, Paul J. "How Epistemology Matters to Theology." *JR* 79 (1999): 1–18.

Groenewald, Alphonso. "The Ethical 'Way' of Psalm 16." In *The Composition of the Book of Psalms*, ed. Erich Zenger, 501–11. BETL 238. Leuven: Uitgeverij Peeters, 2010.

Grohmann, Marianne. "Metaphors of God, Nature and Birth in Psalm 90,2 and Psalm 110,3." In *Metaphors in the Psalms*, eds. Pierre van Hecke, and Antje Labahn, 23–33. BETL 231. Leuven: Uitgeverij Peeters, 2010.

——. "The Imagery of the 'Weaned Child' in Psalm 131." In *The Composition of the Book of Psalms*, ed. Erich Zenger, 513–22. BETL 238. Leuven: Uitgeverij Peeters, 2010.

Grund, Alexandra. *"Die Himmel erzählen die Herrlichkeit Gottes": Psalm 19 im Kontext der nachexilischen Toraweisheit*. WMANT 103. Neukirchen-Vluyn: Neukirchener Verlag, 2004.

Gunton, Colin E. *The Actuality of Atonement: A Study of Metaphor, Rationality and the Christian Tradition*. Edinburgh: T&T Clark, 1988.

Habel, Norman C. "The Symbolism of Wisdom in Proverbs 1–9." *Int* 26 (1972): 131–57.

Hamlyn, D. W. "Empiricism." In *Encyclopedia of Philosophy*, 2nd ed., ed. Donald M. Borchert, 3. 213–21. New York: Thomson Gale, 2006.

——. "Epistemology, History of." In *Encyclopedia of Philosophy*, 2nd ed., ed. Donald M. Borchert, 3. 281–319. New York: Thomson Gale, 2006.

Hasker, William. "Epistemology, Religious." In *Encyclopedia of Philosophy*, 2nd ed., ed. Donald M. Borchert, 3. 320–23. New York: Thomson Gale, 2006.

Hayes, Elizabeth. "Where is the Lord? The Extended great Chain of Being as a Source Domain for Conceptual Metaphor in the Egyptian Hallel, Psalms 113—118." In *Metaphors in the Psalms*, eds. Pierre van Hecke, and Antje Labahn, 55–69. BETL 231. Leuven: Uitgeverij Peeters, 2010.

Healy, Mary, and Robin Parry, eds. *The Bible and Epistemology: Biblical Soundings on the Knowledge of God*. Milton Keynes, UK: Paternoster, 2007.

Heß, Ruth and Martin Leiner, eds. *Alles in allem: eschatologische Anstösse: J. Christine Janowski zum 60. Geburtstag*. Neukirchen-Vluyn: Neukirchener Verlag, 2005.

Höffken, Peter. "Das Ego des Weisen." *TZ* 4 (1985): 121–34.

Høgenhaven, Jesper. "The Opening of the Psalter: A Study in Jewish Theology." *JSOT* 15 (2001): 169–80.

Holladay, William L. *The Root SUBH in the Old Testament: With Particular Reference to its Usage in Covenantal Contexts*. Leiden: Brill, 1958.

Hossfeld, Frank-Lothar. "Die Metaphorisierung der Beziehung Israels zum Land im Frühjudentum und im Christentum." In *Zion: Ort der Begegnung: Festschrift für Laurentius Klein zur Vollendung des 65. Lebensjahres*, eds. Ferdinand Hahn, Frank-Lothar Hossfeld, Hans Jorissen, and Angelika Neuwirth, 19–33. BBB 90. Bodenheim, Athenäum, 1993.

——. "Die unterschiedlichen Profile der beiden Davidsammlungen: Ps 3—41 und Ps 51—72." In *Der Psalter in Judentum und Christentum*, eds. Hans-Josef Klauck and Erich Zenger, 59–73. Herders Biblische Studien 18. Freiburg: Herder, 1998.

——. "Der Elohistische Psalter Ps 42—83: Entstehung und Programm." In *The Composition of the Book of Psalms*, ed. Erich Zenger, 199–213. BETL 238. Leuven: Uitgeverij Peeters, 2010.

Hossfeld, Frank-Lothar, and Till Magnus Steiner. "Problems and Prospects in Psalter Studies." In *Jewish and Christian Approaches to the Psalms: Conflict and Convergence*, ed. Susan Gillingham, 240–58. Oxford: Oxford University Press, 2013.

Hossfeld, Frank-Lothar, and Erich Zenger. "Neue und Alte Wege der Psalmenexegese: Antworten auf die Fragen von M. Millard und R. Rendtorff." *Biblical Interpretation* 4 (1996): 332–43.

Howard, David M., Jr. *The Structure of Psalms 93–100*. Biblical and Judaic Studies 5. Winona Lake, IN: Eisenbrauns, 1997.

——. "Recent Trends in Psalms Study." In *The Face of Old Testament Studies: A Survey of Contemporary Approaches*, eds. David W. Baker and Bill T. Arnold, 329–68. Grand Rapids: Baker Academic, 1999.

——. "The Proto-MT Psalter, the King, and Psalms 1 and 2: A Response to Klaus Seybold." In *Jewish and Christian Approaches to the Psalms: Conflict and Convergence*, ed. Susan Gillingham, 182–89. Oxford: Oxford University Press, 2013.

Hunter, Alastair G. *Psalms*. London: Routledge, 1999.

Hurvitz, Avi. "Wisdom Vocabulary in the Hebrew Psalter: A Contribution to the Study of 'Wisdom Psalms.'" *VT* 38 (1988): 41–51.

Irsigler, Hubert. *Psalm 73 – Monolog eines Weisen: Text, Programm, Struktur*. ATSAT 20. St. Ottilien: EOS, 1984.

——. "Die Suche nach Gerechtigkeit in den Psalmen 37, 49, und 73." In *Vom Adamssohn zum Immanuel: Gastvorträge Pretoria 1996*, 71–100. ATSAT 58. St. Ottilien: EOS, 1997.

——. "Psalm 90: Der vergängliche Mensch vor dem ewigen Gott." In *Vom Adamssohn zum Immanuel: Gastvorträge Pretoria 1996*, 49–69. ATSAT 58. St. Ottilien: EOS, 1997.

Jackendorff, Ray, and David Aaron. Review of *More Than Cool Reason*, by George Lakoff and Mark Turner. *Language* 67 (1991): 320–38.

Jacobson, Rolf A. "'The Faithfulness of the Lord Endures Forever': The Theological Witness of the Psalter." In *Soundings in the Theology of Psalms: Perspectives and Methods in Contemporary Scholarship*, ed. Rolf A. Jacobson, 111–38. Minneapolis: Fortress, 2011.

Jacobson, Rolf A., ed. *Soundings in the Theology of Psalms: Perspectives and Methods in Contemporary Scholarship*. Minneapolis: Fortress, 2011.

Janowski, Bernd. *Konfliktgespräche mit Gott: Eine Anthropologie der Psalmen*. Neukirchen-Vluyn: Neukirchener Verlag, 2003.

——. "Das Licht des Lebens: Zur Lichtmetaphorik in den Psalmen." In *Metaphors in the Psalms*, eds. Pierre van Hecke, and Antje Labahn, 87–113. BETL 231. Leuven: Uitgeverij Peeters, 2010.

——. "Ein Tempel aus Worten: Zur Theologischen Architektur des Psalters." In *The Composition of the Book of Psalms*, ed. Erich Zenger, 279–306. BETL 238. Leuven: Uitgeverij Peeters, 2010.

Janowski, Bernd, and Kathrin Liess. "Gerechtigkeit und Unsterblichkeit. Psalm 73 und die Frage nach dem 'ewigen Leben'." In *Alles in allem: eschatologische Anstösse: J. Christine zum 60. Geburtstag*, eds. Ruth Heß and Martin Leiner, 69–92. Neukirchen-Vluyn: Neukirchener Verlag, 2005.

Jarick, John. "The Four Corners of Psalm 107." *CBQ* 59 (1997): 270–87.

Jellicoe, Sidney. "The Interpretation of Psalm lxxiii. 24." *ExpTim* 67 (1956): 209–10.

Jens, Walter. "Psalm 90 on Transience." *LQ* 9 (1995): 177–89.

Jeppesen, Knud. "The Psalter in the Canon." *Hervormde Teologiese Studies* 59 (2003): 793–810.

Jindo, Job Y. *Biblical Metaphor Reconsidered: A Cognitive Approach to Poetic Prophecy in Jeremiah 1—24*. HSM 64. Winona Lake, IN: Eisenbrauns, 2010.

Jones, Scott C. "Wisdom's Pedagogy: A Comparison of Proverbs VII and 4Q184." *VT* 53 (2003): 65–80.

Kalimi, Isaac, ed. *Jewish Bible Theology: Perspectives and Case Studies*. Winona Lake, IN: Eisenbrauns, 2013.

Kaltner, John, and Louis Stulman, eds. *Inspired Speech: Prophecy in the Ancient Near East. Essays in Honour of Herbert B. Huffman*. JSOTSup 378. London: T&T Clark, 2004.

Kearney, Michael. *World View*. Novato, CA: Chandler & Sharp, 1984.

——. "World View." In *Encyclopedia of Cultural Anthropology*, 4. 1380–83. New York: Henry Holt, 1996.

Keefe, Rosanna. *Theories of Vagueness*. Cambridge: Cambridge University Press, 2000.

Kellenberger, James. *The Cognitivity of Religion: Three Perspectives*. Berkeley and Los Angeles: University of California Press, 1985.

——. "Wittgenstein's Gift to Contemporary Analytic Philosophy of Religion." *Philosophy of Religion* 28 (1990): 147–72.

——. "The Fool of the Psalms and Religious Epistemology." *International Journal for Philosophy of Religion* 45 (1999): 99–113.

Kelly, Brian E. "David's Disqualification in 1 Chronicles 22:8: A Response to Piet B. Dirksen." *JSOT* 80 (1998): 53–61.

Kimelman, Reuven. "Psalm 145: Theme, Structure, and Impact." *JBL* 113 (1994): 37–58.

King, Philip D. *Surrounded by Bitterness: Image Schemas and Metaphors for Conceptualizing Distress in Classical Hebrew*. Eugene, OR: Pickwick, 2012.

Klein, Anja. "Half Way between Psalm 119 and Ben Sira: Wisdom and Torah in Psalm 19." In *Wisdom and Torah: The Reception of 'Torah' in the Wisdom Literature of the Second Temple Period*, eds. Bernd U. Schipper, and D. Andrew Teeter, 137–55. JSJSup 163. Leiden: Brill, 2013.

Klein, Christian. *Kohelet und die Weisheit Israels: Eine Formgeschichtliche Studie*. BWANT 132. Stuttgart: Kohlhammer, 1994.

Klein, Ralph W. *Textual Criticism of the Old Testament: From the Septuagint to Qumran*. Philadelphia: Fortress, 1974.

——. "David: Sinner and Saint in Samuel and Chronicles." *Currents in Theology and Mission* 26 (1999): 104–16.

Klingbeil, Martin. "Metaphors that Travel and (Almost) Vanish: Mapping Diachronic Changes in the Intertextual Usage of the Heavenly Warrior Metaphor in Psalms 18 and 144." In *Metaphors in the Psalms*, eds. Pierre van Hecke, and Antje Labahn, 115–34. BETL 231. Leuven: Uitgeverij Peeters, 2010.

Knoppers, Gary K. "Images of David in Early Judaism: David as Repentant Sinner in Chronicles." *Bib* 76 (1995): 449–70.

Koenen, Klaus. *Jahwe wird kommen, zu herrschen über die Erde: Ps 90–110 als Komposition.* BBB 101. Weinheim: Beltz Athenäum Verlag, 1995.

Koh, Yee Von. "G. H. Wilson's Theories on the Organization of the Masoretic Psalter." In *Genesis, Isaiah and Psalms: A Festschrift to Honour Professor John Emerton for his Eightieth Birthday*, eds. Katharine J. Dell, Graham Davies, and Yee Von Koh, 177–92. VTSup 135. Leiden/Boston: Brill, 2010.

Kornblith, Hilary, ed. *Epistemology: Internalism and Externalism.* Oxford: Blackwell, 2001.

Kövecses, Zoltán. "Metaphor: Does It Constitute or Reflect Cultural Models?" In *Metaphor in Cognitive Linguistics*, eds. Raymond W. Gibbs, Jr. and Gerard J. Steen, 167–88. Amsterdam Studies in the Theory and History of Linguistic Science 175. Amsterdam: John Benjamins, 1999.

——. *Metaphor in Culture: Universality and Variation.* Cambridge: Cambridge University Press, 2005.

——. *Language, Mind, and Culture: A Practical Introduction.* Oxford: Oxford University Press, 2006.

——. "Conceptual Metaphor Theory: Some Criticisms and Alternative Proposals." Annual Review of Cognitive Linguistics 6 (2008): 168-84.

——. "Metaphor, Culture, and Discourse: The Pressure of Coherence." In *Metaphor and Discourse*, eds. Andreas Musolff and Jörg Zinken, 11–24. Basingstoke: Palgrave MacMillan, 2009.

——. *Metaphor: A Practical Introduction.* 2nd ed. New York: Oxford University Press, 2010, Nook.

Kratz, Reinhard Gregor. "Die Tora Davids : Psalm 1 und die Doxologische Fünfteilung des Psalters." *ZTK* 93 (1996): 1–34.

——. "Das Sch°ma° des Psalters: Die Botschaft vom Reich Gottes nach Psalm 145." In *Gott und Mensch im Dialog: Festschrift für Otto Kaiser zum 80. Geburtstag*, ed. Markus Witte, 623–38. BZAW 345/II. Berlin: de Gruyter, 2004.

——. "'Blessed Be the Lord and Blessed Be His Name Forever': Psalm 145 in the Hebrew Bible and in the Psalms Scroll 11Q5." In *Prayer and Poetry in the Dead Sea Scrolls and Related Literature: Essays in Honor of Eileen Schuller on the Occasion of Her 65th Birthday*, eds. Jeremy Penner, Ken M. Penner, and Cecilia Wassen, 229–43. STDJ 98. Leiden: Brill, 2012.

Krüger, Thomas. "Psalm 90 und die 'Vergänglichkeit des Menschen.'" *Bib* 75 (1994): 191–219.

Kselman, John S., S.S. "Psalm 146 in Its Context." *CBQ* 50 (1988): 587–99.

——. "Psalm 36." In *Wisdom, You Are My Sister: Studies in Honor of Roland E. Murphy, O. Carm., on the Occasion of His Eightieth Birthday*, ed. Michael L. Barré, 3–17. CBQMS 29. Washington: Catholic Biblical Association of America, 1997.

Kuntz, J. Kenneth. "The Canonical Wisdom Psalms of Ancient Israel – Their Rhetorical, Thematic, and Formal Dimensions." In *Rhetorical Criticism: Essays in Honor of James Muilenburg*, ed. Jared J. Jackson and Martin Kessler, 186–222. PTMS 1. Pittsburgh: Pickwick, 1974.

——. "Engaging the Psalms: Gains and Trends in Recent Research." *Currents in Research: Biblical Studies* 2 (1994): 77–106.

——. "Biblical Hebrew Poetry in Recent Research, Part I." *Currents in Research: Biblical Studies* 6 (1998): 31–64.

——. "Biblical Hebrew Poetry in Recent Research, Part II." *Currents in Research: Biblical Studies* 7 (1999): 35–79.

——. "Wisdom Psalms and the Shaping of the Hebrew Psalter." In *For a Later Generation: The Transformation of Tradition in Israel, Early Judaism, and Early Christianity*, eds. Randal A. Argall, B. A. Bow, and R. A. Werline, 144–60. Harrisburg, PA: Trinity Press International, 2000.

——. "Reclaiming Biblical Wisdom Psalms: A Response to Crenshaw." *Currents in Biblical Research* 1 (2003): 145–54.

Lack, Rémi. "Le psaume 1 – Une analyse structurale." *Bib* 57 (1976): 154–67.

Lakoff, George. "The Embodied Mind, and How to Live with One." In *The Nature and Limits of Human Understanding: The 2001 Gifford Lectures at the University of Glasgow*, ed. Anthony Sanford, 47–108. London: T&T Clark, 2003.

——. "The Neural Theory of Metaphor." In *The Cambridge Handbook of Metaphor and Thought*, ed. Raymond W. Gibbs, Jr., 17–38. Cambridge: Cambridge University Press, 2008.

Lakoff, George, and Mark Johnson. *Metaphors We Live By*. Chicago: University of Chicago Press, 1980.

——. *Philosophy in the Flesh: The Embodied Mind and Its Challenge to Western Thought*. New York: Basic Books, 1999.

Lakoff, George, and Mark Turner. *More Than Cool Reason: A Field Guide to Poetic Metaphor*. Chicago: University of Chicago Press, 1989.

Lambert. W. G. "Some New Babylonian Wisdom Literature." In *Wisdom in Ancient Israel*, eds. John Day, Robert P. Gordon, and H. G. M. Williamson, 30–42. Cambridge: Cambridge University Press, 1995.

Lasine, Stuart. *Knowing Kings: Knowledge, Power, and Narcissism in the Hebrew Bible*. SBLSS 40. Atlanta: Society of Biblical Literature, 2001.

Lehrer, Keith. "Personal and Social Knowledge." *Synthese* 73 (1987): 87–107.

Lemaire, André. "The Sage in School and Temple." In *The Sage in Israel and the Ancient Near East*, eds. John G. Gammie and Leo G. Perdue, 165–81. Winona Lake, IN: Eisenbrauns, 1990.

Lemke, Warner E. "The Synoptic Problem in the Chronicler's History." *HTR* 58 (1965): 349–63.

Lemos, Noah. *An Introduction to the Theory of Knowledge*. Cambridge: Cambridge Univeristy Press, 2007.

Leuenberger, Martin. *Konzeptionen des Königtums Gottes im Psalter. Untersuchungen zu Komposition und Redaktion der theokratischen Bücher IV-V innerhalb des Psalters*. ATANT 83. Zürich: Theologischer Verlag, 2004.

Lichtheim, Miriam. *Late Egyptian Wisdom Literature in the International Context: A Study of Demotic Instructions*. OBO 52. Göttingen: Vandenhoeck & Ruprecht, 1983.

Liess, Kathrin. "Von der Gottesferne zur Gottesnahe: Zur Todes-und-Lebensmetaphorik in den Psalmen." In *Metaphors in the Psalms*, eds. Pierre van Hecke, and Antje Labahn, 167–95. BETL 231. Leuven: Uitgeverij Peeters, 2010.

Lioy, Dan. "Teach Us to Number Our Days: An Exegetical and Theological Analysis of Psalm 90." *Conspectus* 5 (2008): 89–102.

Lipinski, E. "Macarismes et psaumes de congratulation." *RB* 75 (1968): 321–67.

Liu, Dilin. *Metaphor, Culture, and Worldview: The Case of American English and the Chinese Language.* Lanham, MD: University Press of America, 2002.

Lohfink, Norbert. "Ist Kohelets הבל-Aussage Erkenntnistheoretisch Gemeint?" In *Qohelet in the Context of Wisdom*, ed. A. Schoors, 41–59. BETL 136. Leuven: Leuven University Press, 1998.

Lohfink, Norbert, and Erich Zenger. "Das Weltenkönigtum des Gottes Israels (Ps 90–106)." In *Der Gott Israels und die Völker: Untersuchungen zum Jesajabuch und zu den Psalmen*, 151–78. SBS 154. Stuttgart: Verlag Katholisches Bibelwerk, 1994.

Luyten, Jos. "Psalm 73 and Wisdom." In *La Sagesse de l'Ancien Testament*. Nouvelle édition mise à jour, ed. Maurice Gilbert, 59–81. BETL 51. Leuven: Leuven University Press, 1990.

MacCormac, Earl R. *Metaphor and Myth in Science and Religion.* Durham, NC: Duke University Press, 1976.

——. *A Cognitive Theory of Metaphor.* Cambridge, MA: MIT Press, 1985.

Machinist, Peter. "Fate, *miqreh*, and Reason: Some Reflections on Qohelet and Biblical Thought." In *Solving Riddles and Untying Knots: Biblical, Epigraphic, and Semitic Studies in Honor of Jonas C. Greenfield*, eds. Z. Zevit, S. Gitin, and M. Sokoloff, 159–75. Winona Lake, IN: Eisenbrauns, 1995.

Macintosh, Alexander A. "The Spider in the Septuagint Version of Psalm XC.9." *JTS* 23 (1972): 113–17.

Macleod, Donald. "Faith Beyond the Forms of Faith: An Exposition of Psalm 73." *Int* 12 (1958): 418–21.

Mannati, Marina. "Sur le quadruple *avec toi* de Ps. LXXIII 21–26." *VT* 21 (1971): 59–67.

——. "Les adorateurs de Môt dans le Psaume LXXIII." *VT* 22 (1972): 420–25.

Markie, Peter. "Rationalism vs. Empiricism." in *The Stanford Encyclopedia of Philosophy (Fall 2004 Edition)* [database online; article at <http://plato.stanford.edu/archives/fall2004/entries/rationalism-empiricism/> SEP; ed. Edward N. Zalta; Stanford: Stanford University; accessed June 2, 2008].

Martens, Elmer A. "Psalm 73: A Corrective to a Modern Misunderstanding." *Direction* 12 (1983): 15–26.

Martin, Francis. "The Word at Prayer: Epistemology in the Psalms." In *The Bible and Epistemology: Biblical Soundings on the Knowledge of God*, eds. Mary Healy and Robin Parry, 43–64. Milton Keynes, UK: Paternoster, 2007.

Martin, Lee Roy. "Delighting in the Torah: The Affective Dimension of Psalm 1." *OTE* 23 (2010): 708–27.

Marttila, Marko. *Collective Reinterpretation in the Psalms: A Study of the Redaction History of the Psalter.* FAT 2.13. Tübingen: Mohr, 2006.

——. "The Deuteronomic Heritage in the Psalms." *JSOT* 37 (2012): 67–91.

Mathiesen, Kay. "The Epistemic Features of Group Belief." *Episteme* 2 (2006): 161–75.

Matthews, Victor H., and Don C. Benjamin. *Old Testament Parallels: Laws and Stories from the Ancient Near East.* 3rd rev. ed. New York: Paulist, 2006.

Mays, James Luther. "The Place of the Torah-Psalms in the Psalter." *JBL* 106 (1987): 3–12.

McCann, J. Clinton. "Psalm 73: A Microcosm of Old Testament Theology." In *The Listening Heart: Essays in Wisdom and the Psalms in Honor of Roland E. Murphy, O. Carm.*, eds. Kenneth G. Hoglund, E. F. Huwiler, J. T. Glass, and R. W. Lee, 247–57. JSOTSup 58. Sheffield: JSOT Press, 1987.

——. "The Psalms as Instruction." *Int* 46 (1992): 117–28.

——. "Books I–III and the Editorial Purpose of the Hebrew Psalter." In *The Shape and Shaping of the Psalter*, ed. J. Clinton McCann, 93–107. JSOTSup 159. Sheffield: JSOT Press, 1993.

——. "Wisdom's Dilemma: The Book of Job, the Final Form of the Book of Psalms, and the Entire Bible." In *Wisdom, You Are My Sister: Studies in Honor of Roland E. Murphy, O. Carm., on the Occasion of His Eightieth Birthday*, ed. Michael L. Barré, 18–30. CBQMS 29. Washington: Catholic Biblical Association of America, 1997.

——. "The Shape of Book I of the Psalter and the Shape of Human Happiness." In *The Book of Psalms: Composition and Reception*, ed. Peter W. Flint and Patrick D. Miller, 340–48. VTSup 99. Leiden: Brill, 2005.

——. "The Single Most Important text in the Entire Bible: Toward a Theology of the Psalms." In *Soundings in the Theology of Psalms: Perspectives and Methods in Contemporary Scholarship*, ed. Rolf A. Jacobson, 63–75. Minneapolis: Fortress, 2011.

McCann, J. Clinton, ed. *The Shape and Shaping of the Psalter*. JSOTSup 159. Sheffield: JSOT Press, 1993.

McFague, Sallie. *Metaphorical Theology: Models of God in Religious Language*. Philadelphia: Fortress, 1982.

McGlone, Matthew S. "Concepts as Metaphors." In *Understanding Figurative Language: From Metaphors to Idioms*, ed. Sam Glucksberg, 90–107. Oxford Psychology Series 36. Oxford: Oxford University Press, 2001.

——. "What is the Explanatory Value of a Conceptual Metaphor?" *Language & Communication* 27 (2007): 109–26.

Mejía, Jorge. "Some Observations on Psalm 107." *BTB* 5 (1975): 56–66.

Merendino, Rosario Pius. "Sprachkunst in Psalm I." *VT* 29 (1979): 45–60.

Michel, Diethelm. "Ich aber bin immer bei dir: Von der Unsterblichkeit der Gottesbeziehung." In *Im Angesicht des Todes: Ein interdisziplinäres Kompendium*. 2 vols., eds. H. Becker, B. Einig, and P.-O. Ullrich, 1. 637–58. Pietas Liturgica 3. St. Ottilien: EOS, 1987.

Mihaila, Corin. "The Theological and Canonical Place of Psalm 73." *Faith and Mission* 18 (2001): 52–59.

Millard, Matthias. *Die Komposition des Psalters: Ein Formgeschichtlicher Ansatz*. FAT 9. Tübingen: Mohr, 1994.

——. "Von der Psalmenexegese zur Psalterexegese: Anmerkungen zum Neuansatz von Frank-Lothar Hossfeld und Erich Zenger." *Biblical Interpretation* 4 (1996): 311–28.

——. "Zum Problem des elohistischen Psalters: Überlegungen zum Gebrauch von יהוה und אלהים im Psalter." In *Der Psalter in Judentum und Christentum*, eds. Hans-Josef Klauck and Erich Zenger, 75–100. Herders Biblische Studien 18. Freiburg: Herder, 1998.

Miller, Patrick, D. Review of *Werden und Wesen des 107. Psalms*. BZAW 153, by W. Beyerlin. *VT* 32 (1982): 253–56.

——. "The Beginning of the Psalter." In *The Shape and Shaping of the Psalter*, ed. J. Clinton McCann, 83–92. JSOTSup 159. Sheffield: JSOT Press, 1993.

——. "Kingship, Torah Obedience, and Prayer: The Theology of Psalms 15–24." In *Neue Wege der Psalmenforschung: Für Walter Beyerlin*, eds. Klaus Seybold and Erich Zenger, 127–42. Herders Biblische Studien 1. Freiburg: Herder, 1994.

——. "The End of the Psalter: A Response to Erich Zenger." *JSOT* 80 (1998): 103–10.

——. "Deuteronomy and Psalms: Evoking a Biblical Conversation." *JBL* 118 (1999): 3–18.

Miller, Robert D. "The Origin of the Zion Hymns." In *The Composition of the Book of Psalms*, ed. Erich Zenger, 667–75. BETL 238. Leuven: Uitgeverij Peeters, 2010.

Mitchell, David C. "Lord, Remember David: G. H. Wilson and the Message of the Psalter." *VT* 56 (2006): 526–48.

Morgan, Donn F. *The Making of Sages: Biblical Wisdom and Contemporary Culture.* Harrisburg, PA: Trinity Press International, 2002.

Moser, Paul K., ed. *The Oxford Handbook of Epistemology.* Oxford: Oxford University Press, 2002.

——. "Propositional Knowledge, Definition of." In *Encyclopedia of Philosophy*, 2nd ed., ed. Donald M. Borchert, 8. 86–88. New York: Thomson Gale, 2006.

——. *The Elusive God: Reorienting Religious Epistemology.* Cambridge: Cambridge University Press, 2008.

Mowinckel, Sigmund. "Psalms and Wisdom." In *Wisdom in Israel and in the Ancient Near East. Presented to Professor Harold Henry Rowley by the Society for Old Testament Study in Association with the Editorial Board of Vetus Testamentum in Celebration of His Sixty-Fifth Birthday, 24 March 1955*, ed. M. Noth and D. Winton Thomas, 205–24. VTSup 3. Leiden: Brill, 1955.

——. *The Psalms in Israel's Worship.* 2 vols. Translated by D. R. Ap-Thomas. 1962. Reprint, Biblical Resource Series. Grand Rapids: Eerdmans, 2004.

Müller, Hans-Peter. "Der 90. Psalm: Ein Paradigma exegetischer Aufgaben." *ZTK* 81 (1984): 265–85.

Murphy, Roland E. "A Consideration of the Classification 'Wisdom Psalms.'" In *Congress Volume: Bonn 1962*, ed. J. A. Emerton, 156–67. VTSup 9. Leiden: Brill, 1963.

——. "Assumptions and Problems in Old Testament Wisdom Research." *CBQ* 29 (1967): 407–18.

——. "Qohelet's 'Quarrel' with the Fathers." In *From Faith to Faith: Essays in Honor of Donald G. Miller on his Seventieth Birthday*, ed. Dikran Y. Hadidian, 235–45. PTMS 31. Pittsburgh: Pickwick, 1979.

——. "The Personification of Wisdom." In *Wisdom in Ancient Israel*, eds. John Day, Robert P. Gordon, and H. G. M. Williamson, 222–33. Cambridge: Cambridge University Press, 1995.

Murphy, S. Jonathan. "Is the Psalter a Book with a Single Message?" *BSac* 165 (2008): 283–93.

Nasuti, Harry P. "The Interpretive Significance of Sequence and Selection in the Book of Psalms." In *The Book of Psalms: Composition and Reception*, ed. Peter W. Flint and Patrick D. Miller, 311–39. VTSup 99. Leiden: Brill, 2005.

——. "God at Work in the Word: A Theology of Divine-Human Encounter in the Psalms." In *Soundings in the Theology of Psalms: Perspectives and Methods in Contemporary Scholarship*, ed. Rolf A. Jacobson, 27–48. Minneapolis: Fortress, 2011.

Naugle, David K. *Worldview: The History of a Concept.* Grand Rapids: Eerdmans, 2002.

Nicolau, Olga. "'Ciertamente, es Bueno para Israel, Dios': Estudio del Sal 73 en su Contexto." *RevistB* 71 (2009): 133–47.

Niditch, Susan. *Oral World and Written Word: Ancient Israelite Literature*. Louisville: Westminster John Knox, 1996.

Nielsen, Eduard. "Psalm 73: Scandinavian Contributions." In *Understanding Poets and Prophets; Essays in Honour of George Wishart Anderson*, ed. A. Graeme Auld, 273–83. JSOTSup 152. Sheffield: JSOT Press, 1993.

Nielsen, Kirsten. *There is Hope for a Tree: The Tree as Metaphor in Isaiah*. JSOTSup 65. Sheffield: Sheffield Academic Press, 1985.

——. "Metaphors and Biblical Theology." In *Metaphor in the Hebrew Bible*, ed. P. Van Hecke, 263–73. BETL 187. Leuven: Leuven University Press, 2005.

——. "Metaphorical Language and Theophany in Psalm 18." In *Metaphors in the Psalms*, eds. Pierre van Hecke, and Antje Labahn, 197–207. BETL 231. Leuven: Uitgeverij Peeters, 2010.

Nogalski, James D. "From Psalm to Psalms to Psalter." In *Introduction to Wisdom Literature and the Psalms: Festschrift Martin E. Tate*, eds. H. Wayne Ballard, Jr. and W. Dennis Tucker, Jr., 37–54. Macon, GA: Mercer, 2000.

Nordin, John P. "'There is Nothing on Earth That I Desire': A Commentary on Psalm 73." *Currents in Theology and Mission* 29 (2002): 258–64.

Odell, Margaret S. "History or Metaphor: Contributions to Old Testament Theology in the Works of Leo G. Perdue." *RelSRev* 24 (1998): 241–45.

O'Dowd, Ryan P. "A Chord of Three Strands: Epistemology in Job, Proverbs and Ecclesiastes." In *The Bible and Epistemology: Biblical Soundings on the Knowledge of God*, eds. Mary Healy and Robin Parry, 65–87. Milton Keynes, UK: Paternoster, 2007.

——. "Memory on the Boundary: Epistemology in Deuteronomy." In *The Bible and Epistemology: Biblical Soundings on the Knowledge of God*, eds. Mary Healy and Robin Parry, 3–22. Milton Keynes, UK: Paternoster, 2007.

——. *The Wisdom of Torah: Epistemology in Deuteronomy and the Wisdom Literature*. FRLANT 225. Göttingen: Vandenhoeck & Ruprecht, 2009.

Ortony, Andrew. *Metaphor and Thought*. 2nd ed. Cambridge: Cambridge University Press, 1993.

Packer J. I., and Sven K. Soderlund, eds. *The Way of Wisdom: Essays in Honor of Bruce K. Waltke*. Grand Rapids, MI: Zondervan, 2000.

Patrick, Dale. "The Translation of Job XLII 6." *VT* 26 (1976): 369–71.

Penner, Jeremy, Ken M. Penner, and Cecilia Wassen, eds. *Prayer and Poetry in the Dead Sea Scrolls and Related Literature: Essays in Honor of Eileen Schuller on the Occasion of Her 65th Birthday*. STDJ 98. Leiden: Brill, 2012.

Pepper, Stephen C. *World Hypotheses: A Study in Evidence*. Berkeley: University of California Press, 1961.

Perdue, Leo G. *Wisdom and Cult: A Critical Analysis of the Views of Cult in the Wisdom Literatures of Israel and the Ancient Near East*. SBLDS 30. Missoula, MT: Scholars, 1977.

——. "Liminality as a Social Setting for Wisdom Instructions." *ZAW* 93 (1981): 114–26.

——. "Cosmology and the Social Order in the Wisdom Tradition." In *The Sage in Israel and the Ancient Near East*, eds. John G. Gammie and Leo G. Perdue, 457–78. Winona Lake, IN: Eisenbrauns, 1990.

——. *Wisdom in Revolt: Metaphorical Theology in the Book of Job*. JSOTSup 112. Bible and Literature Series 29. Sheffield: JSOT Press, 1991.

——. *Wisdom and Creation: The Theology of Wisdom Literature*. Nashville: Abingdon, 1994.

——. "Wisdom Theology and Social History in Proverbs 1–9." In *Wisdom, You Are My Sister: Studies in Honor of Roland E. Murphy, O. Carm., on the Occasion of His Eightieth Birthday*, ed. Michael L. Barré, 78–101. CBQMS 29. Washington: Catholic Biblical Association of America, 1997.

——. *Wisdom Literature: A Theological History.* Louisville/London: Westminster John Knox, 2007.

——. *The Sword and the Stylus: An Introduction to Wisdom in the Age of Empires.* Grand Rapids: Eerdmans, 2008.

Pettegrew, Larry D. "'Is There Knowledge in the Most High?' (Psalm 73:11)." *The Master's Seminary Journal* 12 (2001): 133–48.

Pettit, Philip. "Groups with Minds of Their Own." In *Socializing Metaphysics: The Nature of Social Reality*, ed. Frederick F. Schmitt, 167–93. Lanham, MD: Rowman & Littlefield, 2003.

——. "When to Defer to Majority Testimony – and When Not." *Analysis* 66 (2006): 179–87.

Phillips, W. Gary, William E. Brown, and John Stonestreet. *Making Sense of Your World: A Biblical Worldview.* 2nd ed. Salem, WI: Sheffield Publishing, 2008.

Provan, Iain, and Mark J. Boda, eds. *Let Us Go Up to Zion: Essays in Honour of H. G. M. Williamson on the Occasion of his Sixty-Fifth Birthday.* VTSup 153. Leiden: Brill, 2012.

Rabinowitz, Isaac. "The Existence of a Hitherto Unknown Interpretation of Psalm 107 Among the Dead Sea Scrolls." *BA* 14 (1951): 50–52.

Rad, Gerhard von. *Wisdom in Israel.* Translated by James D. Martin. Harrisburg, PA: Trinity Press International, 1972.

——. "Der 90. Psalm." In *Gottes Wirken in Israel: Vorträge zum Alten Testament*, 268–83. Neukirchen-Vluyn: Neukirchener Verlag, 1974.

Rae, Murray. "'Incline Your Ear So That You May Live:' Principles of Biblical Epistemology." In *The Bible and Epistemology: Biblical Soundings on the Knowledge of God*, eds. Mary Healy and Robin Parry, 161–80. Milton Keynes, UK: Paternoster, 2007.

Ray, J. D. "Egyptian Wisdom Literature." In *Wisdom in Ancient Israel*, eds. John Day, Robert P. Gordon, and H. G. M. Williamson, 17–29. Cambridge: Cambridge University Press, 1995.

Reif, Stefan C. "Ibn Ezra on Psalm I 1–2." *VT* 34 (1984): 232–36.

Reisenauer, A. M. "The Goodness of God in Psalm 73." *Anton* 86 (2011): 11–28.

Renaud, Bernard. "Le psaume 73, méditation individuelle ou prière collective?" *RHPR* 59 (1979): 541–50.

Rendtorff, Rolf. "Anfragen an Frank-Lothar Hossfeld und Erich Zenger: Aufgrund der Lektüre des Beitrages von Matthias Millard." *Biblical Interpretation* 4 (1996): 329–31.

——. "The Psalms of David: David in the Psalms." In *The Book of Psalms: Composition and Reception*, ed. Peter W. Flint and Patrick D. Miller, 53–64. VTSup 99. Leiden: Brill, 2005.

Reynolds, Kent Aaron. *Torah as Teacher: The Exemplary Torah Student in Psalm 119.* VTSup 137. Leiden: Brill, 2010.

Rice, Gene. "An Exposition of Psalm 73." *JRT* 41 (1984): 79–86.

Richards, I. A. *The Philosophy of Rhetoric.* New York: Oxford University Press, 1965.

Richardson, H. Neil. "Some Notes on ליץ and Its Derivatives." *VT* 5 (1955): 163–79.

Ringgren, Helmer. "Einige Bemerkungen zum LXXIII. Psalm." *VT* 3 (1953): 265–72.

Roberts, J. J. M. "Of Signs, Prophets, and Time Limits: A Note on Psalm 74:9." *CBQ* 39 (1977): 474–81.

Roffey, John W. "Beyond Reality: Poetic Discourse and Psalm 107." In *A Biblical Itinerary: In Search of Method, Form and Content. Essays in Honor of George W. Coats*, ed. Eugene E. Carpenter, 60–76. JSOTSup 240. Sheffield: Sheffield Academic Press, 1997.

Ross, James F. "Psalm 73." In *Israelite Wisdom: Theological and Literary Essays in Honor of Samuel Terrien*, eds. J. G. Gammie, W. A. Brueggemann, W. L. Humphreys, and J. M. Ward, 161–75. New York: Union Theological Seminary, 1978.

Rudman, Dominic. "The Anatomy of the Wise Man: Wisdom, Sorrow and Joy in the Book of Ecclesiastes." In *Qohelet in the Context of Wisdom*, ed. A. Schoors, 465–71. BETL 136. Leuven: Leuven University Press, 1998.

Sailhamer, John H. "A Wisdom Composition of the Pentateuch?" In *The Way of Wisdom: Essays in Honor of Bruce K. Waltke*, eds. J. I. Packer and Sven K. Soderlund, 15–35. Grand Rapids, MI: Zondervan, 2000.

Sanders, Paul. "Five Books of Psalms?" In *The Composition of the Book of Psalms*, ed. Erich Zenger, 677–87. BETL 238. Leuven: Uitgeverij Peeters, 2010.

Sanford, Anthony, ed. *The Nature and Limits of Human Understanding: The 2001 Gifford Lectures at the University of Glasgow*. London: T&T Clark, 2003.

Scaiola, Donatella. "The End of the Psalter." In *The Composition of the Book of Psalms*, ed. Erich Zenger, 701–10. BETL 238. Leuven: Uitgeverij Peeters, 2010.

Schindler, D. C. "Mystery and Mastery: Philosophical Reflections on Biblical Epistemology." In *The Bible and Epistemology: Biblical Soundings on the Knowledge of God*, eds. Mary Healy and Robin Parry, 181–98. Milton Keynes, UK: Paternoster, 2007.

Schipper, Bernd U. *Hermeneutik der Tora: Studien zur Traditionsgeschichte von Prov 2 und zur Komposition von Prov 1–9*. BZAW 432. Berlin: de Gruyter, 2012.

——. "Afterword: Wisdom and Torah: Insights and Perspectives." In *Wisdom and Torah: The Reception of 'Torah' in the Wisdom Literature of the Second Temple Period*, eds. Bernd U. Schipper, and D. Andrew Teeter, 307–19. JSJSup 163. Leiden: Brill, 2013.

——. "When Wisdom is Not Enough! The Discourse on Wisdom and Torah and the Composition of the Book of Proverbs." In *Wisdom and Torah: The Reception of 'Torah' in the Wisdom Literature of the Second Temple Period*, eds. Bernd U. Schipper, and D. Andrew Teeter, 55–79. JSJSup 163. Leiden: Brill, 2013.

Schipper, Bernd U., and D. Andrew Teeter, eds. *Wisdom and Torah: The Reception of 'Torah' in the Wisdom Literature of the Second Temple Period*. JSJSup 163. Leiden: Brill, 2013.

Schmid, Konrad. "The Canon and the Cult: The Emergence of Book Religion in Ancient Israel and the Gradual Sublimation of the Temple Cult." *JBL* 131 (2012): 289–305.

Schmitt, Frederick F. "Socializing Epistemology: An Introduction Through Two Sample Issues." In *Socializing Epistemology: The Social Dimensions of Knowledge*, ed. Frederick F. Schmitt, 1–27. Lanham, MD: Rowman & Littlefield, 1994.

——. "The Justification of Group Beliefs." In *Socializing Epistemology: The Social Dimensions of Knowledge*, ed. Frederick F. Schmitt, 257–87. Lanham, MD: Rowman & Littlefield, 1994.

Schmitt, Frederick F., ed. *Socializing Epistemology: The Social Dimensions of Knowledge*. Lanham, MD: Rowman & Littlefield, 1994.

Schmitt, Frederick F., ed. *Socializing Metaphysics: The Nature of Social Reality*. Lanham, MD: Rowman & Littlefield, 2003.

Schnocks, Johannes. "Ehe die Berge geboren wurden, bist du." *BK* 54 (1999): 163–69.

——. *Vergänglichkeit und Gottesherrschaft: Studien zu Psalm 90 und dem vierten Psalmenbuch*. BBB 140. Berlin/Vienna: Philo Verlagsgesellschaft, 2002.

——. "Mose im Psalter." In *Moses in Biblical and Extra-Biblical Traditions*, eds. Axel Graupner and Michael Wolter, 79–88. BZAW 372. Berlin: de Gruyter, 2007.

Schoors, A., ed. *Qohelet in the Context of Wisdom*. BETL 136. Leuven: Leuven University Press, 1998.

Schreiner, Stefan. "Erwägungen zur Struktur des 90. Psalms." *Bib* 59 (1978): 80–90.

Schwienhorst-Schönberger, Ludger. "'Bis ich eintrat in die Heiligtümer Gottes' (Ps 73,17): Ps 73 im Horizont biblischer und theologischer Hermeneutik." In *"Gerechtigkeit und Recht zu üben" (Gen 18,19): Studien zur altorientalischen und biblischen Rechtsgeschichte, zur Religionsgeschichte Israels und zur Religionssoziologie. Festschrift für Eckart Otto zum 65. Geburtstag*, eds. Reinhard Achenbach and Martin Arneth, 387–402. Beihefte zur Zeitschrift für Altorientalische und Biblische Rechtgeschichte 13. Wiesbaden: Harrassowitz, 2009.

Sciumbata, M. Patrizia. "Peculiarità e motivazioni della struttura lessicale dei verbi della 'conoscenza' in Qohelet." *Henoch* 18 (1996): 235–49.

Seow, C. L. "'Beyond Them, My Son, Be Warned': The Epilogue of Qohelet Revisited." In *Wisdom, You Are My Sister: Studies in Honor of Roland E. Murphy, O. Carm., on the Occasion of His Eightieth Birthday*, ed. Michael L. Barré, 125–41. CBQMS 29. Washington: Catholic Biblical Association of America, 1997.

Seybold, Klaus. *Die Psalmen: Eine Einführung*. 2., durchgesehene Auflage. Stuttgart: Kohlhammer, 1991.

——. "Zu den Zeitvorstellungen in Psalm 90." *TZ* 53 (1997): 97–108.

——. *Studien zur Psalmenauslegung*. Stuttgart: W. Kohlhammer, 1998.

——. "Dimensionen und Intentionen der Davidisierung der Psalmen: Die Rolle Davids nach den Psalmenüberschriften und nach dem Septuagintapsalm 151." In *The Composition of the Book of Psalms*, ed. Erich Zenger, 125–40. BETL 238. Leuven: Uitgeverij Peeters, 2010.

——. "Psalm 90 und die Theologie der Zeit (Zeiten)." In *Studien zu Sprache und Stil der Psalmen*, 129–43. BZAW 415. Berlin: de Gruyter, 2010.

——. "Zur Geschichte des vierten Davidpsalters (Ps 138–145)." In *Studien zu Sprache und Stil der Psalmen*, 221–43. BZAW 415. Berlin: de Gruyter, 2010.

——. "The Psalter as a Book." In *Jewish and Christian Approaches to the Psalms: Conflict and Convergence*, ed. Susan Gillingham, 168–81. Oxford: Oxford University Press, 2013.

Seybold, Klaus, and Erich Zenger, eds. *Neue Wege der Psalmenforschung: Für Walter Beyerlin*. Herders Biblische Studien 1. Freiburg: Herder, 1994.

——. *Studien zu Sprache und Stil der Psalmen*. BZAW 415. Berlin: de Gruyter, 2010.

Sheppard, Gerald T. *Wisdom as a Hermeneutical Construct: A Study in the Sapientializing of the Old Testament*. BZAW 151. Berlin: de Gruyter, 1980.

Shupak, Nili. "The 'Sitz im Leben' of the Book of Proverbs in the Light of a Comparison of Biblical and Egyptian Wisdom Literature." *RB* 94 (1987): 98–119.

——. *Where Can Wisdom Be Found? The Sage's Language in the Bible and in Ancient Egyptian Literature*. OBO 130. Göttingen: Vandenhoeck & Ruprecht, 1993.

——. "Learning Methods in Ancient Israel." *VT* 53 (2003): 416–26.

Siegel, Harvey. "Epistemology and Education: An Incomplete Guide to the Social-Epistemological Issues." *Episteme* 1 (2004): 129–37.

Simkins, Ronald A. *Creator and Creation: Nature in the Worldview of Ancient Israel*. Peabody, MA: Hendrickson, 1994.

Sire, James W. *Naming the Elephant: Worldview as a Concept.* Downers Grove, IL: InterVarsity, 2004.

Slomovic, Elieser. "Toward an Understanding of the Formation of Historical Titles in the Book of Psalms." *ZAW* 91 (1979): 350–80.

Smart, Ninian. *Worldviews: Crosscultural Explorations of Human Beliefs.* New York: Charles Scribner's Sons, 1983.

Smith, Terry L. "A Crisis in Faith: An Exegesis of Psalm 73." *ResQ* 17 (1974): 162–84.

Snaith, Norman, H. *Five Psalms (I, XXVII, LI, CVII, XXXIV): A New Translation with Commentary and Questionary.* London: Epworth, 1938.

——. "The Prosperity of the Wicked: A Study of Psalm 73." *Religion in Life* 20 (1951): 519–29.

——. "Psalm I 1 and Isaiah XL 31." *VT* 29 (1979): 363–64.

Soggin, J. Alberto. "Zum ersten Psalm." *TZ* 23 (1967): 81–96.

Solomon, Miriam. "Social Epistemology." In *Encyclopedia of Philosophy*, 2nd ed., ed. Donald M. Borchert, 9. 83–87. New York: Thomson Gale, 2006.

Sommer, Benjamin D. "Psalm 1 and the Canonical Shaping of Jewish Scripture." In *Jewish Bible Theology: Perspectives and Case Studies*, ed. Isaac Kalimi, 199–221. Winona Lake, IN: Eisenbrauns, 2013.

Sosa, Ernest. *A Virtue Epistemology: Apt Belief and Reflective Knowledge.* Vol. 1. Oxford: Clarendon Press, 2007.

Sosa, Ernest, Jaegwon Kim, Jeremy Fantl, and Matthew McGrath, eds. *Epistemology: An Anthology.* 2nd ed. Oxford: Blackwell Publishing, 2008.

Soskice, Janet Martin. *Metaphor and Religious Language.* Oxford: Clarendon Press, 1985.

Steen, Gerard. "From Linguistic to Conceptual Metaphor in Five Steps." In *Metaphor in Cognitive Linguistics*, eds. Raymond W. Gibbs, Jr. and Gerard J. Steen, 57–77. Amsterdam Studies in the Theory and History of Linguistic Science 175. Amsterdam: John Benjamins, 1999.

Steen, Gerard, and Raymond W. Gibbs, Jr. "Introduction." In *Metaphor in Cognitive Linguistics*, eds. Raymond W. Gibbs, Jr. and Gerard J. Steen, 1–8. Amsterdam Studies in the Theory and History of Linguistic Science 175. Amsterdam: John Benjamins, 1999.

Stolz, Fritz. *Psalmen im nachkultischen Raum.* Theologische Studien 129. Zürich: Theologischer Verlag, 1983.

Strong, John T., and Steven S. Tuell, eds. *Constituting the Community: Studies on the Polity of Ancient Israel in Honor of S. Dean McBride Jr.* Winona Lake, IN: Eisenbrauns, 2005.

Süssenbach, Claudia. *Der elohistische Psalter: Untersuchungen zur Komposition und Theologie von Ps 42–83.* FAT 2.7. Tübingen: Mohr, 2005.

Tanner, Beth LaNeel. *The Book of Psalms Through the Lens of Intertextuality.* SBLMS 26. New York: Peter Lang, 2001.

Tanner, Beth. "Rethinking the Enterprise: What Must Be Considered in Formulating a Theology of the Psalms." In *Soundings in the Theology of Psalms: Perspectives and Methods in Contemporary Scholarship*, ed. Rolf A. Jacobson, 139–50. Minneapolis: Fortress, 2011.

Thomas, D. W. "A Note on זרמתם שנה יהיו in Psalm XC 5." *VT* 18 (1968): 174–83.

Tournay, Raymond-Jacques. "Le psaume LXXIII: Relectures et interprétation." *RB* 92 (1985): 187–99.

Tov, Emmanuel. *Textual Criticism of the Hebrew Bible.* 2nd rev. ed. Minneapolis: Fortress, 1992.

——. *Text-Critical Use of the Septuagint in Biblical Research*. 2nd rev. ed. Jerusalem Biblical Studies 8. Jerusalem: Simor, 1997.

Troxel, Ronald L., Kelvin G. Friebel, and Dennis R. Magary, eds. *Seeking Out the Wisdom of the Ancients: Essays Offered to Honor Michael V. Fox on the Occasion of His Sixty-Fifth Birthday*. Winona Lake, IN: Eisenbrauns, 2005.

Trublet, Jacques. "Approche Canonique des Psaumes du Hallel." In *The Composition of the Book of Psalms*, ed. Erich Zenger, 339–76. BETL 238. Leuven: Uitgeverij Peeters, 2010.

Tsevat, Matitiahu. *A Study of the Language of the Biblical Psalms*. SBLMS 9. Philadelphia: Fortress, 1955.

——. "Psalm XC 5–6." *VT* 35 (1985): 115–17.

Tucker, Dennis, Jr. "Empires and Enemies in Book V of the Psalter." In *The Composition of the Book of Psalms*, ed. Erich Zenger, 723–31. BETL 238. Leuven: Uitgeverij Peeters, 2010.

Tuell, Steven S. "Psalm 1." *Int* 63 (2009): 278–80.

Turner, Mark, and Gilles Fauconnier. "Metaphor, Metonymy, and Binding." In *Metaphor and Metonymy at the Crossroads: A Cognitive Perspective*, ed. Antonio Barcelona, 133–48. Trends in Linguistics. Berlin: de Gruyter, 2003.

Turner, Mark. "The Way We Imagine." In *Imaginative Minds*, ed. Ilona Roth, 213–36. *Proceedings of the British Academy* 147. Oxford: Oxford University Press, 2007.

Turner, Victor W. *The Ritual Process: Structure and Anti-Structure*. Chicago: Aldine, 1969.

Urbrock, William J. "Mortal and Miserable Man: A Form-Critical Investigation of Psalm 90." In *SBLSP 1974*. 2 vols. 1. 1–34. Atlanta: Scholars, 1974.

——. "Psalm 90: Moses, Mortality, and … the Morning." *Currents in Theology and Mission* 25 (1998): 26–29.

Van Hecke, Pierre J. P. "Conceptual Blending: A Recent Approach to Metaphor. Illustrated with the Pastoral Metaphor in Hos 4,16." In *Metaphor in the Hebrew Bible*, ed. P. Van Hecke, 215–31. BETL 187. Leuven: Leuven University Press, 2005.

——. "Metaphors in the Psalms: An Introduction." In *Metaphors in the Psalms*, eds. Pierre van Hecke, and Antje Labahn, xi-xxxiv. BETL 231. Leuven: Uitgeverij Peeters, 2010.

Van Hecke, Pierre J. P., ed. *Metaphor in the Hebrew Bible*. BETL 187. Leuven: Leuven University Press, 2005.

Van Hecke, Pierre J. P. and Antje Labahn, eds. *Metaphors in the Psalms*. BETL 231. Leuven: Uitgeverij Peeters, 2010.

Van Leeuwen, Raymond C. "Proverbs 30:21–23 and the Biblical World Upside Down." *JBL* 105 (1986): 599–610.

——. "Liminality and Worldview in Proverbs 1–9." *Semeia* 50 (1990): 111–44.

——. "The Sage in the Prophetic Literature." In *The Sage in Israel and the Ancient Near East*, eds. John G. Gammie and Leo G. Perdue, 295–306. Winona Lake, IN: Eisenbrauns, 1990.

——. "Wealth and Poverty: System and Contradiction in Proverbs." *HS* 33 (1992): 25–36.

——. "Form Criticism, Wisdom, and Psalms 111–112." In *The Changing Face of Form Criticism for the Twenty-First Century*, eds. Marvin A. Sweeney and Ehud Ben Zvi, 65–84. Grand Rapids: Eerdmans, 2003.

Van Wolde, Ellen. "In Words and Pictures: The Sun in 2 Samuel 12:7–12." *Biblical Interpretation* 11 (2003): 259–78.

——. *Reframing Biblical Studies: When Language and Text Meet Culture, Cognition, and Context*. Winona Lake, IN: Eisenbrauns, 2009.

Van Wolde, Ellen, ed. *Job 28: Cognition in Context*. BIS 64. Leiden: Brill, 2003.

Vassar, John S. *Recalling a Story Once Told: An Intertextual Reading of the Psalter and the Pentateuch*. Macon, GA: Mercer, 2007.

Vawter, Bruce. "Postexilic Prayer and Hope." *CBQ* 37 (1975): 460–70.

Vogels, Walter. ""A Structural Analysis of Ps 1." *Bib* 60 (1979): 410–16.

Wahl, Harold-Martin. "Psalm 90,12: Text, Tradition und Interpretation." *ZAW* 106 (1994): 116–23.

Wälchli, Stefan. "Zorn JHWHs im Psalter—eine Metapher des Leidens?" In *Metaphors in the Psalms*, eds. Pierre van Hecke, and Antje Labahn, 269–77. BETL 231. Leuven: Uitgeverij Peeters, 2010.

Walker, Simon. "Grounding Biblical Metaphor in Reality: The Philosophical Basis of Realist Metaphorical Language." *Churchman* 112 (1998): 214–24.

Wallace, Robert E. The Narrative Effect of Book IV of the Hebrew Psalter. Studies in Biblical Literature 112. New York: Peter Lang, 2007.

——. "The Narrative Effect of Psalms 84–89." *Journal of Hebrew Scriptures* 11 (2011): 2–15.

Waltke, Bruce K. "Superscripts, Postscripts, or Both." *JBL* 110 (1991): 583–96.

Waltke, Bruce K., and David Diewert. "Wisdom Literature." In *The Faces of Old Testament Studies: A Survey of Contemporary Approaches*, eds. David W. Baker and Bill T. Arnold, 295–328. Grand Rapids: Baker Books, 1999.

Washington, Harold C. *Wealth and Poverty in the Instruction of Amenemope and the Hebrew Proverbs*. SBLDS 142. Atlanta, GA: Scholars, 1994.

Watson, Wilfred G. E. *Classical Hebrew Poetry: A Guide to Its Techniques*. JSOTSup 26. Sheffield: Sheffield Academic Press, 1984.

——. *Traditional Techniques in Classical Hebrew Verse*. JSOTSup 170. Sheffield: Sheffield Academic Press, 1994.

Weber, Beat. "Der Beitrag von Psalm 1 zu einer 'Theologie der Schrift.'" *Jahrbuch für Evangelikale Theologie* 20 (2006): 83–113.

——. "Psalm 1 als Tor zur Tora JHWSs: Wie Ps 1 (und Ps 2) den Psalter an den Pentateuch Anschliesst." *SJOT* 21 (2007): 179–200.

——. "'Dann wird er sein wie ein Baum…' (Psalm 1,3): Zu den Sprachbildern von Psalm 1." *OTE* 23 (2010): 406–26.

——. "Die Buchouvertüre Psalm 1—3 und ihre Bedeutung für das Verständnis des Psalters." *OTE* 23 (2010): 834–45.

——. "Von der Psaltergenese zur Psaltertheologie: Der nächste Schritt der Psalterexegese?! Einige Grundsätzliche Überlegungen zum Psalter als Buch und Kanonteil." In *The Composition of the Book of Psalms*, ed. Erich Zenger, 733–44. BETL 238. Leuven: Uitgeverij Peeters, 2010.

Weeks, Stuart. *Early Israelite Wisdom*. Oxford Theological Monographs. Oxford: Oxford University Press, 1994.

——. "Wisdom Psalms." In *Temple and Worship in Biblical Israel*, ed. John Day, 293–307. Library of Hebrew Bible/Old Testament Studies (formerly JSOTSup) 422. London: T&T Clark, 2005.

Weinfeld, Moshe. *Deuteronomy and the Deuteronomic School*. Oxford: Clarendon, 1972. Reprint, Winona Lake, IN: Eisenbrauns, 1992.

Weiss, Andrea L. *Figurative Language in Biblical Prose Narrative: Metaphor in the Book of Samuel*. VTSup 107. Leiden: Brill, 2006.

Wendland, Ernst. "Introit 'into the Sanctuary of God' (Psalm 73:17): Entering the Theological 'Heart' of the Psalm at the Centre of the Psalter." *Old Testament Essays* 11 (1998): 128–53.

Wénin, André. "Le Psautier comme Livre. Quelques Signes d'Unification." In *Psaumes de la Bible, psaumes d'aujourd'hui.* Jean-Marie Auwers, Elena Di Pede, Dany Nocquet, Jacques Vermeylen, Catherine Vialle, and André Wénin. Lira la Bible. Paris: Cerf, 2011.

Westermann, Claus. *Praise and Lament in the Psalms.* Translated by Keith R. Crim and Richard N. Soulen. Atlanta: John Knox Press, 1981.

——. *Roots of Wisdom: The Oldest Proverbs of Israel and Other Peoples.* Translated by J. Daryl Charles. Louisville: Westminster John Knox, 1995.

White, Alan R. "Coherence Theory of Truth." In *Encyclopedia of Philosophy*, 2nd ed., ed. Donald M. Borchert, 2. 308–13. New York: Thomson Gale, 2006.

Whiting, Mark J. "Psalms 1 and 2 as a Hermeneutical Lens for Reading the Psalter." *EvQ* 85 (2013): 246–62.

Whitley, Charles F. "The Text of Psalm 90,5." *Bib* 63 (1982): 555–57.

Whybray, R. N. *The Intellectual Tradition in the Old Testament.* BZAW 135. Berlin: de Gruyter, 1974.

——. "The Social World of the Wisdom Writers." In *The World of Ancient Israel: Sociological, Anthropological and Political Perspectives*, ed. R. E. Clements, 227–50. Cambridge: Cambridge University Press, 1989.

——. "The Sage in the Israelite Royal Court." In *The Sage in Israel and the Ancient Near East*, eds. John G. Gammie and Leo G. Perdue, 133–39. Winona Lake, IN: Eisenbrauns, 1990.

——. "The Wisdom Psalms." In *Wisdom in Ancient Israel*, eds. John Day, Robert P. Gordon, and H. G. M. Williamson, 152–60. Cambridge: Cambridge University Press, 1995.

——. *Reading the Psalms as a Book.* JSOTSup 222. Sheffield: Sheffield Academic Press, 1996.

——. "Psalm 119: Profile of a Psalmist." In *Wisdom, You Are My Sister: Studies in Honor of Roland E. Murphy, O. Carm., on the Occasion of His Eightieth Birthday*, ed. Michael L. Barré, 31–43. CBQMS 29. Washington: Catholic Biblical Association of America, 1997.

——. "Qoheleth as a Theologian." In *Qohelet in the Context of Wisdom*, ed. A. Schoors, 239–65. BETL 136. Leuven: Leuven University Press, 1998.

Williams, James G. *Those Who Ponder Proverbs: Aphoristic Thinking and Biblical Literature.* Bible and Literature Series 2. Sheffield: Almond Press, 1981.

Willis, John T. "Psalm 1 – An Entity." *ZAW* 91 (1979): 381–401.

Wilson, Gerald H. "The Qumran Psalms Manuscripts and the Consecutive Arrangement of Psalms in the Hebrew Psalter." *CBQ* 45 (1983): 377–88.

——. "Evidence of Editorial Divisions in the Hebrew Psalter." *VT* 34 (1984): 337–52.

——. *The Editing of the Hebrew Psalter.* SBLDS 76. Chico, CA: Scholars, 1985.

——. "The Qumran Psalms Scroll Reconsidered: Analysis of the Debate." *CBQ* 47 (1985): 624–42.

——. "The Use of the Royal Psalms at the 'Seams' of the Hebrew Psalter." *JSOT* 35 (1986): 85–94.

——. "The Shape of the Book of Psalms." *Int* 46 (1992): 129–42.

——. "Shaping the Psalter: A Consideration of Editorial Linkage in the Book of Psalms." In *The Shape and Shaping of the Psalter*, ed. J. Clinton McCann, 72–82. JSOTSup 159. Sheffield: JSOT Press, 1993.

—. "Understanding the Purposeful Arrangement of Psalms in the Psalter: Pitfalls and Promises." In *The Shape and Shaping of the Psalter*, ed. J. Clinton McCann, 42–51. JSOTSup 159. Sheffield: JSOT Press, 1993.

—. "King, Messiah, and the Reign of God: Revisiting the Royal Psalms and the Shape of the Psalter." In *The Book of Psalms: Composition and Reception*, ed. Peter W. Flint and Patrick D. Miller, 391–406. VTSup 99. Leiden: Brill, 2005.

Wilson, Lindsay. "On Psalms 103—106 as a Closure to Book IV of the Psalter." In *The Composition of the Book of Psalms*, ed. Erich Zenger, 755–66. BETL 238. Leuven: Uitgeverij Peeters, 2010.

Witte, Markus, ed. *Gott und Mensch im Dialog: Festschrift für Otto Kaiser zum 80. Geburtstag*. 2 Vols. BZAW 345/I, II. Berlin: de Gruyter, 2004.

Witte, Markus. "Auf dem Weg in ein Leben nach dem Tod: Beobachtungen zur Traditions- und Redaktionsgeschichte von Psalm 73." In *Von Ewigkeit zu Ewigkeit: Weisheit und Geschichte in den Psalmen*, 95–115. BThSt 146. Neukirchen-Vluyn: Neukirchener Verlag, 2014.

Woozley, A. D. "Universals, A Historical Survey." In *Encyclopedia of Philosophy*, 2nd ed., ed. Donald M. Borchert, 9. 587–603. New York: Thomson Gale, 2006.

Wright, Benjamin G.. "Torah and Sapiential Pedagogy in the Book of Ben Sira." In *Wisdom and Torah: The Reception of 'Torah' in the Wisdom Literature of the Second Temple Period*, eds. Bernd U. Schipper, and D. Andrew Teeter, 157–86. JSJSup 163. Leiden: Brill, 2013.

Wright, John W. "The Innocence of David in 1 Chronicles 21." *JSOT* 60 (1993): 87–105.

Wright, N. T. *The New Testament and the People of God*. Vol. 1 of *Christian Origins and the Question of God*. Minneapolis: Fortress, 1992.

Würthwein, Ernst. "Erwägungen zu Psalm 73." In *Wort und Existenz: Studien zum Alten Testament*, 161–78. Göttingen: Vandenhoeck & Ruprecht, 1970.

—. *The Text of the Old Testament*. 2nd rev. ed. Translated by Erroll F. Rhodes. Grand Rapids: Eerdmans, 1995.

Yob, Iris, M. "Religious Metaphor and Scientific Model: Grounds for Comparison." *RelS* 28 (1992): 475–85.

Young, James O. "The Coherence Theory of Truth." In *The Stanford Encyclopedia of Philosophy (Summer 2001 Edition)* [database online; article at <http://plato.stanford.edu/archives/sum2001/entries/truth-coherence/> SEP; ed. Edward N. Zalta ; Stanford: Stanford University; accessed June 2, 2008].

Zakovitch, Yair. "The Interpretive Significance of the Sequence of Psalms 111—112.113—118.119." In *The Composition of the Book of Psalms*, ed. Erich Zenger, 215–27. BETL 238. Leuven: Uitgeverij Peeters, 2010.

Zenger, Erich. "Der Psalter als Buch: Beobachtungen zu seiner Entstehung, Komposition und Funktion." In *Der Psalter in Judentum und Christentum*, eds. Hans-Josef Klauck and Erich Zenger, 1–57. Herders Biblische Studien 18. Freiburg: Herder, 1998.

—. "The Composition and Theology of the Fifth Book of Psalms, Psalms 107–145." *JSOT* 80 (1998): 77–102.

—. "'Es segne dich JHWH vom Zion aus...' (Ps 134,3): Die Gottesmetaphorik in den Wallfahrtspsalmen Ps 120—134." In *Gott und Mensch im Dialog: Festschrift für Otto Kaiser zum 80. Geburtstag*, ed. Markus Witte, 601–21. BZAW 345/II. Berlin: de Gruyter, 2004.

——. "Theophanien des Königsgottes JHWH: Transformationen von Psalm 29 in den Teilkompositionen Ps 28–30 und Ps 93–100." In *The Book of Psalms: Composition and Reception*, ed. Peter W. Flint and Patrick D. Miller, 407–42. VTSup 99. Leiden: Brill, 2005.

——. "Psalmenexegese *und* Psalterexegese: Eine Forschungsskizze." In *The Composition of the Book of Psalms*, ed. Erich Zenger, 17–65. BETL 238. Leuven: Uitgeverij Peeters, 2010.

Zenger, Erich, ed. *The Composition of the Book of Psalms*. BETL 238. Leuven: Uitgeverij Peeters, 2010.

Zevit, Ziony. *The Religions of Ancient Israel: A Synthesis of Parallactic Approaches*. London/New York: Continuum, 2001.

Zięba, Zbigniew. "The Meaning of the Expression לבב חכמה 'The Heart of Wisdom' (Ps 90:12) in the Context of the Transitory and Frail Life of Human beings in Psalm 90." *Polish Journal of Biblical Research* 7 (2008): 113–24.

Zinken, Jörg, and Andreas Musolff. "A Discourse-Centered Perspective on Metaphorical Meaning and Understanding." In *Metaphor and Discourse*, eds. Andreas Musolff and Jörg Zinken, 1–8. Basingstoke: Palgrave MacMillan, 2009.

Bible Reference Index

Author Name Index

Subject Index